WE PEAKED AT PAPER

WE PEAKED AT PAPER

An Oral History of British Zines

Gavin Hogg and Hamish Ironside

BOATWHISTLE BOOKS

First published in 2022
by Boatwhistle Books
22 Gloucester Road
Twickenham
London TW2 6NE
United Kingdom

www.boatwhistle.com

© Gavin Hogg and Hamish Ironside 2022

Typeset by Boatwhistle in Joanna
with a little bit of Apparat
and a little bit of Octynaz

ISBN 978-1-911052-07-4

Printed in the United Kingdom by TJ Books of Padstow,
on FSC-certified 80 gsm Munken Premium paper

Sheffield
16/10/22

To Marco,
Hope you enjoy reading this here book what is in yer hands.
Thank you for all the happiness your music's given me over the years.
Grandi abbracci,
Gavin
X

CONTENTS

PREFACE

All the interviews in this book were carried out between March 2018 and March 2022. We felt it was important to do all interviews face to face, as written interviews lose spontaneity and are too considered. Even though the period during which we carried out our interviews encompassed the entire Covid pandemic, which saw a huge increase in the use of video communication software (especially Zoom and Microsoft Teams), we eschewed resorting to that for any of our interviews, as even that seemed a poor substitute for real old-fashioned conversation. We wanted to be able to look our interviewees in the eye, drink their tea, buy them a beer if necessary and rummage through their zine collections if the opportunity presented itself.

The interviews are transcribed in dialogue form, and are edited as minimally as possible, in true fanzine tradition.* In fact this whole book has been put together in the same spirit as a fanzine. We have had no funding and are affiliated to no academic institutions, and Boatwhistle as a publisher is similarly independent. Nor did we set out to construct a thesis – if it sometimes seems like that is what we are doing (particularly in the Afterword), we humbly apologise, and submit that our opinions should be taken in much the same spirit as John Torode and Gregg Wallace discussing politics on *Question Time*, if you can imagine how that might go.

---

* However, see the 'Note on the text' below for a pedantic explanation of exactly how we edited the interviews, among other things. We realise that this is very much contrary to fanzine tradition, but our scruples got the better of us.

Accordingly, throughout the interviews, our main aim was to let the editors speak for themselves in their own words. In particular, although we often found ourselves debating whether a certain publication is or isn't a zine, we do not set out any hard and fast rules in this preface. There is one exception to this: as the title of this book suggests, we feel that a zine must be made of paper. If you see anything described as an e-zine, we would contend that it is a website or a blog.

We spent a fair amount of time travelling to interviews (often hampered by Covid restrictions), as we aimed to cover as wide a range of geographical locations as possible. The opening of each chapter includes a small map indicating where the interview took place. The rationale for this is perhaps dubious, as in some cases the location of the interview is not where the editor lived when they produced the zine, or not where they live now. This simply reflects the extent to which people move around, and the introductions to each interview go into more detail about this. So the little maps could be considered totally redundant, but we decided to retain them anyway just because we really like them. We think they look cool.

In addition to covering as wide a range of locations as possible, we also wanted to aim for similar diversity in terms of the subject matter of the zines, as well as when they were published. The latter aspect determines the order of the chapters, based on when the interviewees published their first zine. Conveniently, for Chapter 1, Rob Hansen was not only the first of our interviewees to begin his own zine publishing, but is also a historian of the form. This book can therefore be seen as very loosely tracking the chronology of the development of zines in the UK, from the science fiction zines of the 1930s, via the flourishing of music zines in the wake of punk and football zines from the mid-eighties onwards, to the zines that continue to emerge in the present day, despite (and sometimes abetted by) the advent of the internet. Note that the order in which the interviews were recorded bears no relation to the chapter order, which means it's quite possible you will find us ignorant of something in a later chapter that we seemed to have known in an earlier one.

Another aspect of diversity that we wanted to incorporate was to do with the size of the print run/readership for each zine. A lot of the existing literature on zines focuses on titles such as *Sniffin' Glue*, *Ripped*

& Torn, *Vague* – exceptionally successful zines that earned a reader-ship in the thousands across the whole country, and even overseas. While we acknowledge the importance of these zines, and did want to represent one or two of them in this book, we were also keen to reflect the fact that the majority of zines are read in much smaller numbers and leave little trace. We contend that some of the best fanzines are known to perhaps fewer than a hundred people, and their limited sales are typically due to the editor lacking the sort of gregariousness needed to approach strangers at gigs, or shops that might stock it.

Note on the text

The interviews are presented in dialogue form, with the interviewer's turn in bold type and the interviewee's in regular weight. Names are added at the start of each turn where there is more than one inter-viewer or interviewee.

The dialogue has been painstakingly transcribed by the interviewer from an audio recording in each case. We have retained broken sen-tences, shonky grammar and any other verbal idiosyncrasies that give a flavour of the way someone speaks. However, having said two pages ago that we've edited 'as minimally as possible', we should admit that we've freely omitted words, sentences or whole chunks of conversation that we deemed redundant, repetitive or boring. We have even moved a few passages from their true position to earlier or later in the conversation, where it helped to make it flow more logically, although we did that as little as possible. Occasionally the recording was unclear and we gave our best guess. When we had finished our transcription we gave all interviewees an opportunity to see the resulting text (including the introduction), and made further edits in some places where they were able to correct or clarify something, but there were very few changes of this sort.

Where we quote from another source (usually a zine), which doesn't happen often, we reproduce the text exactly as in the original, includ-ing any errors of punctuation, spelling, etc. This is not done to present the author of the source in a bad light, and we hope it does not come over that way. It's rather an acknowledgement that these things matter very little in zines, and can even be taken as a virtue (like the misspell-ings in Billy Childish's poems, for example).

Note on the photographs

The photographs of the zine editors near the start of each chapter became an important part of our project, although it was something that developed as we went along rather than having been planned from the start. Most of them were taken by the interviewer at the time of the interview; for the four that weren't, we credit the photographers in the caption.

ACKNOWLEDGMENTS

Our first thanks must go to the twenty-one zine editors who were interviewed for this book. Every one of them has provided help and encouragement that went well beyond what we could have expected. Some travelled long distances to meet us; several went to considerable trouble to provide images of their zines; one even recorded the interview for us on his mobile phone, when our own ancient tape recorder twirled its final spool. For the early interviews we couldn't be certain when (or even if) the book would appear, but we have met with nothing but kindness throughout.

Gavin gives particular thanks to Lyn – for putting up with me disappearing every now and again, for listening to me quacking on about fanzines, and for her unstinting support (even if she was inwardly stinting); and to Mum – for her positivity and passing on her belief in just getting on with things. Thanks also to various people who have helped along their way with general encouragement, leads to follow, friendship, inspiration, kindness and smiles: Simon Galloway, Michael Johnson, Poppy and Ellis, Ian Moss, John Peel, Richard Ashbridge, Mark Ellen, Rob Freeman, Bob Fischer, Jonathan Wilkins, David Hepworth, Ciaran Humphries, Simon Mitchell, John Naughton, Jude Rogers, Andrew Willshaw, Dave Griffiths, Mark Ritchie, Jennifer Smith, Julie Hamill, Greg Sestero, Ivor and Phyllis, Steve Smith, Andrew Harrison, David Marlow, Nige Tassell and Ros, whose surname I can't recall but who started the ball rolling in the first place all those years ago by selling me a copy of *Perturbed*.

Hamish would like to offer special thanks to Katrina Dixon, for being the first person to make me believe this book could work; it would not have happened without your encouragement. I'm also deeply grateful to Julia and Aspen for their patience and support; to Peter Doherty, Teal Triggs and Matthew Worley for their enthusiastic responses to advance proofs of the book; to Liam Duggan for providing images of All Quiet on the Western Avenue; and to my Ford Ka for driving me hundreds of miles through foul weather, without complaint, to get to several interviews in the north of England.

This book is dedicated to Angus Barclay, who compiled its magnificent index. If the work of zine editors is too seldom given the acclaim it deserves, this is doubly true for indexers. Angus's indexes are brilliantly crafted, and any book that contains one is a lucky book.

1

ROB HANSEN

interviewed by Hamish Ironside

When we first had the idea for this book, the plan was to begin with *Sniffin' Glue*, the theory being that zines began with punk; *Sniffin' Glue* was the first punk zine; therefore *Sniffin' Glue* was the first zine. It's a neat little syllogism. The only problem is that it's wrong!

While I still feel that *Sniffin' Glue* deserves some sort of honorary position, the main flaw in the theory is that it ignores the tradition of science fiction fanzines, which began more than 40 years before punk. Yet, while I would expect almost any zine editor (certainly music zine editors) to be aware of *Sniffin' Glue* and its significance, I don't think many of them would know about the science fiction fanzines. Moreover, while there is the odd figure (such as Jonh Ingham) who has had a foot in both camps, by and large the music zines and the SF zines developed quite separately, rather than the former evolving as an off-shoot of the latter.

If you will indulge a rather laboured analogy: it is as if SF fandom evolved on its own island, like the animals of Madagascar, while the rest of the world of zines developed, a lot later, sometimes crossing continents, sometimes interbreeding, always evolving, but largely separate from the SF zines. Why was this? Well – let's not get into that now, because it's covered pretty well in the interview!

Much of the rest of this book is devoted to music (and other) zines, but once we became aware of the SF fanzine tradition, we felt it important to begin the book by covering that. So we were rather fortunate in finding, in Rob Hansen, a man who had not only edited his own SF zine, but who has also spent a great deal of time investigating the history of SF fandom in Britain.

Rob's main zine was *Epsilon*, publishing 18 issues between 1976 and 1985, with the first three issues being A4 size (297 × 210 mm) and the rest quarto (10 × 8 inches / 254 × 204 mm). *Epsilon* won the awards for best British fanzine and best British fan artist at the Nova Awards in 1982, and in 1984 it won the European Science Fiction Award for best British fanzine.

As well as producing *Epsilon*, Rob has undertaken numerous other activities within the world of SF fandom, including editing or co-editing smaller-scale zines such as *Skwelsh, Fish Helmet, Taffeta, Crank, Chuch, Pulp, The Fanhattonite, Licks* and *Born in the UK*. His major work, researched over many years, is a very chunky book entitled *Then: Science Fiction Fandom in the UK 1930–1980* (Ansible Editions, 2016). *Then* is available to order from https://ae.ansible.uk in both print and e-book formats, and earlier iterations are freely available online.

Rob's research is assisted by the fact that he has a vast archive of fanzines in his own home in East Ham (London), including many ultra-rare zines from the 1930s up to the present day, filling every space from the cellar right up to Rob's bijou office on the top floor. A large amount of the collection was inherited from his friend Vince Clarke (not the one from Depeche Mode / Yazoo / Erasure), another important figure in British SF fandom, who died in 1998.

In case you are already thinking 'I'm not really interested in science fiction, I might skip this chapter', hold your horses! I'm not a science fiction fan myself, but when you actually read Rob's fanzine, the main thing that strikes you is how similar it is to, say, a music zine from the 1990s, in many respects. That's evolution for you! The animals of Madagascar are, after all, not so different from their cousins on the mainland, even if they do have different names. Indeed, given the imaginative flights of fancy that characterise SF literature, it is ironic that the SF zines are so grounded in the quotidian. *Epsilon* issue 7, for example (which appeared after a three-year hiatus), includes Rob's regular 'Odzunsodz' column, which is a droll diary of his own life; this is followed by 'The Move', a detailed account of Rob's move from Wales to London; after this is 'Bodily Functions', which is

Rob Hansen in his basement, East Ham, December 2021.

indeed a piece about bodily functions . . . Even when SF does intrude, it is never about the literature, but rather the business of fandom: what was eaten after a day at an SF convention, or whether politics has any place in 'the British body fannish' – the sort of question a music zine might be just as likely to consider.

In fact my favourite piece in *Epsilon* 7 makes this very point. 'The Death of a Metaphor (by Flogging)' is a rather brilliant one-page pastiche, not of SF but of hard-boiled detective fiction. In this story a 'broad' confronts Rob (who is spooning down baked beans and stroking his Gestetner) about 'an insidious plot by the more degenerate editors to expunge SF from their fanzines and thus, by example, foster a movement away from Science Fiction'. When she asks Rob what he's going to do about it, he replies: 'As little as possible. That's fandom.'

I visited Rob at his home in December 2021, and he allowed me to rummage freely through his archive – a real delight to one besotted with all aspects of print publishing. To me, these self-produced publications, with their paper degrading, staples rusting and inks fading, are as precious as any of the contents of the British Museum. While you can't feel the rusty staples, sniff the pages, and so on, you can see everything in the archive (along with many other fans' collections) in digital form at https://fanac.org (a US site, but one to which Rob has contributed a substantial amount of the British fanzines). This painstaking cataloguing and archiving work is another thing that characterises SF zines, being done in such a scattered and random fashion for other types of zine. For anyone interested in what we discuss below, an excellent repository offering further information is Rob's own site at www.fiawol.org.uk.

I want to start by asking you about the history of science fiction fanzines, because obviously they have been going for so much longer than the other fanzines that I was aware of. They began in the 1930s – was that in America? Would they have started there a lot earlier than they started here?

They did, yeah. Basically, the very first fanzines in the US were about 1930. If you want to give a birthday for American fandom, the first meeting of the first American fan group was 1929, in New York. The first meeting of *our* [i.e. Britain's] first fan group was October the 27th 1930, in Ilford. So we were a year later. But we were very slow getting into fanzines. I don't know whether that was because people at the time didn't have access to means of production – because, remember, we were a lot poorer than the Americans, generally speaking.

Yeah. Although this is Depression era, isn't it?

That as well, yeah, but I mean, they had more access for some reason.

Anyway, the fan groups preceded the fanzines.

Yes.

But how did the fan groups come about? Was it just people with an interest in the literature . . . socialising?

Ah! No! The thing is, they had to – because people were so thinly spread then, people who were fans – not like today, when everybody seems to read science fiction – back then, there used to be a saying: 'It's a proud and lonely thing to be a fan!' Because it's like, people could think they were the only person in their given city or location who was a fan. So therefore, how they first got in touch with each other in America, there was an SF magazine called *Amazing Stories* that started publishing in 1926. It started running letters by readers, and – crucially and importantly – printed full addresses. Therefore, people who bought this then had addresses that they could write to other people, and that's how the first communication between people started. And this eventually evolved into the first fan groups.

The same happened over here, to some extent, in that our very first fan group was the Ilford Science Literary Circle. It started in Ilford. And Walter Gillings, who was then 18 years old [and a junior reporter for *The Ilford Recorder*], convinced his editor to let him put an advert in the paper on the local groups page – because there was a page about the local groups, you know? The local horticultural society, the local Darby and Joan, whatever. And he put one in saying 'I want to start this group for people who are interested in science fiction. And fantasy.' Which is what he did, and that's how the first group started.

He mentioned this in letters to the American prozines – because we didn't have any professional magazines of our own over here –

and so the addresses of Brits started to appear in the letter pages of American prozines. And when they came over here, that's how you started getting contacts, et cetera.

So these groups would be groups of people actually corresponding rather than meeting, is that right?

At first, but then they would meet. As I say, the Ilford Science Literary Circle – that was our first actual in-person meeting groups. And then, what really sparked it open – there were one or two ... there were two or three isolated groups across the country prior to 1935. What happened round about then was that *Wonder Stories* magazine started something called the Science Fiction League. You could write to them, and they would let you form a chapter if you got together three or more people. And therefore, lots of local groups started with people getting together, getting addresses from people writing in to the magazines, et cetera, and they started local chapters. And so, the first one in this country was in Leeds. And for a long time, Leeds Science Fiction League was the biggest group in this country.

And what would they actually do when they met up?

They would talk about science fiction, for the most part.

Yeah. And that would be, like, mainstream science fiction, would it?

Yeah. The fiction that was appearing in the magazines.

And that would then develop in the fanzines in terms of, someone would think, 'Well, we like writing letters to each other, but we could organise this in a way where everyone sees everyone else's letters'?

Exactly, yeah. I mean, the very first fanzines were very *serious*. You know, they were very gung-ho about science fiction. It took a while for a sense of SF fandom as a community to develop. As soon as that happened, then people started writing about the community. I mean, as soon as you have the first convention – and the very first convention *anywhere* was held in this country, in January 1937 (the Americans claim that they did something earlier, but it wasn't a convention) – so we had the first one, and it was in Leeds. Not surprisingly; biggest group in the country. And then the next two years – '38 and '39 – they were in

London, in the Ancient Order of Druids Memorial Hall.

So . . . yeah! The thing about conventions is as soon as you write a report on a convention, you're writing basically about the social aspects of fandom. So that's – you know, that's how it all started. And then the more fanzines there were, the more people commented on other fanzines, and they commented on each other, and . . . yada yada yada . . . you know, a sense of community develops.

And could we identify something as the very first British fanzine?

Yes.

What would that be?

Novae Terrae. The very first one was in March 1936, the first issue. There are other things people sometimes claim were the first fanzine, but, you know, it's a bit dubious. So that's the first one generally acknowledged.

Okay, so let's say, *Novae Terrae* number one –

March 1936.

Do you know what the print run would have been for that, for example?

Nnnnno. It would have been –

Or would you have a rough guess?

Double figures, not triple figures. Because, again, who would they have sent it to?

Well, I thought you might even say single figures, to be honest.

No, no, no, no, no, definitely double figures. But again, we're talking . . . I would imagine, the first issue . . . 40 or 50 copies, perhaps?

I mean, actually that's pretty typical for a fanzine from the eighties.

Really?

Well – the ones I used to read! Not the likes of *Sniffin' Glue* . . . Although I must say, *Sniffin' Glue*, when it started it did 50. I mean, of course, if you sell them all you can always print some more.

Ah! That's another thing. Eventually SF fanzines developed to the point where we didn't sell them anywhere, we just traded them and gave them away. So basically, the profit – the selling of the thing just completely went away.

But when it started, *Novae Terrae*, would that be – it would have had a little price on it?

Oh yeah, yeah. Thruppence.

And how would they have distributed and taken the money, would that be all through the post, do you think?

Yeah, that would have been stamps, for the most part. Because the thing is, while I don't have an original copy of that very first fanzine, I think I *have* got a Xerox. Unless I'm mistaken. So therefore I can show you the very first fanzine that was ever produced in this country. Whoops! Let's, uh ... get the originals ... I should probably be a bit more gentle with these! But still ... let's have a look ... so there's April, that was number two ... Oh! May, number three ... I mean – you can see how ... There are two, let's see if I can find the first one ... Again, these are Xeroxes from somebody who actually had copies ... I could have sworn I had number one in here ... And it was ... they would have distributed them to the names and addresses that they would have got from prozines, because, again, that's all there was ... I could have sworn I had – oh well! So much for that! I was going to proudly show you issue 1, but I don't appear to have it. It's online, anyway.

Yeah, so all of this is online?

Oh yeah, it's all online. There's a complete run of that fanzine online. It took the collections of three of us to put it together, because nobody had a complete run. Which is not surprising, given how old they are.

Ah, well, it says in here, actually, in issue 2, 'The first issue was duplicated and posted to *a few score* science fiction fans throughout the world.' [my emphasis]

Ah, there you go! So, I said forty or fifty, didn't I? That's probably about right.

Yeah. So that's good. So, talking about *Novae Terrae* number one ... how would that have been printed?

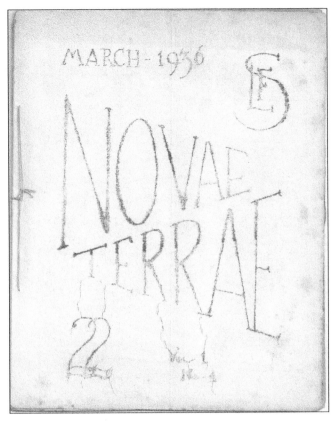

Cover of *Novae Terrae* issue 1, March 1936, edited by Maurice K. Hanson and Denis A. Jacques in Nuneaton: the very first fanzine published in Britain. Like the majority of fanzines up to around 1980, it was printed on a stencil duplicator, aka mimeograph machine (mimeo for short), almost certainly manufactured by Gestetner, who dominated the market for as long as the technology itself was dominant. Stencil duplication is an offset printing method that uses a thin sheet of paper coated with wax as a stencil, with ink forced through gaps in the wax created by either a typewriter or a special stylus used by hand. It meant the entire publishing process could be done by the editor of a fanzine in their own home. After the initial outlay for the machine, the cost of materials was relatively low, and the quality was relatively good. Fanzines produced in the 1930s by this method still look good today.

Novae Terrae produced 29 issues over three years, after which it morphed into a prozine under the title *New Worlds* (a translation of its former name), becoming the country's leading SF magazine. A far cry from this first fanzine, which is bound with hand-tied string! (Subsequent issues were apparently bound using a sewing machine.)

Cover of *The Science Fantasy Fan* issue 2, May 1941, edited by Arthur Williams in London and produced on a spirit duplicator, aka ditto machine (named after Ditto Inc., the leading manufacturer of these machines in the USA; in Britain the main manufacturer was Banda).

Spirit duplication used solvents as inks in a process involving two master sheets, with the top sheet being typed or drawn on and the other sheet being coated with coloured wax; a mirror image of the top sheet was transferred to the waxed sheet, and this then printed the positive image directly onto the paper. The Banda's only advantage over the Gestetner was that it could print in more than one colour (the cover shown here uses purple, red and green-blue inks). But the process could only print on one side of each sheet, and one master could print a maximum of about 500 copies, far fewer than a Gestetner (although probably more than enough for any fanzine). Archived fanzines printed on spirit duplicators have also faded a great deal more than their mimeographed brethren.

He appears to have had an actual duplicator, as far as I can tell. But not necessarily a stapler, as you can tell, because it looks like some of them have been put together with a sewing machine! So, you know . . . seems odd that you'd have one and not the other, but there you go.

Yeah, okay! So, you were saying there were four basic means of printing . . .

At that point in time, yeah. There were the carbonzines, which is basically carbon paper. So in other words you're bashing out the copies on a typewriter. And depending on how hard you hit it, you're going to get maybe five or six copies. So if you had the stamina to do it, you'd then have to type the whole thing again to get more. So that was the first one. The second one was hecto, which was a tray of jelly. And then the other two are spirit duplication – which was spirit duplicators – back when I was in school, the main brand over here was Nig Banda. And then of course there's your regular duplicators, which are Gestetners and Roneos. And although I got rid of mine quite a while ago, I kept some of the actual operating manuals [handing one to me].

Oh, lovely! And I have actually used one of these, because in fact my first fanzine came out on a Gestetner machine, because I knew someone in the village who had one. But would these have been going as long ago as the 1930s and 1940s?

Yeah, I'm fairly certain they were invented earlier than that, yeah. I actually met Jonathan Gestetner, who's the current guy who's . . . the descendant of the guy who invented it. Because . . . fairly recently – within the last three or four years – there's been interest by people in old technology. One of which was duplicators. So although we all got rid of our duplicators about ten years ago, it's like, all of a sudden these guys are interested in duplicators! So there's this group called . . . Alt Går Bra [www.altgarbra.org] . . . which is some kind of Norwegian name . . . and I kind of gave them . . . I gave them all my supplies. Because although I got rid of the duplicator, I still owned the consumables. And although it's quite easy to get hold of an old duplicator now – you can get them on eBay – you try getting hold of the consumables. Again: paper is paper – it's not quite the right quality of paper, but you can get away with it. Ink: not quite the right ink, but again, you can spread it on the drum, et cetera. What you haven't got is stencils.

Yes. Yes.

They're the one thing it's a right pig . . . there's nothing else you can use for a stencil other than a stencil! So I had something like half a dozen quires of stencils. That's what they used to call them, a quire, Q-U-I-R-E. I said 'Here you are, take them away.' Because again, this is all stuff that I was on the point of throwing away when these guys got in touch with me. So I was delighted to give them to somebody who could actually make some use of them. I was never going to use them again.

It's like . . . gold dust, isn't it?

Actually, if you reach up behind you, you see that tube there? At the back?

This?

Yeah. If you give that to me . . . The other thing you could also do . . . There was something called an electro-stenciller. It was a kind of really large thing that sat on the ground, and it had a big drum, and on one side you'd stick a carbon stencil, and on the other you'd stick your actual original artwork. And it would scan it like this, and this side it would be burning into the carbon. And that's how you'd get things like this. These are some leftovers I never used. So there you go: that's . . . an electro-stenciller. And again: if you have an electro-stenciller machine – which are even rarer than duplicators – good luck getting hold of blank electro-stencils!

Is that a later thing, the electro-stencil?

It dates to the fifties, I think, I'm not sure. I could look it up.

So, I guess which one of these you used would come down to economics, is that right? If you could afford a Gestetner, you'd use a Gestetner.

It's whatever you had access to. Hence the reason that – you saw that one spirit-duplicated fanzine, where clearly he had no access to – well, unless it was an artistic choice – he had no access to a typewriter. So he got himself some Ditto masters – or spirit masters, whatever you call them – and he did it by hand. You could, back then. And indeed, you could do stuff by hand on Gestetner stencils as well. I've got an actual

Cover and page 1 of *Macabre* issue 1, December 1939, edited by James P. Rathbone in Edinburgh. *Macabre* is not only the first fanzine to emerge from Scotland, it is also an extremely rare example of a carbonzine – that is, one produced using carbon paper in a manual typewriter. There is an appealing simplicity to this means of production, but the obvious disadvantage is that your maximum print run would be a mere five or six copies, which is why this is the only example Rob is aware of. Only the inner pages are produced this way – the cover appears to be block printed.

A related phenomenon sprang up during the Second World War as SF enthusiasts tried to keep in touch in more restricted conditions. This is *Fan Mail*, a series of chain letters typed up using four carbon papers per letter, producing five copies in total (i.e. including the top copy). Five editors wrote a letter each, and the five batches were themselves passed through five hands, making a total possible readership of 25. The image on the right shows the covering letter of *Fan Mail* issue 3, with addresses of recipients for that particular batch. A more detailed history of *Fan Mail*, plus images of the actual letters, can be found on Rob's website at http://fiawol.org.uk/FanStuff/THEN%20Archive/Fan-Mail/fanmail.htm

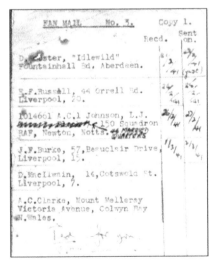

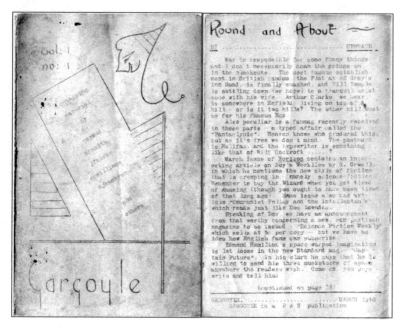

Cover and page 1 of *Gargoyle* issue 1, March 1940, edited by David McIlwain in Liverpool. *Gargoyle* was produced using the hectograph (or hecto) printing process, aka gelatin duplication or jellygraph. This is the last of the four main printing methods Rob mentions that were available to early fanzine producers.

The hecto process involves the transfer of a master copy, prepared with special inks, to a pan of gelatin or a gelatin pad pulled tight on a metal frame. 'Hecto' means a hundred, referring to the fact that you can get around one hundred decent copies at a time, which is enough for most fanzines. The great advantage of this method is that you can produce a reasonable amount of copies in your own home without having to buy an expensive Gestetner or Banda machine. The chemicals required are fairly easily available and not expensive, but the process is more complicated than the other technologies. However, some people might see that as a bonus, especially those who like to develop and print their own photographs, for example. For those prepared to put in the time and effort, this is just as viable a process now as it was eighty years ago.

Eagle-eyed readers may have noticed that *Gargoyle*'s editor, David McIlwain, was one of the recipients of *Fan Mail* issue 3, illustrated on the previous page. He later produced a zine called *Jen*, which lasted two issues – the second of which was entirely in Esperanto!

original somewhere or other of an ordinary wax stencil that some-body has done a hand-illustration on, which you could do, you know, because you had the tools to do it.

Yeah, I saw some of them when I was using the Gestetner, it was my father and his friend produced the village magazine, and there were little sort of magnetic brushes that you'd use to clean up the stencils before they were ... They were kind of baked in, like, a grill, weren't they?

Yeah, somewhere around here, I've no idea where, I've actually got – I've still got a set of stylae for doing wax stencils. And indeed, some-thing I did hang on to – basically, because smell is a powerful sense of nostalgia, so every now and again, I take this [showing me a small bottle] to conventions, I go, you know, 'Remember Gestetners?' I pull this out and they go, 'Oh, great!' Have a sniff. Actually, it doesn't smell that different from nail varnish. I always say to people, if you can get hold of stencils, and you don't have stencil correction fluid, just buy some cheap nail varnish from a shop.

[Sniffing the bottle] Yeah, you're right ...

It's not that different. I'm sure the formulation is a bit different, because nail varnish would probably be a bit thick.

[Reeling from the effects] Blimey!

That's just for correcting mistakes.

But the Gestetner would be the best quality?

Oh yeah, yeah.

But I mean, at that time, was it like buying a small car?

They were incredibly expensive, yeah. You were talking about ... You'd have to spend a month's salary, minimum, to get it. They were very, very expensive. Most of us who had them, later, we had used ones, secondhand ones.

Would you have one for a group? Like, would a group say 'Shall we all chip in for a Gestetner?', or something?

It depends on how they got hold of them. Because these were busi-

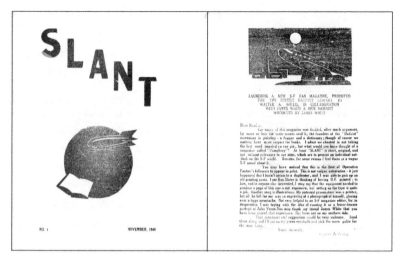

Cover and page 1 of *Slant* issue 1, November 1948, edited by Walter A. Wallis in Belfast. This zine represents a fifth distinct printing technology, which is that of letterpress. This is actually the earliest method of printing text, having been developed by Johannes Gutenberg in the fifteenth century, and it involves inking blocks of type and printing them directly onto paper. It was the chief method of printing books for most of their history, but as editor Wallis notes on the page shown here, 'I may say that the equipment needed to produce a page of this size is not expensive, but setting up the type is quite a job.'

---

ness machines, sometimes you could get them when the company upgraded to a better one. They'd either give you or flog you the old one, cheap. That was one way of doing it. When I got hold of my 466 – which was that machine [pointing to brochure] – which was the first one I had, which is a beautiful machine – it was essentially brand new, but I got it from a used shop, because they'd stopped making them. Remember, they were getting out of the whole – these things were becoming obsolete now. So I got it in the eighties and I used it into the early nineties, and it was basically brand new.

And that's what you did Epsilon on?

Yeah, yeah. Basically it was a used . . . well, a junk shop, in essence. I went in there – well, I couldn't believe it: 'It's brand new!'

And you got it for a really decent price?

Yeah. What was it – fifty quid, maybe? Something like that.

And at that time you could still get all the stencils and stuff . . .

Oh yeah, because there was still an installed user base of business-es that were still using them. It wasn't until they gradually got rid of them all that they stopped making the stencils. I'm told that there's apparently some small manufacturer in Japan, I think, has started doing small runs of stencils.

Well, I was going to say, I was wondering about that, because you'll get just enough demand, won't you? Like what's happened with film, they've started producing more film –

Vinyl!

Yeah, and vinyl.

They junked all those vinyl-producing machines, and then vinyl regained in popularity.

Absolutely.

And there isn't the pressing capacity now that they'd like to meet demand. Because they got rid of all the machines! And it was the same with us, we got rid of all the duplicators.

So, before we leave the duplication, and the technology –

In the seventies, of course, Xerox machines came along. But the early ones were really crap at doing large areas of black. So therefore you'd always get washed-out areas, it was really peculiar. In fact I may have an example here, let's have a look . . . So you had to be careful . . . about . . . Is it that one? Let's have a look . . .

I know what you mean, actually, uh . . .

Well, you've seen them, yeah. Ah, here we are: I made a point of not filling in the blacks – that was black originally – again, self-portrait . . . It didn't print at all. So the very early Xerox machines were rubbish. But by the time you got to 1980, they would do it perfectly. So therefore that point was the point at which the old duplicators were doomed.

But that was the other thing I was wondering, because when I start-ed doing a fanzine, although I did the first one on the Gestetner just because I had access to it, what most people would have done

BANANA WINGS 77 | November 2021

Cover of *Bob* issue 4, October 1992, edited by Ian Sorensen in Hamilton and produced on a photocopier (aka xerox). Photocopying is a dry process that uses electrostatic charges on a light-sensitive photoreceptor to transfer powdered toner onto paper and fix it using heat. It was developed as a working process by 1959, but it was only around the mid-1970s that cost and availability made it a viable option for fanzine producers. It's still a good option for zines produced in very low runs, especially if you have access to an office copier. The downside is that at some point you inevitably leave the original in the copier. Mortification ensues when your colleagues find it, and you can never show your face in the building again.

Cover of *Banana Wings* issue 77, November 2021, edited by Claire Brialey and Mark Plummer, and printed and bound by a commercial litho printer. Litho printing is an offset printing process developed in the late eighteenth century, originally based on the mutual repugnance of oil and water. It involves more sophisticated machinery than stencil duplication and other methods, so the drawback has always been the cost of paying a commercial printer. The early zines that used this method, such as *Operation Fantast* (1949), appear to be more like semipro publications, reflecting the cost involved. But as the technology developed, litho printing from a high street printer became a realistic option for fanzine producers, and by the 1990s it would have been the best option in terms of both quality and cost for runs of about 50 and above.

is gone to either a photocopier or a print shop that did a short run and just got them done litho printed but for quite a low price – but I don't know when those print shops started.

Now – you need to go to ... a website by ... what's his name? Dez Skinn. Because Dez Skinn was somebody who was involved in comics fanzines in the sixties. And the things about comics fanzines, far more than SF fanzines: they need images. SF fans, we don't care, but if you're talking about comics you have to have images. So therefore they needed a means of producing images that was cheap. And there were the print shops back in the late sixties or early seventies – no, sixties – they came up with paper plates that you could do short-run litho on. So it was very cheap, but again, limited. But by limited we mean a couple of hundred – for a lot of commercial purposes, no use. Fanzines? Perfect. So that's why comics fanzines started using them. Again, there's a whole slew about that particular duplication on Dez Skinn's site.

And roughly when did the comics fanzines start?

1960s. Well, no; there's two ways of looking at this. In the 1950s, there was EC Comics fandom in the US, which was specifically devoted to EC Comics. They're the ones that Dr Wertham went after with his *Seduction of the Innocent*, that brought in the Comics Code et cetera, and basically destroyed EC Comics. Except for, the one thing that EC Comics did do, which was *Mad*. Which they then turned into *Mad* magazine, and it kept on going. So that was the end of that particular fandom because EC Comics went away. And then in the early sixties, a guy called Dr Jerry Bails started producing a fanzine devoted to superheroes. And he called it *Alter Ego*.

And that's all Marvel and DC, is it?

Yeah, exactly. He started doing it, and then somebody called Roy Thomas was brought on board as a co-editor, and that started the whole thing rolling there. And that was about '61, I think. Again, we were slower over here, it was about '67 before the first fanzines came out over here.

And just briefly, while we're digressing onto non-SF stuff, one of the very interesting things in your archive is your box of Michael

Moorcock fanzines. It's very interesting because, as you were show-ing me, he did possibly – *probably* – the first British music fanzines –

The earliest I'm aware of – as I say, I can't state for sure that this was the first, because I'm not familiar enough with the field, but yeah, it's the earliest I've found, let's put it that way. From the mid-fifties.

Yeah. And that was *Jazz Fan*, and then that became *The Rambler*.

I can't remember which way round – either *The Rambler* became *Jazz Fan* or *Jazz Fan* became *The Rambler*.

I think it was *Jazz Fan* became *The Rambler*, the chronology makes sense with music history as well.

Basically he just kept the numbering up and changed the title. Fair enough!

And he also did one on Burroughs, and he seemed to be doing them on whatever took his fancy.

Yeah, he was a big fan of Edgar Rice Burroughs. As indeed lots of people were.

Oh, I assumed that was William Burroughs! Okay, that makes sense: Edgar Rice Burroughs.

Who, basically . . . I mean, I make a point in my book of saying that, while Mary Shelley is generally regarded as the start of respectable SF, there's a far more disreputable tradition that basically started in the pulps, and it started with Edgar Rice Burroughs. His Mars books are basically the source of everything that came afterwards.

Yeah. Well, I'm glad you got on to that, because that was actually one of the things in the little book that I didn't bring with me, but I wanted to sort of get on to how this connects with the history of the actual literature, science fiction literature. Because on the Wikipedia page, if you read the history of it, it goes right back to Lucian in the second century AD.

I think that's bollocks, personally!

But it does say a lot of people say *Frankenstein* is the first real SF novel.

Well, it's the first thing that's recognisably science fiction. It's recognisably a science fiction story, because she's using – fair enough, not *real* science – but she's using a scientific approach, kind of, to what she's doing. It's about reanimating – so, yeah, it's the first thing that's recognisably – because some people say, back in sixteen something or other, somebody wrote a story about somebody flying to the moon, being pulled by a chariot pulled by swans. That's not science fiction! The fact that it's got travel to the moon doesn't make it science fiction.

But, I mean, it seems like there were sort of sporadic works that could be considered science fiction in the Victorian era, but as a genre it really started early twentieth century. Would that be fair?

Well – yeah, I mean, as I say, the first thing that could recognisably be called SF is *Frankenstein*, Mary Shelley. Then you've got Wells and Verne with their stuff, which is pre-twentieth century – well, the early stuff is pre-twentieth century. And they were called scientific romances back then. But science fiction *genre* – as a recognisable *genre* – started, basically, with *Amazing Stories*, 1926.

Yeah, so this was, like, magazine publishing, of short stories?

Oh, yeah. For a long time, for a long time, that was science fiction. There weren't science fiction books. Because the first science fiction books, I think, were post-war. And they were basically collections of stories that had first appeared in the magazines. So there weren't science fiction books, as such, other than the scientific romances of Wells and Verne, et cetera. Hence the reason they were considered, 'Yes, this is, kind of, our stuff', but it's *not*, if you see what I mean.

Did those magazines just spring out of nowhere? Or . . . how would that have come about? I know there was a big short story market, and the likes of F. Scott Fitzgerald were . . .

The sheer number of pulp magazines that were being published by then – and they were called pulp magazines because they were printed on cheap pulp paper – was *vast*, in the US. Because, remember, no television – I think this may even have been mostly pre-radio – and people were consuming pulp fiction in vast quantities. There were, you know, westerns, romances, anything you can think of.

Yeah. Crime.

Yes. Aircraft pulps were really big back then, because remember, aircraft was new technology, and people were really fascinated by this. There were all manner of magazines with the air heroes in them. You know, people who would go and – well, the closest thing we have in this country, probably, that remained, was Biggles. He basically started in that era as well.

Yeah. But what I'm curious about is why it seems like it's unique to SF that they created this fandom. I mean that didn't happen with the westerns and the crime pulps, did it?

Exactly. I'm not entirely sure why. I actually think a lot of it came about – it's the old thing about banding together when you get mocked. Because, again, if you were interested in Sherlock Holmes, fine; if you were interested in romance, fine; if you were interested in westerns, fine; but if you thought that men were one day going to fly to the moon you were a nutter. Seriously, people were considered mad.

Covers of *Jazz Fan* issue 5, March 1957, and *The Rambler* issue 10, January 1958, both edited by Michael Moorcock in Norbury, southwest London. Moorcock's are the earliest music zines that we are aware of. It's interesting that in this issue of *Jazz Fan* Moorcock was already using the shortened form 'zine' to describe his publications. Rob also uses the terms 'zine' and 'fanzine' interchangeably in *Epsilon*, confounding my assumption that 'zine' was a much more recent usage.

So that sort of prejudice was around from the very start?

Oh yeah. So it's basically grouping together for mutual support. I think if it hadn't been for that, perhaps it wouldn't have happened.

And so, getting back to the fanzines, the very early ones were discussing that literature primarily.

Very much so. They were what we call 'sercon' fanzines, which means 'serious and constructive'. As opposed to the 'fannish' ones, which are basically about fandom. So the fannish versus sercon, if you come across those terms, that's basically what the distinction is.

Yeah. And at some point the fannish ones developed out of the sercon ones, roughly when would you say that happened?

Early 1950s.

Okay, that took quite a while, then.

It did, yeah. It's not that there weren't the occasional ... I mean, in this country, if I was going to say what the first article in a fanzine that could be considered fannish as opposed to sercon was, it was probably a report on the Second Convention by William F. Temple. He was the first person to actually introduce humour. Because prior to that, good God the fanzines were po-faced and serious! SF was far too serious to joke about. And he was the first person to actually make fun of people. And it went down very well. But he was a bit of an outlier. There were one or two people doing that, but it wasn't until the early 1950s that it really took off, and that the fannish fanzines largely supplanted the sercon ones. I think through most of the fifties, in fact, there were very few sercon fanzines published at all.

Another thing I wanted to just ask you about SF culture, if you like, and about the fanzines, is that at some point it became ... the way you'd distribute, you'd ask for 'the usual'.

Ah, yes!

I like that phrase. And, you know, that seems unique to SF fanzines as well.

Yes, it is. As far as I can tell, almost everybody else sells them.

So, briefly to say what the usual is . . .

The usual means . . . it's usually a trade or letter of comment. For the most part. Or sometimes they just say 'show of interest'. I mean, you send them to your buddies anyway.

And it's very formalised, isn't it? Because 'letter of comment' is often abbreviated to 'LoC', and so you get this kind of jargon that comes in.

Yeah. Any group, over time, is going to develop jargon. Basically, 'fanzine' started as an SF jargon. Because that was a term that was coined by a guy called Louis Russell Chauvenet in 1940. Before that they were 'fanmags'.

So the word 'fan' existed prior to that, but do you know where the word 'fan' came from? Is it 'fanatic'?

Well, yeah, everybody assumes it's short for 'fanatic'. You'd have to look into the etymology of it. I think the first person to apply it to SF fans was probably Hugo Gernsback, in his magazines, because he was the editor of *Amazing* and *Wonder*. So I think he was the first person to do it, but I'm not entirely sure.

And obviously you weren't reading the ones in the thirties and the forties when they came out –

Not born till 1954, so no! So it's the seventies for me, obviously.

Okay, right, so you first started reading them in, what, early seventies?

Yes. By then, whereas in earlier generations SF was the magazines, when I came along, of course, paperbacks had arrived. So therefore, I paid no attention to the magazines and basically just bought – you know, it was the paperbacks for me. So that was an actual generational split there, if you like.

What sort of writers, just to name a few? Asimov?

Yeah, all the basic ones. Have a look at my bookshelves.

Yeah. Well, I can see all sorts of things, including some non-SF stuff.

Well, yeah, there's the fantasy stuff as well, because there was always a

Cover of *Rastus Johnson's Cakewalk* issue 6, June 1994, edited by Greg Pickersgill, produced on a home laser printer.

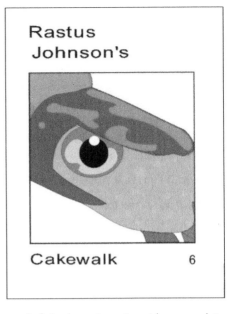

Our review of printing technologies ends with the digital options of inkjet and laser printers, which are distinct from litho in that they do not require a plate from which to offset. As with the old Gestetners, using your own home printer has the main advantage of convenience. A laser printer is reasonably cost-efficient; an inkjet printer much less so (as Arlo of *Pint-Sized Punk* notes in Chapter 20). But commercial online printers now use digital technologies for low runs, even in full colour, at a unit cost low enough to make them probably the best option for most zines. At time of writing, one can get a full-colour 24-page zine printed in a run of 50 with a unit cost of about £1.20 per copy, which goes down to under 80p per copy for a run of 100. Some would call this progress . . . as for me, I say *bring back the Gestetner!*

---

lot of crossover between the fantasy stuff and the SF. Any number of writers wrote both.

Yeah. Presumably you were probably reading comics as well?

Yes.

But when would you have first seen a fanzine? And how would that have come about?

How I got into fandom was, in 1974 – or was it '73? Whatever, there was a magazine printed in this country called *Science Fiction Monthly*. It was this big tabloid-size SF magazine. It's the first SF magazine I bought. It was very very atypical, because it was basically a poster magazine, but in between the glossy poster magazines there were standard newsprint pages put in there, and they printed SF, and they also had a column on fandom. Which I'd never heard of before. And they advertised conventions. And the first one I didn't go to, but the next one was '75, which was in Coventry, and I thought: 'Yeah, I want to go to that.' So I went to it. Again, didn't know anybody, went there as a single individual ... They tended to pair you up with other single people who didn't know anybody, but I'm relatively garrulous, so I got talking to people. They had a fanzine table, and I bought a couple of fanzines, and they had addresses of other people in, so I wrote off for other fanzines, and they sent me fanzines, and it just kind of snowballed from there.

Yeah. And you were nineteen, twenty?

I was twenty at the time.

And what happens at a convention? Are there, like, speeches and things?

Well, you have a guest of honour. And the guest of honour will do a speech at some point or other. But then there are panels, where people talk about various aspects. There's usually films there. Occasionally people will put on a play, et cetera, et cetera, but it's mostly, I would say, panels, more than anything else.

But a lot of ... uh ... drinking ... and socialising?

Oh yeah, a lot of drinking and socialising. Again, the first one I went to, not knowing anybody, I was there for the science fiction. By the time the second and third ones came along I was there for the socialising.

But if you produced a fanzine, presumably you'd bring along a load of copies and hand them out to everybody?

Yes. Because it saved on postage. And the bane of fanzine producers was always postage, which was always too much bloody money!

Yeah, yeah. Well, some people, in the eighties, when I was doing mine, would actually soap stamps. You know? So you could reuse them.

One thing I did – when was that? Would have been the ... eighties. I did a joint fanzine with somebody in America, and what we did, which I think were the only people who ever tried it, was that we would alternate who did the fanzines and typed up the stencils, and if you did it for that month, you'd run off the copies for your country, then you'd roll up the stencils and send them across to him, and he would run off copies for his country.

I see.

We have slightly different paper sizes, so you had to be a bit careful, because they had American quarto and we had regular quarto. But, again, it worked for a bit. Until Ted got arrested and thrown in jail, it worked pretty well!

Oh really? Did he really?

Yeah!

Is that Ted White?

That is Ted White. My co-editor was Ted White. And he wrote a series of articles at the time, 'Letters from Jail', which are actually very entertaining, and then fairly recently he collected them into a book. But yeah, so, he got basically arrested for dealing dope.

Oh, is that right?

Yeah. That's it, he wasn't doing hard drugs, it was basically for his local community. He kind of was their wholesaler. And somebody objected to this and ratted him out, and he ended up in jail.

I want to get on now to talking about your own fanzine, Epsilon. I can see how, having had your first exposure to the whole scene, you then wanted to start one. So, Epsilon – just to briefly do an overview – there were 18 issues between 1976 and 1985. When you produced that very first one, first of all, had you been thinking about it for a long time, about how to produce a fanzine?

No. I did it because it's what everybody else did. It was my way of getting involved. But I didn't really have a clue what I was doing, hence the reason – although it looks very nice – and it cost a fortune, because I didn't realise how much litho was – so that was the first and last one that I ever did [i.e. entirely printed litho] . . . so . . .

And when you say litho, what would that involve? I mean, that involves going to . . .

A proper printer.

A proper printer, yeah.

You give him your pages, and a lot of money! And they print it up for you.

Yeah. I mean, these days – you know, it's really cheap.

I know it is. It wasn't back then. *Jesus* it wasn't!

I mean, can you give me a rough idea in today's money? What would you say one issue would have cost you?

To produce that, as I recall, was more than I earned in a week. Hence the reason – I went a bit mad, which is why I never did it again. But having said that I was only earning £18 a week back then anyway.

Yeah. And what were you doing, while we're talking about that?

Oh, by profession I was an engineering draughtsman.

Oh, okay. And that's what you were for your whole career?

Yeah. I started off in Guest, Keen & Nettlefolds, which was steel, down in south Wales. And I ended working for the Whitechapel Bell Foundry. People always say 'Oh, the Bell Foundry! Really cool!' Because of course it *was*, until it went tits up, the oldest manufacturing company in the country. We had some customers who'd been a customer of ours for centuries. We didn't think in terms of years. Good Lord no!

So you were professionally a draughtsman –

Oh yeah, yeah. But an *engineering* draughtsman, I wasn't doing – you know, the art stuff was just me.

But do you think there's a sort of crossover in being a draughtsman and having an interest in – because one thing that's apparent from looking at Epsilon is that you do like drawing, and sometimes –

Well, you say that, actually what I really always liked was writing. I *love* writing.

Well, I mean, that's apparent as well . . .

I always get more of a sense of accomplishment from writing than I ever do from art. I haven't actually drawn anything in years. Literally, I just stopped doing it.

Most of the fanzines have a little bit of art content, though.

Most fanzines had a cover. In the States they tended to put more art inside. In this country, we'd have a cover, and then we tended to be a bit niggardly about putting art inside because it was a pain in the bum – again, if you're doing a wax stencil, what you could do – you could either use a stylus and do it on the stencil directly, or you get lots of individual bits of art, you get a single electro-stencil of it, and then you could cut out a hole in the wax stencil and you could paste in the bits of the electro-stencil. So therefore you'd have these kind of hybrid stencils that you'd use.

I see.

In fact there's a whole set of . . . I think it's online as well . . . there was something called *Duplicating without Tears!* [archived at https://fanac. org/fanzines/Duplicating_Without_Tears/index.html], and there was another one in the seventies – because that was the fifties, *Duplicating without Tears!* – where it was people collecting the knowledge that they'd acquired about how to do this stuff. You know, all the short cuts, et cetera, et cetera, how you could save money. So there are some fanzines out there that are specifically about duplicating. Which was very useful.

So, getting back to Epsilon, from reading it myself, and coming from totally outside the world of science fiction, the thing I'm struck by is how there is almost no mention of science fiction in there at all!

Exactly.

And it's almost like fanzines I was reading in the nineties . . . there are some where they're writing ostensibly about music, but the ones I really like are where they digress onto other things as well.

Exactly, yeah.

What really strikes me is you wouldn't have to be an SF fan to enjoy an SF zine.

No, and in fact later on we'd have people who would find fandom and weren't SF readers, who would actually become involved in fandom for the sake of fandom. Who actually didn't have much interest in science fiction at all. There weren't very many of them, because –

Covers of *Epsilon* issues 1–9 (this page) and 10–18 (opposite page), representing the entire run edited by Rob Hansen between 1976 and 1985. Cover art is by Rob, with assistance from Harry Bell for issues 11–13 and from Dan Steffan for issues 14 and 16.

They probably wouldn't have heard about it.

Exactly. The doorway into fandom, obviously, is SF, because that's how you hear about it. But occasionally it would happen.

It's funny how there's a curious world where you think it's all talking about travel to other worlds, and actually, it's really about the train journey to a convention and what you ate, and what you drank in the pub.

This is why, whenever I read in the press, somebody writing about SF fanzines who has never read an SF fanzine, they always get it wrong. They say, 'Of course, SF fanzines are full of amateur fiction and poetry.' No they're bloody not!

No, no.

That's not true. I mean, yeah, there are some that do that, but it's very rare.

I mean, just from a quick overview, almost looking at random, some of the things I was seeing, there's this by Ted White [in Epsilon issue 18], he's talking about 'the philosophies of house wiring' between the US and the UK, the differences . . .

Again, he came over for our wedding – because, weirdly enough, it wasn't me that he knew really well, it's my wife. Because she's a fan from the Washington area. So he came over for the wedding, and that's when we decided to do the fanzine together.

And that's a different fanzine – is that Crank? Which is mentioned in the last issue of Epsilon. That was like a more business-like thing, was it? Because I read that it was monthly . . .

Yeah, well – yeah, except that we only ever did five issues because, as I say, Ted got arrested. But – we were relatively compatible in terms of our views of fandom. Though, as it turned out, not in terms of editing each other's work, which we almost came to blows over! But other than that, that was to get around postage. That's the one where we were mailing the stencils back and forth.

What would make you want to have done it as a collaboration rather than just doing your own fanzine?

I'd never collaborated on a fanzine before. I thought it was time I did this.

Just following the chronology – because *Epsilon* covered roughly a decade, mid-seventies to mid-eighties – and then you did a few issues of *Crank*. But was that the end of your fanzine editing career?

No. Because after that – I then went into APAs [pronounced 'appers'] for a while – I told you what APAs were, Amateur Press Associations – there are several of those, and I used to do APA zines for a whole bunch of them.

Could we briefly say what it was? Because you told me in the basement, but we haven't got it on the thing.

Right. Amateur Press Associations started in the Victorian period. What they are is, they were basically amateur journalism groups. And the way they worked is that there would be a set number of people in a given Amateur Press Association, each of whom would put together an amateur magazine. What we'd now call a fanzine, but they didn't call them that then; and there are ways in which they aren't fanzines, but anyway – so they put these together – they'd print off a number of copies equal to the number of people in the Amateur Press Association. They'd send these in to a central editor. He would then collate up packages of all the individual fanzines people had sent in, to send back – so you'd get back a set of a fanzine by everybody in the Amateur Press Association. And so they're self-enclosed things, as opposed to general fanzines that you'd send out to all manner of people. And the first fannish APA was 1937: FAPA, the Fantasy Amateur Press Association, which was started by Donald Wollheim in New York. And that's still going today, so it's been going for a while.

And how did it come about that you went from doing your own fanzine to doing that?

Well – just circumstances. Just a question of what you feel like doing at a given point, you know? And then, uh . . . while this was going on I'd also started looking into the history of British fandom. Because the Americans had a set of books covering quite a few of their earlier decades of fandom. In the 1950s, Sam Moskovitz came out with *The Immortal Storm* – it was serialised first in a fanzine – but that was about

1930s fandom. And then in the 1960s, Harry Warner Jr came up with *All Our Yesterdays*, which is about the 1940s in fandom. And then in the seventies he came up with *A Wealth of Fable*, which is about the fifties. So, I read all these, and the one that actually interested me the most is *that* one.

That's *All Our Yesterdays*.

Yeah. I mean, fair enough, he tried to cover fandom across the world. But he could only do so in the most glancing fashion. So I'd read tantalising bits and pieces about British fandom, but it wasn't . . . not to the extent that I wanted to. So therefore I then started to . . .

Do what he was doing but in more detail, for Britain?

Yeah. Far more detail, yeah. So I started off doing it in fanzines – first of all, it started off as an article. Then that article was expanded and printed for the 1987 Worldcon as a booklet. And then afterwards, I thought 'I can expand this into something bigger.' So therefore, over the next few years, I put it out basically as a part work. There were four bits, all told – there's the fourth one, for instance – that's over a hundred pages. So that kept me busy for the next few years.

And you were producing this yourself . . .

Oh, yeah.

This is lovely . . . on coloured paper . . .

And again . . . by that point I also had a proper golf ball Selectric typewriter. Because, again, *that* is the typewriter there that I produced my early fanzines on, which is actually a manual, and the thing with manuals is you never get quite the same evenness of letters. You use a Selectric and it's exactly the same pressure for every letter, so it's a lot more even.

Yeah. And you've got different fonts, as well.

Yeah, exactly, you could do that as well, which was useful.

But anyway, you're using your Gestetner to print that yourself, and, uh, *staple* it yourself?

Yep! Collated it myself. In fact there's my collating table, because prior to me pulling them off, there were, um – you see these things here? You know, the shelving unit – I basically had strips here, and I had the big – there's one of them there – I had the big ones in, so when I wanted to collate, I'd basically pull them out, stick 'em in, pull that out, stick it down, and there was my collating table! My duplicator was there, I'd run them off, stick 'em on there, and just go along collating.

So it all happened in here.

Yeah. That's the way I used to do it. So that was that. And then eventually – so that was . . .

'93.

'93, yeah, '93. And then it went to an online version for a long time.

This is what I was wondering – so you kind of became aware of the internet pretty early in its, uh . . .

Oh yeah, yeah, I mean I taught myself basic HTML in 1996, I think. So that's pretty early.

This is what I was thinking about the SF world, that it was probably a very early adopter of the internet.

Oh, very early. Yep.

Did an awful lot of the print immediately go online?

No, it was gradual. And, indeed, some people still like print fanzines [holding up a 2021 print SF zine].

Yeah. Good for them!

Oh, yeah, definitely. But, as I say, the vast majority now, if you go to eFanzines [https://efanzines.com] you'll see that it's probably a hundred to one, maybe? People putting out PDF fanzines online as opposed to paper.

But do you feel like it's an acceptable substitute, or has it lost something?

Well, I think it's definitely lost something. As you were saying, I actually like having the tactile experience of having something to read in my hands.

Exactly.

The thing about PDFs is you can print them off if you wish to do so. So there's that. Because, again, it's a forced format: unlike HTML that kind of flows to fit your screen, PDF – that's it. As you see it – that's how it will print.

I hate reading things on screen. I mean, it's what I do for my job, but I love print.

I mean, I've obviously got an e-reader, because, again, why wouldn't I have? Again, I do e-books. But, again, that's, as much as anything, because . . . *yes*, I could do that [holding up book] – that's the final form of *Then*, which is 2016 – which is, you know . . . you could beat somebody to death with that! That's 400-odd pages there . . .

So that's the culmination of your historical work. Presumably you're writing that in quite a different voice to what you're writing your fanzines in, because it's not full of your jokes and things like that?

No . . . I'm trying to think . . . I don't think there are *any* humorous asides in it. Because that's supposed to be – insofar as it *can* be – a work of history. It should work as a narrative: you should be able to start at the beginning and work your way through it. But also, people are going to dip into it. Again, I had to come up with an index, which – Jesus Christ! Doing an index – and that's a fairly detailed index – it took . . . it's me sitting there with the final version, so that I knew what the pagination was, and just going through for about two months, every night after work – and eventually . . . I'm glad I did it – oh, I wouldn't want to do it again!

2

MARK PERRY

interviewed by Hamish Ironside

Sniffin' Glue is the most legendary zine of them all, and its story has been told many times before. But that is not going to stop us from telling it again!

In the traditional telling, the story of *Sniffin' Glue* is bound up with the story of punk, which is another story that has been told many times, and in fact one that has been embellished, rationalised, commodified, Disneyfied, and neatly packaged in TV documentaries and glossy magazines, to the point where it is as familiar (i.e. boring) as the story of Elvis or the Beatles.

It would be hard to tell the story of *Sniffin' Glue* without mentioning punk at all, but there is a lot more to it than that. To cover the basic facts as briefly as possible: the entire run of *Sniffin' Glue* appeared in the course of just over one year, from July 1976 to August/September 1977. It was founded by Mark Perry (always credited as Mark P), and the first few issues were entirely written by Mark. As it grew (which happened rapidly), a few other people contributed writing or photos. The zine appeared monthly, and there were twelve full issues, plus a four-page issue 3½ (dated 28 September 1976) to tie in with the 100 Club Punk Festival, and an unnumbered *Sniffin' Snow* issue for Christmas 1976, making a total run of fourteen issues. (The introduction to issue 12 intro says there are 'fifteen if ya count 3½, 7½ and Sniffin' Snow', but Mark confirms that this mention of issue 7½ is a complete red herring. It was a hoax to bamboozle the collectors, who were evidently already nurturing their archives.)

Mark now lives in Penzance, and I took the opportunity of a relaxing of Covid restrictions in October 2020 to take the amazing train ride down to interview him at the Longboat Inn on a very cold and wet afternoon. I had followed my usual approach of doing a little research, but not too much; which is to say that I knew the outlines of the *Sniffin'* *Glue* story, but had not actually seen a complete issue, and apart from the covers I had seen online, the only actual content I had read was a very entertaining interview with Subway Sect by Steve Mick (Stephen Micalef), who was Mark's earliest contributor to the zine.

Since then I have read the whole run of *Sniffin' Glue*, thanks to Mark having very kindly lent me *Sniffin' Glue: The Essential Punk Accessory*, a book published by Sanctuary Publishing in 2000, which reprints all fourteen issues in their entirety, on suitably coarse paper. The book also has a substantial preliminary section in which Mark gives the story from his own perspective, in conversation with Danny Baker, a schoolfriend of Mark's who had contributed to the last few issues of the fanzine.

Reading the fanzine itself makes the stale story of punk seem fresh again. It has all the attributes of a great zine from the very first issue, being driven by youthful exuberance, forthright opinion, anti-establishment ethos and a special disdain for the weekly music papers. The six-page issue 1 begins with 'Mark P's Sniff':

> The Ramones were in London this month and to realy get into the fact we've put this little mag/newsletter together. It's a bit amatuer at the moment but it is the first go isn't it,I mean we can't be Nick Kents over night can we.

The Ramones were the main band that prompted Mark to do the first issue, but Blue Öyster Cult receive the next largest amount of column inches, and the list of other bands he hopes to cover in future issues includes the likes of Nazz/Runt, the Mothers of Invention and Eddie and the Hot Rods, alongside the more expected names of the Sex Pistols and Stranglers. Indeed, another interesting aspect of reading through the issues is to track how the punk 'scene' was happening alongside other scenes; most notably reggae, but also the tail end of pub rock and the beginning of heavy metal. However, even in the first

Mark Perry in the Longboat Inn, Penzance, October 2020.

issue Mark is writing, on the final page, 'Most British rock is past it but the punk scene isn't. Let's build our own bands up instead of drooling over the NY scene.'

A great deal happened in the year of *Sniffin' Glue*, and more than 40 years later it stills feels exciting to read about it in Mark's original words. As he admits, though, his heart was not really in it for the last couple of issues, by which time he was also involved in running a record label, and had formed Alternative TV, the band that has represented his main activity up to the present day (their early recordings have been packaged in an excellent four-CD set by Cherry Red, under the title *Viva La Rock'n'Roll*, of which the fourth disc is Mark's solo album, *Snappy Turns* – my personal favourite). It's true that the last two issues show a marked downturn in quality, and the enthusiasm of Mark P is largely replaced by somewhat tiresome diatribes from Danny Baker, pieces by random contributors not directly involved with the zine, and a profusion of advertisements. Even though Mark's interests were elsewhere by this point, his contribution to issue 11 (a review of *Rock'n'Roll with the Modern Lovers*) is by far the best thing in it.

Even the Sanctuary book is now something of a collector's item – a lot of copies are on sale online, but expect to pay at least £50. As for the original issues, you are unlikely to find any of them on sale for less than £100, and issue 1 will probably be well over £1000. A complete set of all 14 issues was on sale at the Bonhams 'Punk × Culture' auction just a few days after I met Mark, with a reserve price of £10,000–12,000 (although it didn't sell). Mark himself has no original copies of the fanzine, which perhaps serves as an indication that he was just taking it day by day, without any long-term plan, and just enjoying the experience for as long as it was enjoyable.

I began by asking him about the production side of the fanzine. The first issue of *Sniffin' Glue* was produced on a very small scale, which is always said to be a run of 50 copies, although I had my doubts about how accurate that might be. By the final issue it had grown to a circulation of around 15,000, but still looking very homemade, and determined to avoid *selling out* at all costs, despite the ever-increasing number of adverts.

We didn't use proper printers, so we used to just use photocopiers wherever we could. My girlfriend did some in work, and then I used to do some – because I used to work for a bank at the time – and then a mate would do some, you know? Or there used to be some of these sort of high street xerox places. Some were on shiny paper, all sorts – what I'm saying is there are probably lots of different versions of that first issue. So if someone has got an issue number one . . . I mean, there's probably some doubt about whether it's the real deal. It was always very easy for someone to – because it was always stapled in the top left corner, it was never bound properly –

Is that right?

Single sheets stapled in the top left, it was never a proper bound magazine.

So you always, the whole run, that's the way you did it?

The whole run was that. And someone said 'Why don't we do it as a magazine?' We said 'No, we'll stick to that, that's our style.' And I knew I was going to end it after [issue] 12 anyway. What I'm trying to say is, anybody at the time could have taken that apart and made other copies of it. So if someone's – especially those early ones, there's no guarantee it's actually a real, authentic issue. I probably wouldn't even be able to tell. There's no way of telling. Anyone could have done it, you know? It's truly a – I know I'm talking about me own work here, but it's truly like a DIY, street magazine.

Which is what fanzines should be. But I suppose – my first question about it was going to be, you know, what gave you the idea? Because as far as I'm aware, there wasn't anything like that in existence at the time, so it was quite unusual just to – or did you know of anyone who was already doing things like that?

Yeah, I knew fanzines before that. At the time there was somebody doing, I believe, a reggae fanzine. There were fanzines – I think there was an old rockabilly one that I'd seen . . . because I used to go to this shop to buy a lot of my records – I was really into underground music at the time – and I used to go to a shop called Rock On records. One of their shops was in Camden, and another one was in Newport Court in Soho, which is the one I used to go to. And they used to have a lot of these little alternative fanzines – rockabilly, reggae, blues, that type of thing. There was a British one – a guy from Scotland called Brian Hogg used to do a fanzine called *Bam Balam*. And that used to be about sixties bands and that, and he used to have, like, discographies of bands like the Kinks. So I knew what they looked like. I knew the form, if you like. I knew the form. And what really inspired me directly, I think it was *Punk* magazine, which was a magazine that came out of New York. I think the first issue of *Punk* – I think, you'd have to look it up – was probably late '74, '75.

Because the punk scene in New York started a bit earlier than the UK one. I mean, Patti Smith, her first album come out in '75. Then you had the Ramones, Television . . . So *Punk* had already, I think, by the time I did anything, they'd already had about three or four issues out. Anyway, when I heard about the Ramones and started getting into what I considered, and other people were talking about, this new music – punk or whatever – that was my – because I wasn't a musician of any sort – that was just an idea I had.

What age would you have been in '76?

I was nineteen. I said to the guy in there [Rock On], I said, 'How many people are doing magazines about the Ramones and all of that?' And he said, 'Oh, there's only this New York one.' I said, 'What about in the UK?' 'Oh, no, no one's doing one.' I said, 'It's a shame.' He said, 'Well, why don't you do one yourself?' It was a sort of light-bulb moment! So I did. I went home –

And did you do the first issue all on your own?

Yeah. Totally on my own. I mean, it was only about six pages, as I say. I had an old children's typewriter at home. One of those old ones you got bought for Christmas and never used, sort of thing! I dragged that out, typed away, and . . . the first fanzine was mostly about the Ramones. It was a review of the Ramones first album, plus a review of their first live concert in the UK, which was at the Round-house. July the fourth, 1976! So within a few days after that, by the next week, *Sniffin' Glue* was on the streets. It was on sale in Rock On, the shop that told me to do it. I said, 'I've done this fanzine – are you going to sell it?' And then straight away, they saw it, I gave them about twenty copies, they said, 'Oh, here's some money, go and get some more done.'

As soon as they saw it I think they thought, 'This is a winner!'

Okay, because it says, like, on Wikipedia and everything, there were fifty copies of the first issue . . .

Probably in the end, yeah.

Yeah, but you don't really know, because you would be the only person who could say.

As I say, I wouldn't put it past some of these shops . . . 'We need some more of these' – 'Well, just photocopy that one!'

But you didn't start off thinking 'Right, I'm doing fifty' and then just leave it at that, you did twenty, and then you did another –

Oh no, we just, off the cuff, sort of, you know . . .

So it might not be fifty, it could be . . .

Others could have been . . . I mean, later on, there was a story – actually, Debbie Harry told me this herself, because, once we were established a bit – I know I'm going forward a bit – but once we were established, we became like personalities, everyone wanted to talk to Sniffin' Glue. And Debbie Harry came up to see our offices. Blondie were over here playing. And she said, 'Oh, it's great!' She said, 'I love that you do it on pink paper!' I said, 'Pink paper? What are you talking about?' She said, 'Oh, in New York, Sniffin' Glue is on pink paper.'

Oh, really?

So when I looked into it, there was this bloke called Bleecker Bob who used to run a record shop in New York, and he was a well-known bit of a dodgy dealer, and what he used to do is get Sniffin' Glue and then print off his own ones. On pink paper, some of them! I said [to Debbie Harry], 'We didn't do it on bloody pink paper!' sort of thing . . . Yeah, so that stuff used to happen, this sort of . . . piracy. Bootleg copies, I guess.

I mean, normally, a normal fanzine, people wouldn't go to the trouble, would they? It's cheaper to buy than it is to copy. But I guess . . .

I know. But remember, it took off so quickly – I mean, it's hard for people to get their head around now, the enormity of it. If you cast your mind back – well, you're obviously younger than me, you can't cast your mind back – I take it you're younger than I am . . .

Well, I'm 49. See, I don't remember punk, but . . .

Yeah, so sometimes you have to remind people, the magazines, the main music magazines, they sold a lot of copies. Weekly, NME, Sounds, Melody Maker and Record Mirror, they used to sell, like, 80,000 copies.

Yeah, when I was getting into music in '81, all four were still going then.

That's right, yeah. Well, Sniffin' Glue got written about in those magazines, and within a few months of starting – the first issue came out late July [1976] – by the third or fourth issue – because the first couple of issues we didn't have a photo – by issue 3, the one with the Damned on the front, and then the Clash one – by that time, we'd been in Sounds. They did this round-up of all the punk bands – the Damned, the Clash – and they had Sniffin' Glue! We were included as one of the most, you know – so, of course, suddenly everyone wanted to come to Sniffin' Glue. So all around the country – the UK's not very big, is it? – suddenly everyone wants the Glue, it's the voice of punk. It became that. We became like the spokespeople, if you like. The place to go. If you wanted to know about punk, you had to have Sniffin' Glue. So that's why there was a mad rush to get them.

And it seems like . . . because other people started writing for the magazine as well, so . . .

Yeah, I got a few mates into it. A few schoolmates who were into music and that. And then of course other people – this is the other thing – which I'm sort of proud of, in a way – is that I inspired other people. Like there's a guy, the second UK fanzine, punk fanzine, was a thing called Ripped & Torn. And Tony D [Drayton], he wanted to write for – he come from Glasgow – and he came down, I met him at a gig – again, about September '76, quite early in the punk scene – and he said, 'Oh, I'd really like to write for Sniffin' Glue.' And I told him, I said 'No! Go and do your own fanzine! You're not writing for Sniffin' Glue.' I was just taking the piss out of him, really – some Scottish . . . you know! And a month later he had his own fanzine out. And he still talks about that, they recently did a Ripped & Torn collected edition, and in the thing he said 'Inspired by Mark telling me he didn't want me to [write for his fanzine], "Go out and do your own!"' So you had a lot of that. As soon as people saw how easy it was to produce a magazine, to produce a fanzine, how easy it was to do, you know, a lot of other people started doing it. Within a few months, you had, like, hundreds. It took off, you know?

That was my impression – it was something that worked with punk, because the whole ethos was the same as for forming a band.

Right. It was the perfect music for it. I mean, fanzines have existed in the past. I mean, I don't know how far your research goes, but I believe there were fanzines way back in the early sixties about Marvel comics and that. These comic fans did those sort of things.

They say the actual name 'fanzine' came from, like, science fiction fanzines. And then you're telling me there were these earlier music fanzines, like, Bam Balam and the reggae one . . . but at the same time, if you read about fanzine history now, they always go back to Sniffin' Glue as being the first.

I think it's something about the attitude that we had. I mean, I think one of the problems with a lot of the fanzine people – and I know most of them, you know, especially the early wave of them, like Adrian Thrills who did 48 Thrills, Tony Drayton who did Ripped & Torn, you know, loads of these people – their secret wish was to be writers. And a lot of them did. If you look at the list of contributors to things like Sounds, NME and all that, they were all ex-fanzine people. Like Jon Savage, all that lot, you know – Adrian Thrills ended up writing for the NME. But I had no aspirations for that. I wasn't thinking, 'Well, if I can do a fanzine, maybe the NME will give me a job!' There was that sort of ambition about being a writer with a lot of these fanzines. But with Sniffin' Glue – again, I'm sort of bigging myself up, in a way! But we didn't have that, we had a bit of attitude. Like, we didn't mind slagging people off – we slagged off the Pistols when they needed slagging off. We didn't mind that, we had a bit of – you know what I mean? We didn't sell out in that magazine sense. A good example is when we ended. I mean, we ended at the top of our game. You know, punk was still massive. A lot of fanzines were still going. But we decided to call it a day.

Sniffin' Glue issue 1, July 1976.   *Sniffin' Glue* issue 2, August 1976.

And you said you only ever planned to do twelve issues, so did you think of it like that: 'I'll do this for a year . . .'

I've always been sort of, like – I don't know if it's my background – being true to my belief, never selling out, that sort of thing. And I think events then confirmed my idea about keeping it limited. Because to me, once punk was being written about by *Sounds*, *NME*, as we've described, there was no need for the fanzine anymore. *Sniffin' Glue* was there when it needed to be there. And the last couple of issues, it's just like . . . wanking! It's not important anymore.

Were there not other things that you wanted to write about?

No, not really. By that time, by the time we did issue 12, September '77 or something, I had me band going, Alternative TV; and I was working on a record label, putting records out. So I was . . . when I started *Sniffin' Glue* I was working in a bank. But of course a year later I'm in the music industry. I'm in a band and I run a record label. It wasn't like I didn't want to be involved any more – I was involved. And a lot of it, to tell you the truth, I was up to here with it. Because *Sniffin' Glue* . . . it's alright at first – 'Go to *Sniffin' Glue*, ring Mark P up', you know, 'Ask him what he thinks about this, that and the other' . . . it's like, I don't want

Sniffin' Glue issue 3, September 1976.   *Sniffin' Glue* issue 3½, 26 September 1976.

---

to talk about this any more. You know, you get fed up with . . . this idea of being spokesman, you don't want it after a while. You know, at first it's 'Ooh, I'm in the papers! I'm on telly!' You know . . .

But do you like that there is still continued interest, 40 years later?

Yeah, because now I can say I'm proud of that, because that was my work. That's something I created, so I'm proud that it had such an effect.

Yeah, well you should be.

People are still talking about it, writing about it. Yeah, so now, in retrospect, I look back . . . I'm certainly glad we ended it when we did. Because there's nothing worse – whether you're a band, a magazine – to sort of outstay your welcome. I hate that, I hate bands that do that.

So you were doing about one a month, you did the whole thing over the course of a year, twelve issues – but I saw one cover that was issue 3½ – so does that mean there's really thirteen issues?

Uh, fourteen, because there was a Sniffin' Snow as well. Yeah, so that [pointing to cover in book] was number 3, where we had the first photo and all that, where we had to start using a printer's. Because

Sniffin' Glue issue 4, October 1976.   *Sniffin' Glue* issue 5, November 1976.

---

we couldn't photocopy any more so what we used to do was, pages with photos on, we used to get them printed – we found this printer in Cambridge, of all places – and then the others we used to photocopy. By this time I had my mates helping with me.

I see. Why could you not . . .

Well, to do photographs properly, you obviously had to get them properly printed, you couldn't photocopy them, it'd just look like shit.

Just for quality?

Yeah.

But that seems like a bit of a contradiction to me, because, like . . .

I always say, we weren't trying to look shit, we did the best we could. So when we had photos, it was like, 'Well, let's try . . .' It's a learning process. When people ask me, 'Tell me how to do a fanzine', I say, 'Well, the world doesn't need any more fanzines, but for you . . . it might be good for you.' Because you'll learn about publishing, you'll learn about editing, the choice of what photo you're going to use. So when we got to the point where a photographer, Michael Beal, said 'Oh, here's some photos you can use in your fanzine', we were like, 'Oh shit, it's going

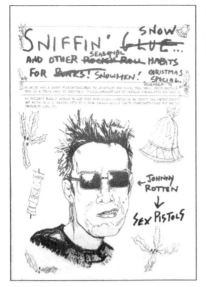

Sniffin' Snow, December 1976.　　　　*Sniffin' Glue* issue 6, January 1977.

to look shit! Let's look into how we can do that, and we can make that look good.' So that's what happened, you know. As we're going through it, we're learning, we're finding a printer's. We used a guy in Cambridge for ages, right through to the end. Good deal on that, we used to get the old van out there . . .

I know someone who's a photographer, and they use a photocopier to produce photos, deliberately, because they like all the little streaks you get, things like that.

Yeah, you can use that as an effect. But we were never – I think a lot of people, again, they get this wrong, they think that Sniffin' Glue looks grungy because we wanted to look grungy, but I always did the best I could. It happened to catch the zeitgeist of the time – the punk aesthetics, if you like – but we didn't do it on purpose, I didn't say, 'Well, I could do this really good, but I'll do it looking shit!'

But at the same time, you didn't want it to look like the NME, did you?

Oh no, no, because – well, I'd've given up, wouldn't I? If I'd set the bar that high . . . 'How am I gonna do that?' I'd have given up. I mean, I couldn't even bother with Letraset. Someone said, 'You can make the

Sniffin' Glue issue 7, February 1977.

Sniffin' Glue issue 8, March 1977.

heading look better by using Letraset.' I said, 'Don't worry, I want it to be my writing.' And if you look, all the way through it's got that Sniffin' Glue heading – you know, the Sniffin' Glue logo . . . it's my writing. That's the look!

I like the fact that you did a new one every issue. Rather than just re-using the same bit of paper, you know? Because if you wanted to – I mean if you really wanted to – you could have spent a couple of hours doing it as a . . . like more like a typeface or something . . .

Yeah, yeah . . .

You know? And just kept re-using that, couldn't you?

Absolutely, yeah.

But I like the fact that you didn't do that, you just did each cover completely differently.

[Looking at the book] If you look, see the way it's typed? It's not set, it's typed on the typewriter. You know, I'd do one column, and then set the margins again and do the next column, so . . . because – I don't know, I always liked columns. A lot of fanzines at the time, you'd see they'd start typing at the top and go down, that'd be it. So I had this

Sniffin' Glue issue 9, April/May 1977. *Sniffin' Glue* issue 10, June 1977.

---

idea of what a magazine should look like and feel like, you know what I mean?

I think you're right. I mean, I like A5 as a format. But I think, if it's A4, it should be two columns.

I think, later on, when other people were doing it – like Danny Baker got involved . . . and we had a lot of ads towards the end as well. That was my other – What happened was, I never wanted to have ads in it. Again, my – I don't want to sell out. Not taking any ads. My partners in it – Harry Murlowski came on board, he was taking photos, he was doing the driving up to Cambridge and all that. He said, 'Let's have some ads', you know?

So how did he get involved?

Oh, he was a friend of a friend. The first person to get involved was a guy called Steve Micalef, who I went to school with.

The only thing I could find on the internet was by Steve Mick, this interview with Subway Sect. It was brilliant, I loved it.

It's great fun.

Sniffin' Glue issue 11, July 1977.

Sniffin' Glue issue 12, August/September 1977.

He starts talking about . . .

The grapes!

This thing about grapes, yeah!

But that's the first mention ever about boycotting that I've ever read. Because at the time I thought, 'What is this? It's mad, but we'll put it in!' But years later it's like this – you know, he was so aware of this grape situation . . .

The thing is, I'd heard of the Subway Sect and Vic Godard but I'd never actually heard them. But it was the grape story that made me want to listen to them! It wasn't, like, talking about their music or anything, it was just thinking, 'That's so great, he was boycotting the grape sellers.'

That's right . . . Yeah, so Steve Micalef, he was like me, he was really into his music, and he could write a bit as well, he was a better writer than me.

Whereabouts was that school?

West Greenwich Secondary School. So Steve Micalef, he's started going to college. And he had a friend there, Harry Murlowski. And Harry had a camera. So it was 'Oh, get Harry in!' 'Anyone got a camera?' 'Yeah, Harry's got a camera, get him to take photos!' Whoever's got a decent camera – the old Pentax, you know – that was it! So Harry was involved. But what Harry brought, as well as being able to take photographs, he was also quite good at getting stuff done. He was that sort of bloke. It was like, 'How are we going to get to Cambridge?' 'I'll do it! I'll borrow me mate's van.' So it was good to have a sort of jack of all trades. Harry would never – he never wrote a word. But he became like the manager. When we finally got an office, he became like the office manager. It just built up like that.

How did Danny Baker get involved?

Another school friend. I went to school with Dan. Danny started sniffing around: 'What's this magazine you're doing?' You know, and he knew Steve as well. I said 'Oh, it's about punk . . .' 'What's punk?' Danny was . . . he was into his prog and all that, his Nick Drake and all that. So he started coming down to see what the punk thing was about. And he started wanting to get involved. So he did, he wrote a few reviews.

Was he really into punk or was it more like he wanted to be involved in the fanzine?

The way he tells it is that he was going out with a girl called Sharon at the time, and she said 'Oh, you seen what that Mark's doing? It's marvellous! You ought to get involved, Danny.' Danny was thinking, 'Oh Christ, my girlfriend thinks what Mark's doing is marvellous . . .' It was one of those sort of things! So that's it. But it's made Danny's career. Because Danny at the time was knocking around, he was working in a record shop and that . . . Course he went from *Sniffin' Glue*, then he worked for the NME, and then he ended up with the BBC and all that, on telly and stuff, so he done alright out of that. But, yeah, it was mostly school mates. Other people contributed to it as well, but the main people were me, Steve Micalef, Harry Murlowski, and then later on Danny Baker.

But it was always your fanzine.

Oh, absolutely.

And so – because it seemed like you were sort of saying that in the last couple of issues you were feeling like it was going a bit – it wasn't quite like your original vision.

No, no, because punk was being written about by everybody, it was in the charts – it had just lost it. Some of the last articles I write [in Sniffin' Glue], they're just full of self-loathing, almost. You can tell I've had it up to here. It's like nothing mattered any more. I don't want to use the term 'selling out', because that seems quite naive, because every band wants to sell records, you want people to listen to your music, you know – even me. But I just thought it had lost its purpose. It was just like any other music. And I thought, 'Well, if it is that, then I'll just carry on with my band, doing what I can musically, putting out records that I love. There's no use writing about it anymore.' But of course, Danny Baker, at the time, actually wanted to keep it going.

That's what I was thinking – the other people you were involved with, they might not want to finish at that time.

Danny told me, years later – because at the time he was trying to be all like, 'Yeah, fine, yeah, end it now' – but he admits to me, he thought 'Oh, shit, what am I going to do now?' You know, because when you were working for Sniffin' Glue, you were getting into gigs for nothing, you were getting free beer, you were, like, going on the road with the Clash and people like that . . . But, obviously, he didn't argue about it. I knew it was the right thing to do. Luckily, he had lots of mates on the NME, and they invited him to work there. I don't know if you know but on the last issue –

There was a flexi.

That's right. So I used that – and it was a conscious thing to use that – to introduce my band. So it was like, 'This is what I've been doing . . . and now this is what I'm going to be doing from now on.'

I wanted to get on to that. Just a pedantic, silly little question: they were all 30p up to that point, was the last one 30p as well? Or was it more because of the flexi?

[Laughing] I can't even remember how much they were.

I was just curious because they all have 30p on except that one.

54

I really don't know. If you'd've asked me what price did you sell it for, I wouldn't even have been able to remember. The first one was 15p, though, wasn't it?

Oh! Well, it doesn't say on there . . . the first one that's got a price on, actually, is issue 7, and that's 30p . . .

I think a lot of the time shops would put their own price on. You can imagine . . . there's no barcode or anything!

What I also wanted to ask about was the formation of Alternative TV. That was something presumably that was happening in the course of the same year that you were doing Sniffin' Glue?

Yeah, because once '77 had started, I think it was up to number 7, Sniffin' Glue 7? I think number 7 was January or something?

Yeah – that's February '77, yeah.

Yeah, by then I'd been asked to be A&R for this label, punk label. So I formed a punk label called Step Forward Records. We put out Chelsea, we put out the first Fall records – their first four singles, two albums.

Oh right, I never knew that.

Yeah. And Sham 69, their first things . . . anyway, so I did that, so by March '77 I was doing the label, and then about the same time I formed the band. I had some ideas about different music and that, you know?

And all this time, were you working at the bank?

Oh no, nooooo! No, I left the bank in September '76. Yeah, much to my . . . it upset my mum. [Laughs] 'Oh, why are you leaving your job?' You know, 'You got a job at the bank! You're going to be a bank manager one day!', and all that.

And what were you saying to her, 'I'm going to make money out of the fanzine!'?

Doing the magazine! 'Surely this is not . . .' Can you imagine it?

But I guess the sales it got – I mean, I don't know when it started selling in the thousands, but maybe . . . presumably you were making enough money to just be doing that?

To get by, but we were spending it as quick as we were making it! It wasn't a money-maker. I mean, if I had done it properly . . . there was a point, I said – you know, when it got to issue 12 – if we'd have said, 'Right, let's get a proper . . .' We could probably have gone to one of – I mean, there was talk of that – you know, Harry, who had a bit more of a business head, he was saying, 'Well, let's talk to one of these publishers, they might take it on.' They probably would have done.

Yeah, they probably would have.

You know, the main punk magazine. And just, like, done all the production side, and we could have just knocked out the copy, sort of thing. So there was potential for me to become a sort of . . . 'professional writer/editor' . . .

You definitely did the right thing.

That's right, because, to me . . . it wouldn't have been that touchstone of street, you know, street cred, if I'd've kept on going, and sort of petered out in the eighties, you know . . . But getting back to what I was saying, there was one point in mid-'77 where I was doing Sniffin' Glue, the label and the band. It was all happening. It was great! My whole life was the music business.

But how were you able to launch a label? Did someone give you some funding for that?

Yeah, yeah, a guy called Miles Copeland.

Oh, yeah – brother of Stewart Copeland.

At the time, early '77, he was running this label called BTM Records, and they had a lot of old prog rock acts. Renaissance . . . Curved Air . . . Climax Blues Band . . . He was quite a music fan, Miles, and he wanted to get into this 'new music' happening – he wanted part of it. So he came directly to me – good on him, really – he said, 'Look, Mark, I've read your fanzine' – and he's seen the press and that – 'do you want to do a label? You could put out the music you like . . .' So he got me to do that, and he was also managing Squeeze, who were sort of local mates of mine, because they're from southeast London as well, so I knew them . . . There was me, there was Squeeze . . . and the third . . . Yeah, I did Step Forward Records, Squeeze had Deptford Fun City Records, and then his brother Stewart, who I suddenly met – this was before the Police – he formed Illegal Records. So they were three punk/new wave labels.

So the Fall was one of the first bands you did on Step Forward?

Well, yeah, we did Cortinas, band called Chelsea . . . band called the Models, who ended up being Rema-Rema – Marco [Pirroni] was in the Models. I know Marco, I go way back with Marco, who ended up with Adam and the Ants.

But how was it you came across the Fall?

Well, funnily enough – this is the odd one – Danny Baker saw the Fall. He was touring around with Sham, because Sham 69 were one of their bands . . . we had this office, up in Oxford Street. We were in the centre of Oxford Street, doing the Glue . . . you know, a band would come in and say, 'We're doing a gig in Birmingham – anyone want to come?' 'Yeah, I'll come with you, get the beers in!' You can imagine it . . . so Danny Baker went up to Birmingham with the Sham once, and supporting was the Fall. Supporting Sham. And Danny Baker come back and said, 'I saw this great band from Manchester, the Fall.' He said, 'They haven't got a record deal – you should do them.' And that's how it happened. He had a phone number scratched on a bit of old paper – that was it. After us they went with Rough Trade. Yeah, we had some good bands . . . we had the Cramps. It was a really good environment, brilliant environment. I think that was what helped Sniffin' Glue – although I started independent, DIY, you know, within six months I was right at the centre of it all. Still in touch with my roots, but I was able to get stuff done – that's the key thing, get stuff done, you know? So, Sniffin' Glue, we could always interview the best people, the people we wanted to interview. There was never any problem with access. Because a lot of things, I've found – subsequently, trying to help other people, when they come up with these ideas – is how do they get to talk to people? And I do feel sorry for people nowadays – 'I want to start this fanzine, what do I do?' Email someone, email someone's manager . . . and because we were there at the start, we didn't have that problem. If we wanted to talk to the Clash we'd just go up to Joe Strummer in a club. You see what I'm saying?

I think now it's probably quite a good environment again, because people are making music in their bedrooms, and they're just putting them on the internet, and people are quite . . . they're quite accessible again. When I did my fanzine it was '89/'90, it was still quite easy . . .

What was the focus of your zine, then?

Well, it was music, but . . . I would write about anything. But there was a scene going on that I was interested in, which was what they called hardcore at the time, and there were bands like Silverfish – you know Silverfish?

Oh, yeah! I know Lesley [Rankine].

. . . and there were American bands like Fugazi and stuff like that. But at the same time I was getting into They Might Be Giants, who are not part of any scene. And I was just writing about . . . anything. I started writing about poetry and things like that . . .

Oh, right, right. What was it called, your fanzine?

It was called *Saudade*. But it never . . . had any sort of . . . sales. Because this was the problem – and this is what I have been asking a lot of people about – *Sniffin' Glue* is a bit of an unusual one, because it had such incredible success. But most people's fanzine experience is, you put an awful lot of work into it, and no one's interested.

No, that's the problem. Yeah. I think that's why the *Sniffin' Glue* story is so unique. It's not like what normally happens . . . but it's like what I was saying earlier, you'll learn a lot of stuff by actually doing it. You might not sell any, but by actually doing it, you're going to learn stuff.

You learn loads of stuff. And you learn something about the world – about how uninterested they are in what you're doing! Which I think is a good lesson to learn.

One of the problems I've got is I'm a bit blasé about it. Because once you've done the fanzine – 'the number one fanzine' – it's like you haven't got anything to prove. I was involved in this thing a few years ago called the Punk Congress. It was in Germany. And everyone was being very academic about punk and all that. And of course I was sailing through thinking, 'What's all the fuss about?' And one of the things they had there was a fanzine workshop. And people were just coming in – fans, people who'd bought tickets – sat there, doing their own fanzine . . . and I was like, 'Oh, give us a break!' Because to me, the idea is the most important thing – why are you doing it? If you're just doing it as some sort of cut-and-paste exercise, to tick a box, what's the point of that? It's about that motivation for doing it. A true fanzine has to be done by one person, sitting in front of a typewriter in their bedroom.

Exactly.

You know, that's the pure . . . it's one person's voice. And doing the best they can. And that's why it ends up like I was saying before, DIY: it's the best they can, you know what I mean? Not because they're sitting in some university-arranged workshop.

No, I know, it's a bit false, isn't it?

It is a bit false, yeah. So that's why – that idea that it's one person who hasn't got any other way of expressing themselves about the music they love, or the poetry they love, or the football club they love – they choose that way of doing it to get it out there. You know, that's the purist. That's the fanzine – the fan using that as their mouthpiece, if you like.

I think the classic fanzine editor is someone who's quite . . . um . . . shy and introspective . . .

Possibly . . .

And that's why they're inclined to be in their bedroom behind the typewriter. There definitely are a lot of them like that. I mean, that's what I was like.

Well, for me, it was a way of getting involved. I wasn't a musician, I wasn't about to put on gigs. 'How can I be involved in this new punk scene everyone's talking about?' I mean, when you went to see Led Zeppelin there was no way you would think 'I want to be involved in this!' It's like, Led Zeppelin, they can play properly, and all these big labels, but there was something about punk, you just thought 'I could get involved in this, it's not that hard.' Because it was basic, street level.

You could get your foot in the door. It's like, I've always felt, with football . . . you know football fanzines, I used to pick up a few of those, because I used to knock around with this guy and we used to go and see a lot of non-league stuff. We used to go up to, like, Enfield and all that. Basically, we got fed up with the big clubs, you get fed up with going to Stamford Bridge and all that. It was better sometimes standing with a couple of hundred people, and I always felt the most interesting fanzines were the ones with the smaller clubs. Because, in a way, it's like what I said about music: Liverpool don't need any publicity, do they? Because it's being written about – pick up any paper, they're writing about Liverpool. But who's writing about Barnet?

My mouthpiece, if you like, up to '77, was *Sniffin' Glue*. That was the way I communicated. But once I got the band going – once I saw the band as a valid way of communicating my ideas – that was why I didn't need *Sniffin' Glue* anymore. I mean, like I said earlier, it was also to do with, everyone was writing about punk, what was the point of *Sniffin' Glue*? But for me personally, I already had another way of getting my ideas out. I didn't need to use the fanzine, I had the band.

But it's quite a different medium, isn't it? I mean, writing songs, is, sort of, um . . .

Yeah! I just found it . . . again . . . I don't know, more free, in a way. Because I mean . . . I was never quite into – because I noticed, a lot of the fanzines that we've discussed, especially the ones that got into, you know, issue 20, 30, 40, hundreds – you start getting into this format that you can't get out of. You start interviewing bands – you imagine *Sniffin' Glue*, it goes into '78, '79, the Buzzcocks have just put out their third album: 'Ooh, he's interviewing Pete Shelley from the Buzzcocks!' 'So what you doing at the moment?' 'Well, we're working on . . .' It just becomes like the standard – the treadmill of putting magazines out. You've got to have your interviews, got to have your live gigs, got to have – how can you be groundbreaking? You're just reviewing records! And if you slag a record off . . . what I've found, which is why I would never want to run a magazine, is that people buying the magazine, all they want to read is people who echo their own opinions. People don't want to read *Sniffin' Glue* and have us say 'Oh, punk is shit now, it's all sold out, punk is dead.' They'll think, 'Fucking hell, that's cheery!' They want to read a magazine that's saying 'Punk has got some great stuff going to happen in the new year! There's going to be a punk festival!' You know, they want enthusiasm. I didn't have that for punk anymore.

Like I say, I think you did the right thing. Because the bands that are really adulated from punk now – like, the Sex Pistols I see as being the number one punk band, and I think it is because they had a short career. They ended at the right time.

That's right. Absolutely.

And like you were saying, I think the Clash went on a bit too long.

Oh, just thinking about it is weary! See, the thing is, with a lot of the other bands . . . like I said to you earlier, I met my wife when we played Pontins holiday camp. You know, we're all there playing Pontins, and, you know, it's fun, it's quite fun playing music, talking to people about punk. But you look at it from a negative, you think, 'I'm playing a fucking holiday camp – what the hell are we doing, for God's sake?'!

Oh, I don't think it matters. I mean you take yourself very seriously when you're young, but when you're a bit older you sort of think, 'Well, it's something to do, why not?'

The problem is, that's when I call it out, because I've had a bit of a thing going with this – I don't know if you know it – the Rebellion punk festival?

No.

Well, there's this big thing that takes place every year in Blackpool. And basically, I mean, from my point of view it's cabaret. It literally is cabaret. The Damned play there every year, and when Pete Shelley was alive the Buzzcocks, and Sham 69. And you've got Sham 69 singing 'If the Kids Are United' and all that, and it's like . . . it is cabaret. It might as well be Liberace up there. And it's a shame – if I was putting my ultra-serious hat on – it's a shame that punk has become that. But as you've said, when you're young, you have all these ideals about what stuff means – what rock means, what punk means – and then later on in life it all gets put in perspective. Maybe it is just a bit of music we liked when we were young, you know . . .

When I was younger, I was quite, sort of, earnest. I was very earnest in my – early Alternative TV, I was very earnest in my approach. We'd always be serious about this, or serious about punk and that. I couldn't stand any sort of jollity. Like the Rezillos – people who treated punk in a sort of funny way, I hated all that sort of nonsense. There wasn't any time for that. It was serious business, you know what I mean? I was quite po-faced, if you like. I mean, I've met people who've said 'Oh, I never wanted to talk to you in the early days.' I said 'Why?' 'Oh, we didn't want to approach you, you seemed so aggressive.' 'Really?' I had this reputation for being unapproachable. I mean, God knows how I got any friends or girlfriends! Because I was so serious in my approach to it all, you know? To me, it was a time for that. I think we reacted particularly when – you know the Sex Pistols, you know the Bill Grundy incident?

Yeah.

And then the gigs started getting cancelled … there was almost a sort of, like, we were behind the barricades and all that. You know, we became very protective of punk. There was a time, maybe a couple of months during that era – late '76 – when it seemed like a really serious thing to be involved in. A real choice: you know, are you into punk or not? It seemed like a lifestyle choice that mattered.

3

MICK MIDDLES

interviewed by Gavin Hogg

Mick Middles has been writing about the music scene in Manchester since punk shambled into town in 1976. *Ghost Up*, the fanzine he put together with his friend Martin Ryan, was short-lived, with only three A4 issues appearing between April and July 1977. Mick explains where the name came from:

> When we were teenagers, we would frequent a pub – the Lamb Inn in Gee Cross, Hyde. When somebody became unduly inebriated, the locals would say 'Oh he's gassed up'. A few years later, we were looking for a fanzine title and I suggested *Bourbon Gorilla*, a play on the Hawkwind song 'Urban Gorilla'. Martin thought this was a bit too close to the troubles in Belfast. So he asked for another suggestion. I said *Gassed Up*. He kind of misheard me and wrote it as *Ghost Up*. Somehow I looked at that spelling and loved it. It seemed a bit Beefheart/Buzzcocks. Years later, while talking to Paul Morley and Kevin Cummins, this exact question came up. I have the same answer. Morley looked astounded and said, 'That's the greatest fanzine name ever.'

In our interview it's clear that Mick finds some of his early writing a little embarrassing, but I rather like the fact that when they went to interview Buzzcocks they hadn't actually thought of any questions to ask and the first one was 'Do you do your own material?' You could call it naivety, but I think it captures the excitement of those days, where the access to bands was suddenly available and what you were actually going to ask Pete Shelley was way down your list of priorities.

A typical issue might feature live reviews of bands like Slaughter and the Dogs or the Drones, reviews of albums by the Jam and the Stranglers, a couple of band interviews and a think piece about new wave by Paul Morley, writing as Modest Young.

After *Ghost Up* Mick went on to write for *Sounds* and had a regular weekly column in the *Manchester Evening News*. He's also written books on many of the Manchester artists who flourished in the aftermath of punk: *The Fall* (co-written with Mark E. Smith, Omnibus, 2003), *The Smiths* (Omnibus, 1985; the first biography of the group, published before *The Queen Is Dead* had been released), *Red Mick* (Headline, 1993; a biography of Mick Hucknall of Simply Red) and *Out of His Head* (Empire, 2014; the story of Chris Sievey, the man behind Frank Sidebottom).

I first met Mick in 2015 at the Foresters Arms in Romiley to discuss his forthcoming appearance on Charity Shop Classics, a community radio show I present. We got on well, and several years later, when I mentioned that I was working on a book about zines, he told me about *Ghost Up*. Never one to pass up on an opportunity like that, I swiftly made the necessary arrangements to interview him. We met in March 2019 at the Globe, an excellent vegan pub in Glossop, this being about halfway between Mick's home in Sale and mine in Sheffield.

Tell me a bit about the genesis of *Ghost Up*. How old were you when you started it and what inspired you to do it?

Well, in 1976 I moved from Manchester to Silverdale in the Lake District, that well-known enclave of punk rock. It was just as everything started happening so I missed a lot of it and moved back to Manchester in December.

What took you to Silverdale?

My parents bought a restaurant and I was cooking there. There were the weekly music papers so I knew about Television and the Ramones, I knew something was happening. I got back just before the Sex Pistols played at the Electric Circus so I went to that. I'd never seen anything like it before.

Myself and my friend Martin were on our way down to the Ranch Bar, the hangout for the Manchester punk people. Steve Shy [fanzine editor] was there selling *Shy Talk* at the bar and we were chatting to people. We suddenly realised that the people we were talking to were actually from bands like the Buzzcocks, Ed Banger, Slaughter and the Dogs. Until this point, a rock star was Robert Plant and someone who wrote for the NME would be travelling the world with Led Zeppelin, living in a different world. Now it was Paul Morley from Stockport who was trying to scrounge a pint off me.

It brought everything into your world.

Yeah, it had all changed and suddenly, without even trying, we knew everybody. It was quite a small scene really, there were only about thirty people involved. You'd go and see the Buzzcocks and know everyone there.

Mick Middles (left) with Gavin Hogg at ALL FM in Manchester in 2015 for the recording of Gavin's Charity Shop Classics show (photo by Lyn Lockwood).

By January 1977, Kevin Cummins was sending photos to the NME, Paul was writing for them and there was a guy called Ian Wood who was writing for *Sounds*, it just felt like everyone was doing something. We thought 'Oh, let's do a fanzine!' It seemed like an obvious thing to do. *Sniffin' Glue* had been out for about a year by then. Strangely we used to go and buy it at Paperchase in Manchester. Back then you could sell your fanzines there, you can't imagine it now. It's mostly birthday cards for £4.50.

We had no idea how to do a fanzine, but we thought we should interview somebody. We'd met the Buzzcocks and *Spiral Scratch* was out. Martin wrote a letter asking Pete Shelley and got a phone call from him, telling us to come and meet them that Saturday. We thought that Howard Devoto was the lead singer, so when we turned up and he wasn't there we asked where he was.

'Oh, he's left.'

'And who's that?' It was Garth, this huge, quite fearsome-looking guy on bass.

They took us down to the pub and Pete came down. Although we'd met him once before, we thought punks would at least have bondage trousers, if not a Mohican; he turned up in flares and an orange cagoule. It wasn't quite what we were expecting.

'Come on then, ask us some questions.' We'd forgotten about that bit, I'm not exaggerating!

I think we asked if they were a political band or something. It was a start anyway. So, we photocopied a hundred copies, took the fanzine down to the Electric Circus and sold them for 20p, which in 1977 was pretty good.

We were walking through Ashton-under-Lyne soon after and we saw this old printing machine with rollers in the window of an antique shop. We bought it and then thought 'How are we going to get this home?' We lived four miles away in Stockport and had to carry it onto the bus. It was spilling green ink all over the place. We managed to get it back to Martin's parents' house and it ruined the front room carpet immediately. We slowly typed out the fanzine, which took about three months. We had to type it onto this cylinder and to print it out you had to manually rotate it at an even speed; if you went too fast the ink was faint. It got reviewed by Richard Boon in *New Manchester Review*

All three issues of *Ghast Up*, published within a few short months in 1977.

saying the green ink was an innovation!

Looking back now, I'm embarrassed by the writing. It was really naive but it was what it was. We only did three issues, it all got too laborious in the end. It did get us in the centre of things.

And was it what propelled you into your writing career?

Yeah, I'd always wanted to be a journalist, there were a lot in the family. Although Dad wasn't a journalist, he worked for the *Sunday People* in Manchester so he used to take me down there and I'd see the late-night printing on the rollers on Saturday nights. He did the plates for the football reports. It seemed so romantic back then. It was kind of in my blood. Martin was different, he was a civil servant and had no particular ambitions in that area. It was something I always wanted to do but I didn't do the fanzine to start a career, it just happened.

But once you had, did it set you on that path?

Yeah, we did things for quite a few other zines too. There was a network of them. We sent some copies of Ghast Up to Geoff Travis at Rough Trade and he was lovely. He sold them and used to send us nice letters. We went down there with these paper badges with Ghast Up on. He saw the badges we were wearing and went 'Is that your mag? I owe you some money don't I?' and gave us about thirty quid. We were surprised we'd sold any! I think because it had 'The Buzzcocks' on the front of that first issue – pity it had that rather than 'Buzzcocks', but there we go.

There were a few people that used to keep in touch. Morrissey was one, not so much with us, more with Steve Shy. There were only our two zines in the Manchester scene then and he was doing it before us. Both the zines got mentioned in the NME and Melody Maker round-ups. Things just rolled on from there and people started to know who you were from it. Around the same time Paul Morley did a one-sheet zine he used to give out called Girl Trouble.

So you had Buzzcocks in the first one – who else did you manage to interview?

I remember going round to Mark E. Smith's flat in Prestwich to interview the Fall. They were very much a fanzine band; they picked up on fanzines quickly and were keen to talk to zines from different areas of the UK. They understood that the writers would end up working for the NME or Sounds – which they did. There were zines like Alternative Ulster, written by Dave McCullough who went to Sounds and Gavin Martin who went to the NME.

I don't know how many of those interviews made Mark E. Smith any money – but he kept going for forty years, so . . .

I guess that in the early days those interviews helped to spread the word about the band.

Also the artwork of the Fall's singles was very 'fanzine-ish' – lo-fi, part naive, part intellectual, part street slang.

We used to go to the Electric Circus all the time and we saw AC/DC there with Bon Scott. We didn't know whether they were punks or not, we had no idea. They didn't sell out but they were phenomenal. We put them in the zine and people were saying, 'What are you putting them in for? They're not a punk band.'

The orthodoxy of punk rock?

It was going back to the time when people only seemed to listen to one type of music, when it was more tribal. You were a soul fan, a blues fan, a progger or a punk and if you did anything a bit off-kilter you'd get criticised for it. 'You can't put that in there, Blondie aren't punk, Television aren't punk!'

We did write about the Saints who'd just come over to London from Melbourne. What a fantastic band they were, really friendly too. We just turned up at Manchester Poly and went backstage. We did the same with the Vibrators. It wasn't strictly a punk zine.

Paul Morley used to write for us under the pseudonym Modest Young and he called it a 'pop zine'. It wasn't the same as Shy Talk, not as hardcore, more poppy. Bands like the Vibrators were regarded as a band who were cashing in a little bit. As were the Drones I have to say, though I liked them.

Did you get in touch with bands beforehand or would you just go on the night and see what happened?

Sometimes we'd get in touch beforehand but sometimes just turn up. Before the zine we'd only go to the Apollo or the Free Trade Hall, we wouldn't have thought of going to the Poly or other places. Doing the zine made it easier to do that and we started to get to know people at those venues.

Was there a camaraderie among the Mancunian bands?

No, they were ferociously competitive, all that stuff about collectives and being in the scene together was bollocks! We learnt quite quickly that they all hated each other. If you wrote something positive about one of the groups, all the others would hate it. To this day that goes on. Also, the music press back then was quite negative. You were there to criticise things you didn't like and make a point. It was a bit edgy, if you said that Slaughter and the Dogs were just glam rock you'd have three big lads from Wythenshawe coming round your house. These days it's all happy and people seem to think there's no point reviewing an album if they don't like it.

We didn't know quite where to go with the zine after a while so I started sending reviews to Sounds. They started printing them even though what I wrote was a bit naive. You'd speak to them in the week and say what gigs were coming up and they'd tell you which ones to review. It was a slow process but it was great to actually get paid. It would take a week to write it up, you'd post it, they'd get it three days later, a few weeks after that it would be in the paper and a month later you'd get paid.

How many issues of Ghost Up did you produce?

We had three, the same as Shy Talk. We also did one called Punctate which we only did a hundred copies of. It was more Martin doing that one really because we had this stupid printing machine and we had to do it in dots. It was a whole zine of pictures of the Clash and Buzzcocks in dots but people seemed to like it! It was so laborious.

How many copies of each did you do? You said you'd done a hundred of the first one, did you make more when you had your own press?

Good question . . . I think it was still about a hundred of each one. They sold pretty well.

Where did you sell them?

We'd sell some at gigs and also swap them with other people. Glenn Gregory would bring copies of Gun Rubber from Sheffield and swap zines with us at the Electric Circus. That spread the network out from Manchester.

So people in other places start to find out what's going on?

Yeah. There were loads in London and Glasgow too. It was a nice little thing. I think what happened was that Sounds looked at this and thought that they should bring some of the fanzine writers on board because they knew who knew what was going on in different pockets of the country. It was in their interests to do it. They had an enormous circulation at that point, it was phenomenal, 200,000 a week.

There was a magazine that I did something for that was written exclusively by zine writers, called National Rock Star. They printed your review and at the bottom they'd put the name of the zine you wrote for. There was only one issue I think but it sold well.

What were your favourite memories from the fanzine days?

I started doing some stuff for City Fun. That was a collective which was around for a while, there were about 40 issues altogether. Who in Manchester didn't write something for City Fun? I don't think there's ever been another fanzine quite like it. The whole of the Manchester scene were involved.

Were Cath Carroll and Liz Naylor part of it?

That's right, Jon Savage and Rob Gretton were involved too. Jon had just moved up to Manchester to work at Granada. I'd only known him from Sounds which I never quite got as I always thought he was more of an NME person really. He loved Manchester and used to go driving round the Trafford Park estate to soak up the industrial vibe.

Andy Zero 'edited' it, but it was all quite loose. There was also a guy called Bob Dickinson involved. He went on to deliver lectures on fanzines and wrote a book about them called Imprinting the Sticks.

Later on, in the mid-eighties, we did something called Muse, which was a glossy magazine. It ran for about twelve issues. It was part what's-on guide like City Life [Manchester's version of Time Out] and interviews with people like John Lydon. It got sold in WHSmith's and we got paid £70 per week. It became less fun and more serious when we had to sell advertising space.

Actually, we had one full-page advert in Ghast Up from Chrysalis for Generation X's 'Your Generation'. We had to go down to one of their gigs at Rafters to prise £20 off their manager because Chrysalis wouldn't pay us. I never thought Billy Idol would become a massive superstar in America, it still doesn't compute! I went to America once for a few months. I got to LA and the first thing I saw was a Harley-Davidson pull up at the lights – and Billy Idol was riding it!

'Remember me, Billy?'

'Remember Rafters? You got that twenty quid?!'

I was proud of getting the advert but once you start doing that it stops being a fanzine in a way.

What do you think makes a fanzine a fanzine?

I think it's something that's written out of a passion either for a scene or a band. Some of the best ones are just on bands, they go into incredible detail. A lot of those fanzine writers went on to write books about the groups. I guess it's about not doing it out of a commercial sense or to further a writing career. In a sense it did for me but that wasn't why I did it: it was the sheer joy of doing it.

Later on the football fanzines started and they were a bit too sincere I think. The punk zines were different.

Were they more irreverent?

Yeah, it was more about being involved. Some amazing things happened like getting letters from Adam and the Ants and people like that.

Did you interview them?

No, but we got a letter from Andy Warren who went on to be in Monochrome Set. He said Adam had liked a review I'd written. Until then music was us and them, either you were a fan or involved in the music business, there was no grey area in-between. You'd got to the bar and the lead singer's standing next to you and you have a chat. That hadn't happened before in rock. The Peter Gabriels of this world didn't want to be knocking around with the fans!

How did you divide the labour for the zine?

Martin was the editor really and he did the front page and the layout. I did most of the writing.

Of all the interviews you did, which one were you most excited about or sticks in your memory the most?

None of them were very good it has to be said! The Drones one was interesting.

That was Paul Morley's band wasn't it?

Yeah, he was managing them. We met at the Smithfield pub next to the Band on the Wall venue. We didn't really know them but we knew Paul was behind them. It was a really odd interview, I reread it a few months ago and wondered what we were thinking. Morley was pushing them like they were the Clash. He turned against them quite nastily not long afterwards. When he was at the NME someone gave him the job of reviewing their record, Manchester's first punk album. He destroyed them. They wanted to kill him. Their first bit of national publicity was their ex-manager slagging them off!

How did you make the artwork in the zine?

We took take pictures at gigs with a Polaroid camera which cost about £4.50. Sometimes Martin would do a drawing from the photo and he did it with some of Kevin Cummins's pictures too, which really pissed him off. 'What are you doing that for? That's my copyright!'

'It's not, because I've drawn it.'

It turns out he was right. Paul said it was good, it was 'artlessness'. He was putting his intellectual spin on it.

What were your favourite zines, either at the time or subsequently?

I didn't really have a favourite, they all had their own different flavours. Gun Rubber was completely different to Ripped & Torn.

There's one that this guy from Nottingham is doing now which is strangely fascinating. He interviews old punk and new wave bands now and they're all gardeners in Buxton and stuff like that. It's more interesting reading about them now than it would have been then. I love knowing what happened to them. What's interesting is that even if there are bands in there you haven't heard of, it's about little scenes that used to exist in Basingstoke or places like that.

What was the last zine you bought? Was it that one?

Actually he does it for free. He got in touch with me asking if I wanted him to send one.

I'm not sure about the last one I bought. Was ZigZag a fanzine or a magazine?

It was somewhere between the two, wasn't it?

It's difficult to remember but I know people still want to write about music. I was doing a lecture on rock journalism for some students at BIMM [British and Irish Modern Music Institute] and shot myself in the foot by saying they were wasting their time! There aren't any jobs in it now, let's be honest. Go and be a lawyer or something! In the past, if you had a job with the NME you could move to London and just about make a living.

I'm sure there's a lot going on but I don't see fanzines around these days.

Do you still listen to the music you used to write about?

That's a great question. No, not really. I like going back further than that these days, I'll put on a Caravan album quite happily. I wouldn't sit down and listen to a Buzzcocks LP these days, though I might put on a Fall record occasionally. It's odd because I still love the music. I still listen to the Television albums and maybe the Saints but I haven't listened to the Drones in 40 years.

You recently compiled a CD box set for Cherry Red [Manchester, North of England: A Story of Independent Music – Greater Manchester 1977–1993]. Did you have to spend a lot of time listening to it all or was it mostly compiled from memory?

I did listen to every track while I was putting it together but I don't think I've listened to any of it since. Box sets are weird aren't they? I don't know whether people actually play them.

I've got quite a few – they're nice to have but I don't often dig them out and listen to them.

Yeah, they're good to get out and read the sleeve notes. There's too much on them to listen to; that one I did there was about 75 tracks on.

What about writing about music? Do you feel any compulsion to do that?

Yeah, I still do bits for *Record Collector* and a lot for the *Quietus* website. They've chopped things down a bit, you used to be able to write as much as you wanted but it's good that it's instant and you can share it with friends straight away.

The quality of writing there is strong, isn't it? That's why it's well known.

Yeah, I think it will keep doing well. I like writing for them because you're often writing about things that won't be reviewed anywhere else. I did one for a band from New Zealand and it got talked about on the radio over there! I kept getting sent links to it – 'Your review got mentioned again!' It was fantastic.

Websites and blogs have pretty much replaced fanzines– but there are so many of them, is anyone actually reading these things?

There's a tidal wave of them.

It was more polarised in the seventies, everyone read the NME. One front cover could launch a career. Now you can have ten number one singles but a lot of people won't know who you are.

4

STEWART HOME

interviewed by Hamish Ironside

The website of the Stewart Home Society (www.stewarthomesociety. org) avers that 'Stewart Home is the most out there writer on the planet – the only person on earth who is visible to the naked eye from outer space!' Having read his amazing novel *Cunt*, I am inclined to concur. He is chiefly a writer, but has also been somewhat involved with various artistic movements, many having trickster or prankster elements to them: neoism, situationism, plagiarism. His politics are far to the left. Perhaps his most endearing quality is that he doesn't take anything too seriously. As the Stewart Home Society also proclaims, he has been 'radically inauthentic since 1962'.

Stewart's writings have included novels, short stories, poetry and non-fiction for various small publishers, as well as pamphlets and newsletters, often self-published and self-distributed. But his first published work was a music fanzine called *Down in the Street* in the late 1970s. We became aware of this fanzine from a fleeting mention in the second RE/Search volume on zines, where Stewart was referred to in connection with the mail art movement. However, all efforts to find a copy of *Down in the Street* proved fruitless, so this interview was conducted without having even seen an issue of it. After making enquiries on our behalf, Stewart later managed to obtain the images of two covers reproduced in this chapter, but as this book goes to press we have still not seen an actual issue.

Following *Down in the Street*, Stewart occasionally produced other zines, such as *Bitch Bitch* (co-edited with his friend Dave King around

1981), which only ran to one or two issues, and the intriguing *Smile* project that we discuss below.

The interview took place in the gardens of the Barbican complex in east London soon after the first Covid-19 lockdown's restrictions were relaxed in May 2020. Stewart bore my almost total ignorance about *Down in the Street* with the most impeccable grace. He was also kind enough to meet up again about eighteen months later just so I could photograph him, seeing as I'd neglected to do so at the time of the interview.

I'm quite interested in the fact that I've been unable to find a copy of any of your fanzines, and I believe you haven't kept any?

No.

How long would it be since you last saw a copy of any of your fanzines?

Well, it depends which ones, but the main set . . . I had the original artwork, and a musician who is in some of them borrowed them in about 1982. When I retrieved what was left of them, 15 years later or something, what they'd done was marked up every mention of them and thrown away all the other pages, even though it was the original artwork, which they said they'd return in a couple of days, after copying it.

Right.

I didn't keep copies, I kept the original artwork. And then someone with a huge ego and little talent decided . . . they were only interested in themselves.

Yeah. Would that be because you'd managed to sell them all, the ones you'd printed?

Yeah, yeah.

Right, well, that's very unusual for a fanzine.

No, it depends when you were doing it. I mean, I only did a hundred copies, so, in 1979, '80, it was easy to sell a hundred copies. And then

Stewart Home somewhere near St Paul's, London, January 2022.

when I was doing art magazines, or, you know, art–political magazines in the eighties, it was easy to sell two thousand copies, then. But, you know, stuff's changed because the distribution's changed. The fanzines would just go at music gigs.

Well, that's what I was wondering. Okay. First of all, I just want to check that the Wikipedia information agrees with what you can remember. Because they say you did . . . Down in the Street was the main fanzine –

Well, I did seven issues of that, it was multi-page, '79, '80 . . . and then I did a one-sheet one, called *Caught with the Meat in Your Mouth*, so it was like a newsletter-type thing, given out free rather than charged. And . . . I can't remember . . . when was that? '81, '82?

Yeah. So, starting in, probably, '79, you think –

Yeah, well definitely in '79, yeah –

You'd have been 17 then?

Yeah.

You did about seven issues of *Down in the Street* in about a two-year period?

Less than that.

Less than two years – a new issue every three months or so?

No, less than that.

Oh, really?

It was probably about every month, two months . . . I used an old typewriter and Letraset.

And did everything yourself?

Yeah, you know, collage, and then just made up the original artwork and photocopied it.

And what would have been your motivation, was it seeing other fanzines?

I think it was to get into gigs for free, and get free records!

Oh right, they'd let you in for free?

Yeah, and they'd give you records to review. I got into a lot of gigs for free, yeah. Although, it was also . . . you know, I was into playing music as well. Although the bands I was in never did that much. I was just into the music scene and that was . . . something to do.

I wasn't reading fanzines until the late eighties, so for me this is all stuff I know from reading histories of things like that, but they always talk about Sniffin' Glue, like that was the first –

Well, first punk one, but I mean . . . you know, you could argue about what's the first anything . . . It's a kind of genre, how do you define it?

Well, yeah, they say there were, like, science fiction fanzines in the fifties and things . . .

I mean, that was the one, I used to read Sniffin' Glue . . . again, you know, you can see how Mark Perry used that to promote himself. I mean, I know Mark, he's a nice enough guy. I haven't seen him in a while . . . But, you know, he had the Alternative TV flexi-disc on the last one, I think, which had Sham on the front cover, Sham 69?

Right.

But for me, at that time, I'd been into the punk scene, so . . . you know, I got into punk in '76. Summer of '76. And . . . you know, first of my school – there was me and one other into punk, northern soul was more the thing – people would go all the way up from down south to Wigan Casino [laughs] . . . and I liked that music, but, you know, the live music scene was more exciting, because . . . you know, seeing a band rather than hearing a DJ play a record. But I wish I'd gone to it now, I could have done . . .

Wish you'd gone to what?

Wigan Casino. The northern soul scene. Because I just thought 'What's the point of going all that way just to hear people play records?' [laughs] But I think I made the wrong decision, when I was fifteen, sixteen. But I was more into seeing bands around London. That was my thing. So yeah, I mean, I left school in '78, so then I had a bit more money, so I could afford to go to more gigs.

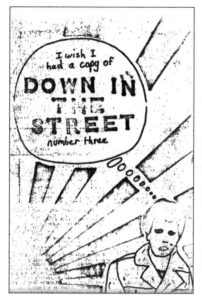

Covers of *Down in the Streets* issues 3 and 4. Stewart tracked down these images, and he remarks: 'The copy of *DITS* 3 is really faded ... Obviously the radiating rays were originally solid black too! I can see I did a drawing of Adam Ant on the cover in his raincoat era. I remembered doing collages and stories for the zine but forgot I did drawings too! And as that's issue 3 it came out just before Adam started having his pop hits... not sure of exact date but presumably around April 80 ... the next one is June/July and the first was definitely done in 79. Less thrillingly perhaps issue 4 has Thatcher in a sniper's target and a mash-up headline of a Tory law and order slogan (short sharp shock) and a Ramones song (Gimme Gimme Shock Treatment) ... oh well, I was teenage at the time.'

You were in the Merton area then?

Southwest London, yeah. But it was easy to get into the West End, you could be there in 30 minutes.

And so you were interviewing bands and reviewing records?

Interviewing bands, reviewing gigs. And then I used to put in other stupid stuff ... um, and I probably started a little bit late, because a lot of the bands I was really into weren't so available then, or changed the line-ups. You know, I'd go through waves of bands; when they became successful I'd stop going to see them. It would be because it was less interesting to see a band in a big venue than in a club.

What would be some of the bands you interviewed?

I mean, it would be little bands . . . I remember covering UK Subs. They were one of the later bands, they were still going then . . . I mean, I used to go and see bands like Chelsea, but I never covered them in the fanzine. Do you remember Chelsea, or Gene October?

No.

The Members I used to see a lot, but they became big before I was doing the fanzine. Um . . . Adam and the Ants. I did some coverage of them, didn't interview them, but I remember speaking to them occasionally.

Right. That was the first band I loved, but I was, like, eleven, it was when *Kings of the Wild Frontier* came out.

Yeah, this was the different line-up, that became Bow Wow Wow. But Adam was always a great performer.

Yeah. Well, I think it was a really good thing, for me, getting into the band at the time, because it does make you think 'I want to get that album he did before', and that sort of leads you in to listening to punk and things like that, and getting more curious about another kind of music that you probably wouldn't have been exposed to if you were just listening to all the chart music.

No, exactly. One of the bands I covered a lot, that I can't stand now because they became fascist, was a band called Crisis. Who were a Rock Against Racism band. I've got no problem with the other members, but the two main songwriters became fascists, from being members of Trotskyist organisations!

You were already left-wing, according to Wikipedia, but was that something that came from your family?

Not from the family so much, just my own opinions.

Just your inclination?

Yeah, my inclination.

Were you writing about politics in the fanzine?

In passing, but not really, it was more music. Because you're trying to figure out your opinions on a lot of it. And I was going to different meetings of different groups, you know, from anarchists to Trotskyists . . . and I never really felt I completely fitted in with any of the groups. So they'd maybe have some things I'd agree with and others that I didn't. The basic things were anti-royalist and anti-racist attitudes, the easy stuff for a teenager to [endorse]. So, you know, it was like, going to see the Ants, some kids I got to know from Paddington were at the Ants. You'd get to know kids from all over London, going to the gigs in the centre. And I remember the last time I saw these kids, at the Ants gig on the *Zerox* tour, at the Lyceum, they told me they'd joined the NF. And I was just, like, 'What are you doing here, then?' And they were like, 'What do you mean? We like the Ants!' And I said 'Well, you know – Dave Barbe' – you know, a mixed-race drummer – great drummer, actually – 'so you're saying you've joined the NF but you want to come and see Dave Barbe' . . . Whether they really had joined the NF I don't know, whether they were saying it for a wind-up . . . Hard to know.

So you'd always bring a few fanzines to the gig and just expect to sell four or five, something like that?

Oh no, you'd get rid of loads more than that.

Would you? Just going up to people and saying 'Would you like to buy a fanzine?'

Yeah. You know, it's 10p!

10p? That is a bargain! The only time I ever tried doing that with my own fanzine was at the Reading Festival, and I did sell loads. But it had never occurred to me to do that before. I was sort of advertising it in *Record Collector* and things like that, and selling . . . fuck all, basically!

No, it would be, you know, whatever bands I had in it, I would go to the gig they were doing and then you'd take, basically, a hundred to one gig and get rid of them all. That was it. Or, you know, you might get rid of fifty . . . most of the gigs I went to, I wasn't selling fanzines because I wanted to watch the band and have a good time! But it would just be, like, a gig or two to get rid of that issue, and then . . . you know, that was it. And I think they'd go in the odd record shop, but that wasn't so good, because they wanted a cut of the money, and I was just putting it as low as possible anyway.

Cover of *Bitch Bitch* issue 1. Stewart writes of this zine: 'I jointly edited it with my friend Dave King between *Down In the Street* and *Smile* so circa 1981 or maybe a year or two later, not before 1981. This was the first publication I did that was offset printed I think. I think we did 500 or 1000. Don't remember if we did more than one issue . . . if we did it didn't go beyond issue 2.'

See the dust jacket of this book for a colour version of this very striking cover design.

I would give mine to postal distributors – I'd just send it off, and it never occurred to me to ask them for any money. I was just so pleased they were taking it at all. That seemed like an end in itself.

Oh right, no, it was good to get some money back, although in the end – I think I paid for the xeroxing when I first started, but then I found a way of ripping it off so I wasn't paying for it –

Like at work, or something?

Yeah, but then it was still a bit of work to put it together. Get some free records, into some gigs for free . . . Yeah, and you would give them away to people you knew as well. But, that was the thing, people would say, 'Oh, you should *print*' [i.e. rather than photocopy], and it was like: 'No, because if you do 500 or 1000 then that's gonna be *work*, to do the distribution.' I mean, later on when I was doing other stuff which wasn't music-related, I *was* printing it, and you could get rid of it, because you had all the radical bookshops around London, and you'd just take stuff around.

Yeah. I mean, when I was doing mine, I was sort of in the country-side, and so I was very rarely getting to gigs or anything. It wasn't so easy . . . But aren't you curious now to have copies of the fanzines and re-read bits of them, to see what you were writing when you were 17 or 18?

Not really.

Not at all?

No, not at all, I really don't care about that stuff, I'd rather just hear some of the tunes. But, you know, what I listen to now is much more the northern soul stuff.

It seems like at some point maybe you became aware or more interested in the general art scene? Because the first thing I read about you in connection with fanzines actually wasn't about *Down in the Street*, it was in – you know the RE/Search book?

Oh, yeah . . .

There was a guy called John Held, a mail art guy –

Oh God, yeah, I know . . .

I think he mentioned you in connection with the *Smile* project, and he was saying – well, I don't know . . . it was already in existence in America but I got the impression you sort of started it going over here?

No, I started it here. I mean, this came about partly through messing around with band names, so . . . I was in some different bands – a ska band called the Molotovs, and then . . . an indie band called Basic Essentials, who broke up because of record company interest – only indie record companies, but it was too much for the band to take! You know, when we had scouts coming to watch us and stuff . . .

And then we had this really stupid band that we kept changing the name of. It was kind of parodic. We were a kind of mix of punk and experimental stuff, and it would be called different names for virtually every gig. So it would be Orchestra of the Academy of the Applied Literary and Dramatic Arts, then it was the Slaves of Freedom, then the Screaming Peasants . . . my joke was that we were gonna advertise ourselves as, like, Led Zeppelin or something, just to get people to come in! [laughs] And then thinking, if a lot of people used the same name for their band . . . then, you know, it would just be very funny! And then, um . . . we had a singer who was really in with Crass and Conflict for a while, which isn't really my kind of music, but we'd do gigs with – not with Crass, but with Conflict. Colin was always – you

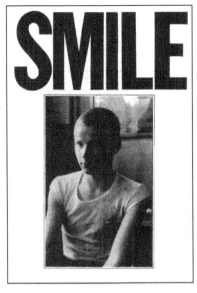

Covers of *Smile* issues 1 and 10. The cover star of issue 1 is Stewart himself at around 18 years of age.

see him slagged off now, but I can only say that my experiences of him were very good.

Colin who?

Colin Conflict. You don't know? Oh, well – when we played with him he always paid us, he offered to put us on his record label, blah di blah di blah . . . Conflict were one of the bigger anarcho bands. Anyway . . .

Just to briefly say what *Smile* was, though . . .

Well, I had a load of poetry and stuff I was writing, so I just decided to print it up and do an art magazine, and say we had an art movement called the Generation Positive. So I did that and I said all magazines should call themselves *Smile*. This had been this idea I'd had with the band, which we'd never really pursued to any great extent. So I did the first issue in January 1984, and then the second one in . . . was it January? March, April – quite quickly after – no, I think the second one was done before April, so maybe it was March . . .

But other people did start doing them?

Oh, yeah, yeah, and then other people did –

And were you sort of encouraging them?

Some of them just did it and some were encouraged, but what happened was in April '84, after I'd started Smile and done the first two issues, I came across this thing called a neoist apartment festival in Kennington, south London. Neoism was this sort of pseudo-art movement. So I wrote them a silly letter, because I thought that if I write a silly letter and they reply they're okay, but if they don't they're po-faced and so I don't want to have anything to do with it. Anyway, so I got involved with them, and that had been started by various people . . . but there was a project associated with that called Monty Cantsin, where everyone used the same name, and this was meant to be for an open pop star, which had been started by a guy called Dave Zack in 1978. Dave Zack was an American mail artist. And this Latvian called Maris Kundzins had been the first person to use the name, but then other people had used it. And at this point a guy called Istvan Kantor, who was a Hungarian living in Canada, was mainly using it. And he'd do these performances where he'd pull out the Monty Cantsin chair and be whacking a stick around him violently and say 'Anyone who wants to be Monty Cantsin can be Monty Cantsin!' So I started using the Monty Cantsin identity as well, which I did for a while. And the Smile and Monty Cantsin stuff took off through the mail art network at the time.

Yeah. Because the thing that it reminded me of which I'd heard of previously was the Luther Blissett thing . . .

Yeah, well Luther Blissett followed on from that.

That was later, was it?

Yeah, it was . . . about mid-nineties, it started?

And was it meant to undermine the cult of the author?

That was one of the things, yeah. With the Luther Blissett, it was some guys in Bologna who started it. And they contacted me because the launch – they convinced this programme *Chi l'ha visto: Have You Seen Them?*, that chase runaways, that this guy Harry Kipper had gone missing – who was spelling out the word 'art' by cycling between different European cities – that he'd gone missing in the Balkans! And

I was his best friend in London, so they came over and filmed me and kind of took me out for meals and stuff, while they were doing that! But, yeah, he didn't actually exist. But that was the way he was spreading the name Luther Blissett while he was doing this, asking everyone to call themselves Luther Blissett. And then there were a whole lot of people involved in Luther Blissett. I mean, I'd say that they improved a lot of the ideas that people had been working with earlier. It was definitely a kind of more successful variant of that same stuff.

But with Smile, it started off probably – you know, I just thought I'd print up a load of these stupid poems I was writing!

Yeah, so it was a vehicle for your own writings.

Yeah. A few manifestoes, but mainly – because in the early eighties there was this kind of poetry revival scene . . . I don't know if you remember people like Anne Clark?

No.

She was big at the time. And they'd go on, and a lot of poets would do these poems about being really depressed and stuff, and how they lived at the top of a thirty-storey tower block, and they'd been burgled two million times in the last five minutes, and their mum had depression and a hysterectomy or something, you know . . . So I'd just get up and do these really stupid poems about fruit and vegetables, really short. Which had just started off as a laugh, and then they ended up in this Smile magazine. So one thing just evolves into another.

Yeah, yeah. And you did just a few issues of Smile?

No, I did eleven issues.

Eleven? And they were numbered?

They were numbered, yeah. I also did two unnumbered xerox editions, in smaller numbers.

Okay – and you don't have any of them?

No, I have some of those.

Oh, you do?

Yeah, yeah, it's only the early fanzines I lost. It kind of evolved, because

I was also around kind of political groups, like the London Workers Group, and then *Workers Playtime* [a magazine], which kind of came out of that. Which I was more involved with than London Workers Group. I was around people with things like compositors, I don't know if you know what an IBM compositor is? It's like a volatile machine with a golf [ball] head . . .

Yeah . . .

You can type in so much and then play it back, and you have to program it to stop where you want to change the typeface with a different golf ball. But because I can touch type, you know, I was quite good at doing stuff like that. So I'd just borrow their machine, and I started typesetting the magazine, so they looked more professional. And also I'd use a spot colour. You know, if you use glossy paper on the cover and then a spot colour it looks more . . . kind of flash?

So did you sort of teach yourself all that? Like touch typing?

No, I learned touch typing in a course. Which was great, because it was twenty-nine girls and me! [laughs]

Like, at school, was that?

Yeah, yeah. So the boys would be saying 'Oh, are you *gay* or something?' *Me* gay? I'm in there with all those girls! Although I have no problem with people who are gay, I'm just – there was a lot of homophobia . . . still is, unfortunately . . . Yeah, so, it looked more professional, and people would wonder how it was paid for. But it was quite feasible to do that kind of stuff, because the typesetting I was doing myself, and I'd do stuff for other people as well, as a favour, not for money.

When I look at fanzines now, the more amateurish they look, the more I like them.

No, well, that's what I was going to say. So, you know, I learned how to do that, and then moved into DTP at the end of the eighties. And then I did a lot of pamphlets, up to about 2005, 2006, when I got bored with trying to distribute them. Because you saw the numbers that you could distribute [going down] . . . in the eighties, you could easily get rid of 2,000 copies of anything, going down to, like, a few hundred . . .

But I decided to move because I realised that people preferred it more rough looking than DTP. I'd set the stuff on Word so it looked more amateur, and it would sell better. Because it's like the audience for that was meant to be underground . . . well, if it looks less professional . . .

Exactly.

You know, so having, in the mid-eighties, managed to look *more* professional than most people, which would have kind of helped you reach people then, later on, after the DTP revolution, the less professional, the better it was, and the more people liked it.

So one of the things I'm wondering, because you mentioned pamphlets, was what's the difference between a fanzine and a pamphlet? Because apart from the fact that fanzines are usually numbered – but some people do one-off fanzines, like I think you were saying you had – so would a one-off fanzine just be a pamphlet?

I think it partly depends on format. I think of a pamphlet as usually being A5 rather than A4.

Ah. Were your fanzines A4?

The fanzines were usually A4. It was A5 . . . no, it was A4 to start with, went A5 because of cost, then went back to A4, with glossy and spot toner and professional-for-the-time typesetting, and then went to A3 as well –

Wow!

So I played around with the formats, just to see what you could do.

Yeah. I always preferred A5. Mine was A5, and then I did the last issue as A6.

Right. Very small.

I like them . . . the smaller the better, really.

I think it's also what the content is, because if it's more 'of the moment' content, it's more like a fanzine than if it's something that is not pitched to any particular time.

Yeah. Because we're sort of asking these questions because we're thinking about who to include in our book, and, you know, there's

all these things that are slightly related, like small press comics as well, self-published comics, and things like that, and you feel like you have to . . . draw the line somewhere. Because otherwise it's just like . . . anything could be included.

No, exactly. I mean, the other thing, if you just take a sheet of A3, treat it as four pages and fold it in half, and give it away for free, it's very easy to format. A lot of people were doing that [in the nineties]. There was London Psychogeographical Association, Association of Autonomous Astronauts – I collected a lot of that stuff in a book called *Mind Invaders* in '97. You know, sometimes people did pamphlets, but there were a lot of what people called newsletters. But I don't know whether you'd count them as fanzines. I mean, when I'm talking about me doing fanzines, I think of the early music stuff I did. I don't really think of Smile as being a fanzine, because I think it had a different audience. I guess fanzine also means fan base, so it's an enthusiast's response to something.

Going back to *Down in the Street*, were you using the name 'Stewart Home' at that point?

No, no. I think I used the name 'Rebel Mantovani'!

So right from the beginning you didn't want to use your own name? What would be the reason for that?

I think it was just to have a funny name!

Yeah.

A joke. And also because I hated the fake rebel thing in the punk scene. You know, you'd see someone who'd sprayed 'Question everything' on the back of their leather jacket. So I'd go up to them and say, 'Why have you got "Question everything" on the back of your leather jacket?' And they'd be really pissed off! [laughs]

And when did you start using 'Stewart Home'?

God, I can't remember . . . I don't think I put it on *Caught with the Meat in Your Mouth* . . . [long pause] You know, it came and went with the bands, but also, Stewart Home wasn't the name I was born with anyway.

No, I know. But you never use the name you were born with?

Yeah, no, I do. Recently, with Zoom, it's got very confusing to people. Because some people who know me as Stewart Home, if I have to see them on Zoom, they see me at a computer that says 'Kevin Callan'. And they say 'Whose computer is that?' And I say 'It's mine! That's my name!' [laughs] And they're like 'But that's not what I know you as . . .' I go, 'Doesn't mean it's not my name!'

One of the things I'm wondering about . . . thinking about fanzines, one of the things is how kind of transient they are, you know, and ephemeral. And the fact that you haven't got any of yours any more, and they're impossible to find, you know –

Some people – I have superfans, and they collect everything. They've told me they've got them. I haven't seen them –

Well, I tried googling, and I've drawn a blank . . .

Yeah. No, I mean, because I didn't know then that you were supposed to deposit stuff at the British Library. Which probably most 17-year-olds don't know.

Well no, most people don't know that, but I mean, if you had known, would you have done that?

Probably not! 'Why should I give these old crusties free magazines?'

That's what I'm wondering about, you know, like . . . whether when you're producing it you're thinking 'This is literature that will last forever!'

No, no, I'm just thinking, 'This is for this week' . . .

5

MARK HODKINSON

*interviewed by Gavin Hogg
and Hamish Ironside*

When you begin researching Mark Hodkinson's output as writer, editor, publisher and broadcaster, the sheer variety and abundance of it are impressive. But when you begin examining it in detail, what is more impressive is how well he does all of it.

At the time of writing, his latest book is *No One Round Here Reads Tolstoy: Memoirs of a Working-Class Reader* (Canongate, 2022), a brilliantly entertaining account of how Mark became a bibliophile despite growing up in a house that contained just one book. Prior to that, Mark has written novels, books about football, music biographies (with subjects including Marianne Faithfull and the Wedding Present), along with journalism for *The Times* and *The Guardian*, among others. His occasional radio programmes for the BBC have included 'J. D. Salinger, Made in England', a fascinating investigation into the Devonian background of 'For Esmé – with Love and Squalor', possibly Salinger's best short story (for that matter, possibly the best short story by anyone, ever!). Finally, Mark's own Pomona Books (www.pomonauk.com) is probably the independent press that feels closest in spirit to what Boatwhistle stands for, publishing books purely based on their literary qualities and regardless of their commercial potential – the same impetus that makes one start a zine, but all the rarer in the book trade. *No One Round Here Reads Tolstoy* goes into agonising detail about some of the consequences of running a publishing house on this basis.

Mark Hodkinson at his home in January 2022 (photo by Kellie While).

Before all of this activity – and arguably the foundation of it all – there was Untermensch. It began in the early 1980s as a band formed by Mark with a group of friends from his school in Rochdale. Mark explains where the name came from:

> We settled on Untermensch after our very first singer (Steven Bridge) found the word in a Sven Hassel book. It means sub-human and we felt, as champions of the underdog and under-privileged and any-one else under-something, that we'd adopt it as an inverted badge of honour. At the time, we weren't aware of its Nazi affiliations – the term was used pejoratively as a catch-all for Jews, Romanies, homo-sexuals etc.

Having started as a band, they began also producing *Untermensch* the fanzine, which ran to four issues in total between late 1981 and early 1983. The first issue was in an unusual 297 × 105 mm format (i.e. as A4 sheets folded not as A5 but along the longer axis), and sold for 15p; the other three issues were A4.

All four issues are true collaborative efforts, and no one is named as editor. This, as well as the overall ethos of the whole enterprise, reflects the influence of Crass, the presiding spirits of many a fanzine in this post-punk period. After the first, mainly music-based issue, subsequent issues of *Untermensch* start to include pieces opposed to war, religion, sexism and vivisection, as well as a strongly local flavour throughout, whether reviewing Rochdale's venues or railing against the apathy of the townsfolk ('Come on Rochdale, get off your arses!'). Special mention must go to a wonderfully ingenuous short interview (by Mark Witty) with Buddy Rich, who was appearing at the Bradford International Jazz Festival. Similarly likeable is the volte-face whereby Untermensch slag off Rochdale College Disco in issue 1, then apologise and run an interview with its organiser, Henry, in issue 3. The frank admission of having made a mistake is endearing.

In due course Untermensch morphed into other bands, and the members diversified into other interests, with Mark going on to study journalism before beginning his career writing for local newspapers. He kept writing for other zines during this time, and produced one more of his own, under the name of *Intense*, in 1987 – a very enjoyable and well-written effort, rather more light-hearted and irreverent in tone than *Untermensch*.

We visited Mark at his home in Littleborough, on the outskirts of Rochdale, in February 2022.

———

GAVIN: Can you tell me a bit about how Untermensch started? How many of you were doing the fanzine, and how old you were you when it started?

We were about 15 when we got together. I don't know . . . even now I find it difficult to say how we embraced what was going on, we just seemed to do it intuitively. I'm talking post-punk really.

GAVIN: So this would have been around 1981?

1980 we formed. I think we were the quiet kids at school, in a very rough school, that gravitated to one another. And then . . . 'Well, let's form a band.' And then the fanzine felt absolutely a natural progression. 'We've rehearsed for three days, what shall we do now? We'll start writing.' We'd had no encouragement whatsoever at school. The literacy we had was one another, and sharing stuff. We're still best friends now, the four or five of us that were in and out of the group.

HAMISH: Could we quickly say who the others are in this group?

There's Dave Taylor, who was the Lord Mayor of York last year. And he puts his hair up like the guy out of Prodigy. Very left wing. I think he left the Labour Party, he's in the Green Party now. He got disillusioned with the Labour Party. This is amazing, considering we were all from very normal working-class backgrounds: he was a dyed-in-the-wool communist by 14. We educated one another and he was part of that.

The singer was called Jim Stringer, he's a graphic designer and copywriter now. The drummer was Robert Taylor, not related to Dave. The keyboard player was called Terry Eves. He was four years older than us and had just arrived back from Tasmania. Brought up in Rochdale, went to Tasmania for four years with his family – came back, had a keyboard and joined the band.

HAMISH: I was wondering how much your novel, *The Last Mad Surge of Youth*, was based on specific people.

Oh God, yeah completely, they're all in there. Have you read it?

Untermensch in 1981(?). Left to right: Mark Hodkinson, Terry Eves, Jim Stringer, Rob Taylor, Dave Taylor (photo by Peter Read).

HAMISH: I'm three-quarters of the way through it at the moment.

It's basically very autobiographical.

GAVIN: Would they recognise themselves in it with things they did and said?

Yeah, it's funny, because they've not read it in much detail. One or two bits I thought they might say, 'Oh God, why did you put that in?' They haven't done, but they are basically the members of the band in the novel.

HAMISH: So was it a band first and then the fanzine idea just came along as a secondary thing?

Yeah. I don't know how we knew to do them even. We weren't aware of a big culture of fanzines.

HAMISH: Had you seen any?

No ... Maybe. I don't remember. Obviously I remember later being sold them at gigs and seeing them around. But it felt just − I hate the word organic because everyone uses it, but it was very organic: 'Let's do some writing now and show it to mates at school.' This idea that we could possibly convert them to being more open-minded − without being pious, because we were never that. We wanted a bigger gang and we also saw it as a way to publicise the group.

We had no idea whatsoever of how the music business worked, how you'd get a press officer and the rest of it, so we thought it was kind of a quasi-pamphlet about the band. 'But we'll do it subtly, so we'll put other groups in as well and make it interesting.' When you look at them they don't fit in with the clichés of how most zines look. That was because we didn't know the clichés. The first one, we said 'Why don't we fold it that way?' I've never seen that done before.

HAMISH: I know, I'm really interested to see this. It's like handling a precious artefact when you get issue 1 of any fanzine. Is it done on a duplicator? It's not photocopied.

Is that where you typed onto it? A Gestetner?

HAMISH: Yeah.

It was one of those we did it on. Once you've done it, it was very difficult to change it, basically.

HAMISH: How did you have access to that Gestetner?

The school was called a community school. Although it was very rough, there was an inclusivity about it where you were meant to be tied in with the local community. We had a community teacher and he would be running under-fives' groups and pensioners' groups, they'd all be coming to the school. That particular department had a duplicator, and we said, 'Can we do this fanzine?' He didn't know what a fanzine was, this bloke, but he was fine with it. He saw the first one and said, 'It's great lads, but can you spread your "fucks" out a little bit? If they're all in one place I'll get in trouble.' He was a typical bearded, corduroy, quasi-liberal school teacher. When I think back, how cute, you know – that was good advice, because I think we were fucking 'fucking' all over the fucking place!

HAMISH: Were they basically treating it like a school project then? You didn't have to pay them to do it for example?

I think he got us the paper for free and gave his time for free but it was not school-endorsed or supported in any way beyond this one man. I think he thought 'Yeah, you lads should be doing stuff like this, I've heard a bit about punk.' I want to make this clear, it was a very unsupportive, hostile school and we'd found the one person that, on the blind side of the rest of the school, would help. It wasn't modern in any way whatsoever, the school. I sound really bitter – well, I am. It did all it could to crush people. We were going to work in mills. Or factories. You can see how strong the clique would be of people that weren't going to do that, and their determination. And when I say we were outside the clichés, when you look at the acts we had on the front of the first issue there was no other fanzine in 1980 that would have Hawkwind, Massagana, a reggae band from Moss Side . . . are Crass on there?

GAVIN: Yeah, and Dead Kennedys and Tractor, a local band.

Because we didn't know, we just thought these lads have sent us a cassette, we'll put them in. I was a bit embarrassed for a while about that because you look at the cool fanzines and . . . it's nice as an older person

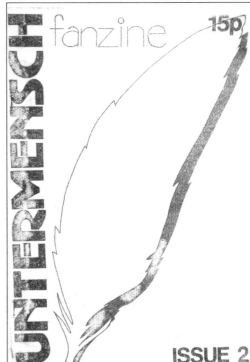

Untermensch issues 1 and 2.

to see that we weren't in with it but at the time I thought, 'God, we're so far out of it, it's not a proper fanzine.' All the covers are a bit odd.

HAMISH: I think they all look quite big names there. They're mostly bands I recognise: Crass, Hawkwind, Dead Kennedys, UK Subs. The last three I don't recognise: Massagana, Tractor, Bizarre Dares.

They were a local group, Bizarre Dares. Tractor were a good band, they were prog rock.

GAVIN: Yeah, they were on your Radio 4 documentary about singles ['Single Life'] weren't they? Tony Crabtree. He sounded like an interesting character.

HAMISH: Do you remember how many you would have printed of issue one?

A ridiculous amount. About five hundred?

Untermensch issues 3 and 4.

HAMISH: And how were you selling them?

At gigs. I loved all the process apart from that bit. We got involved with a poet called Andy Thorley, Andy T, who was released on Crass Records. He's still at it now. He was part of the team but on the edges of it. Without realising, we found out what we were all good at. Me and Dave were the best at writing. Andy was a good seller and he liked talking to people. I was too shy for that, I didn't like it. Terry, the keyboard player, would come back and he'd have sold twenty and I'd done three.

HAMISH: Would you all share the money out and everything?

The money always went into the next one. If we needed more paper because we'd stopped getting it for free we'd use it that way. We'd put gigs on as well. We saw ourselves as a mini-conglomerate really. And incredibly earnest.

GAVIN: You were saying before that you wanted to expand the gang. Did that start to happen through the fanzine and the band?

It did. When I think back we did extremely well because now you can contact people very easily but then it was all hand to hand really or letter writing. Dave Taylor had his address in there and we met some lovely people . . . 'Can I do you the cover?' Or 'I've done this piece . . .' So it grew. Not massively, but the five became twenty, maybe. There was a good scene that developed around it. That's another important thing about fanzines: people gravitate. How old are you? [To both]

HAMISH AND GAVIN: 51.

Similar age to myself then, a bit younger. It was so difficult to gather people. It felt that way. When you think about now, you can run a band from a laptop, make the music, do the pictures, send it everywhere. I don't know how we had the energy. Well, I do know we had the energy, we had lots of it – and the determination, and ambition – of each of us – was extraordinary. The dedication.

HAMISH: So there were four *Untermensch* fanzine issues, is that correct? I see here a *Shunt*. Is that a one-off?

That was a pal of mine [Mark Witty] who wanted to do his own comedy fanzine. I've not opened that for thirty-five years. He's now a producer at Yorkshire TV, the guy that did it. Basically, we lent him contacts and print and all that sort of stuff.

HAMISH: So you basically weren't really much involved with that?

I think he put inside something about that – 'This is brought to you by Untermensch Productions', or something like that.

GAVIN: Yeah, 'Untermensch Productions present'.

A very funny man. But that was the theme of it – umbrella was another term we'd use, 'come and get under this umbrella with us'.

HAMISH: The only one I've had a chance to read is *Untermensch* number two. There you can clearly see there are a lot of different writers. The other one I had was *Intense*, which is later, I think 1987, and I get the impression that it's all your own work. Is that right?

It more or less is, yeah. With bits of stuff by – do you know Tony Michaelides? He was like the Manchester John Peel, he was on Piccadilly Radio. And Tony got access to Julian Cope and Michael Stipe on his programme. I think one or two of his interviews are in there.

HAMISH: That's right, there are some nice interviews in there.

Things I really like are like when you're having a go at Michael Parkinson – a 'Yorkshire twat'. That's the sort of thing I like in fanzines, it's always these little incidental things you probably think of as filler at the time but they're always my favourite bits.

I think that being an iconoclast is really important and fanzines serve that function extremely well. Random targets like Michael Parkinson, he was always scratching his nose and talking about the great era of films in the fifties – well, that's boring, Michael. He was a great interviewer by the way, I'm not completely dissing him, but . . .

HAMISH: I'm not a fan of Michael Parkinson so you don't have to say anything nice about him on my account.

GAVIN: Were you still living in Rochdale or had you moved to Manchester when you did *Intense*?

I've never left Rochdale. I lived in different parts of Rochdale.

I've been lucky, I've always done what I wanted to do. I thought 'Well, if it takes off . . .' My mate Terry from the band was round last night. He brought the fanzines and said 'It started with this [points to *Untermensch* issue 1] and it's ended up with this [points to *No One Round Here Reads Tolstoy*], and daft as it seems, I'd never thought of that. But it did.

HAMISH: That was one of the things I wanted to get on to – it seems like you sort of transitioned to – I don't know if a writing career came first – but you've done like broadcast journalism as well, and then novels and all sorts of things, and publishing now with Pomona. How did that all happen and do you think any of it came out of doing the fanzines?

I think everything came out of the fanzines, yeah. Learning how to interview, getting it all done. The DIY element means that I felt so empowered by my experience that began with fanzines that I did some very formal local newspaper journalism. I could do near enough anything now. Quite a lot of people get stuff dropped on them, don't they? They're very fortunate in life. But to me everything has felt a good struggle, a kind struggle. I still think I'm . . . people often disown their younger selves: 'I'm different now'. I think I'm still the same, I feel very much like I've changed very little.

HAMISH: I'm glad you've said that because I agree. Another thing, getting a bit off the topic a bit here, but the fact that you're obviously a big Salinger fan, which I am as well. But that's one of the things about . . . People look at *Catcher in the Rye* and say, they dismiss it as an adolescent novel, as if adolescence isn't an important time of life, and as if that's not a valid attitude to have.

I cover that in the book. And I did a radio interview with Nihal Arthanayake last week, and I said that very thing. I was on for about an hour. I was really nervous beforehand, but I settled down and I was fine. He said something like, 'Oh, everyone reads that when they're little', and I said that very point. I said it shouldn't be dismissed that way, it's an important piece of work. It indemnifies us from mistakes and childishness if you say 'Oh, that was then and this is now'. But actually I still feel the same way and I still re-read the book. I don't feel . . . my attitude is still very much, 'Do what you want to do and enjoy life, and be in control of your life.' But it came against that background of being told 'You can't have this life.' Again, in that interview I did with Nihal I was saying, 'A lot of people didn't make it through from my background. You see them at 23 and they look 50.' A lot of them are dead now, they stayed in the part-time job in the mill that was meant to last for three months, and they were fucked at 40. But one or two of us kind of drew from it the fight. I'm 57 now, and I've really fought for that book to get to this point and it's all to do with all this stuff [points at the fanzines on the table]. My apprenticeship that started with fanzines has been thorough and sustained. When I look back, I did twenty-five, thirty books on Pomona, each of them was a real . . . well, you'll know, producing a book – it's a long, difficult, time-consuming, often thankless process. But I have that resilience.

HAMISH: Exactly, it's resilience, isn't it? I think you find from doing a fanzine that you're going to get knocked back maybe by every three or four people you ask but then the fifth will respond. I used to write to people, just send them like a questionnaire to fill in. Most of them don't reply but then I got one from Paul Heaton, which was a really nice thing. You sort of realise that it's worth persisting. I don't mind writing to ten people, if one replies that's still a success. And I think that's a good lesson to learn.

If you struggle too long you can turn in on yourself and it can spoil what you're trying to do and make you embittered, but there's a point where you're just about right – you've had enough of the fight and enough commendations from other people to be happy with yourself and you work better for it. Before I got the deal for this book I'd given up and I was happy giving up – thinking I'd just publish on Pomona if I got an idea, and happy doing other people's work. It took me years to reach that stage: 'It's not going to happen for me, I'm not going to get a major publishing deal, this is it.' And that was okay. About two weeks later I got a new agent and he'd had two offers for the book.

All the hustling I've done – because I am a hustler, because I had to be – it goes back to the bands I was in. We very nearly got deals in two or three groups, and didn't quite. I often wondered what patronage is like, what's it like to be in that creative process with other people that can make a difference. I discovered it with Canongate. This is what I wanted to happen with Untermensch, who became the Monkey Run. Then I joined a band called the Last Peach. In 1993 we were the *Melody Maker*'s tip, with Suede and Pulp. We really had the heat behind us and didn't quite get the major deal. I've been the nearly man a few times, and I've reconciled that. Thinking, 'Well, I've not been in a factory, I've not worked in a mill.' And I was told in my careers tutorial that the best I'd be would be a retail manager at Marks & Spencer's. And then they added that they'd got their own free chiropodist that comes every two weeks!

GAVIN: That's a deal-breaker for me!

I went home and told my mum and she said, 'Well, they know best. You'd better pack in this now.'

Sorry, it's a bit deep.

GAVIN: One of the things I really liked with issue of 2 of *Untermensch*, possibly because you'd not really read many fanzines before, is that it is very much grounded in the local area and the town you were from. I'm guessing from what you've said that it wasn't a conscious thing particularly. There's stuff like reviews of different nightspots, at times it's almost like a local newspaper – there's a report about a jumper that is £2 more expensive than it was a few weeks before, or a thing about a pub refurbishment.

Yeah. I think we were quite magnanimous in that we didn't hate other bands particularly, and that's almost like the default setting. It was a little bit ... Christian. And evangelical. Gathering people, and not being horrible to one or another. We would include these bands that were absolutely awful, that weren't really fanziney bands – like, borderline cabaret – but we'd treat them respectfully, with decency, and write about them, and not be nasty. Because we were an isolated group in a very conservative town, we would go out to these pubs, and ... a mate of mine wore eyeliner, so someone broke his arm. It was a rough place to be. So our revenge on the people that were doing this attacking and running these pubs was to say it straight: 'If you get on a train here you can go and watch some brilliant bands in Manchester, or in Leeds. You don't have to go down to Tram Tracks or Scene One and have a fight and beat someone up.' Because it was – I mean I don't know your backgrounds, but this town was rough. There's never been an alternative scene really. So we did all know one another, and look out for one another, and the fanzines were part of that process really. It was lonely as well, as you get more worldly you realise you can go to other places, but I ended up in Tiffs, hating it, but I wanted to meet girls. So you did it and suffered it. 'You go on your own, and you leave on your own ...' – it's classic really.

GAVIN: **There's lots of frustration in the fanzines, with that life and those experiences that you lived.**

But there's another weird thing about places like this: from them come really interesting nutters. And people outside of ... because it's so judgemental, it squeezes from it people that do dream big. Either friends of mine or friends of friends, some real characters, some real personalities. You can see how that would happen in a place like this. You cut yourself off and become more of what you are, because they won't let you in anyway, so you might as well be what you want to be.

HAMISH: **You were also writing for other fanzines – you mentioned** *Tongue in Cheek*, **which is one I know as well. You carried on doing that, but at some point did you stop reading fanzines and sort of lose interest in that whole scene?**

Yeah, I think I did really.

HAMISH: **Too many other things to do?**

I was very unsure, like most people are when they're young, but when I got into newspapers I realised I did have a talent for the whole gamut – you know, for interviewing, for what was a news story, how to deliver and how to write features. You want a bigger framing for what you're doing. That wasn't with arrogance. Because when I'm doing this one here [Intense], I'm not far off joining The Times, when I'm doing that fanzine. I'm steeped in that culture, and I'll dip into it, but I wanted a bigger influence, and my ego wanted more.

HAMISH: **But also it becomes your livelihood, doesn't it? If you want to be a freelance writer and a journalist and everything, you probably get to a sort of conflict where you think, 'Well, I'm going to have to start writing for editors and things that they want to pay for.'**

Yeah, yeah. Very much so. I think now, with the internet . . . when I was doing the Times pieces I'd get five hundred quid a piece, and now you're well paid if you get a hundred and fifty or two hundred quid. The internet feels a bit fanziney, the way it's devalued copy. Have I answered that question?

HAMISH: **Yeah, you have.**

Yeah, it's just a natural . . . I am ambitious. [But] there's something in the punk thing, that you shouldn't have an ego. That was, like, the thing that was preached. And Crass were a big influence on me, where they all wore black and they had false names, and it was a big, fluid group. They were anti-ego. So I carry a little of that with me.

HAMISH: **Actually that was how we came to ask you for this interview, was that I was saying to Gavin, the one period we hadn't covered was the early eighties fanzines, and my impression of that, just from what I'd read, was that they were all about Crass. Because Crass wouldn't do mainstream media so, as a result, I got the impression they were in almost every fanzine that was going around that time.**

Yeah, they were.

HAMISH: **They must have influenced the whole sort of politics of a whole generation of fanzine editors, do you think?**

Not just fanzine editors. To me they were the ultimate rock and roll statement. On their own label. Managed themselves. Did their own roadying. Feminists – girls in the group and boys in the group. They were almost unrecognizable from each other because of these black boiler suits that they wore. They never got paid for a gig, every single gig was a benefit. They sold over a million records on their own label. Didn't do a radio interview, didn't do a press interview. They were what the Pistols should have been. And they did it because they were grafters who were artistic and all the things that we were in our little satellite way. That was the mother ship; they were the people we were trying to emulate. They were saying 'You can do this'. They had their own security. Everything about them was independence and autonomy. What a marvellous example to set. And I happened to love the music.

HAMISH: I've never heard a Crass song. I've spoken to a few people and mentioned Crass, they all know the name but they don't know the music at all. I guess it's like a result of the same thing: that they never get played on the radio, they don't really get attention, even in retrospective articles in the music magazines.

That's the appeal, because it was massive but it was understated. Crass had that appeal, like a secret society. Actually, the branding was incredibly powerful, much like early Joy Division for example, because of the strange art. I don't know if you've seen the artwork – it's all cut-up, surrealist, monochrome covers that fold down. My friend Christian that did all the typesetting for the Pomona books, I think he loves Crass mainly for the artwork.

HAMISH: Yeah. I've seen it in a secondary sort of way, because it's talked about a lot in this book, I don't know if you've seen it, Ripped, Torn and Cut [Manchester University Press, 2018]. It's a really interesting book actually. It's a collection of essays by different writers, so it's got, like, Nicholas Bullen, who used to be in Napalm Death – he did a fanzine when he was about 12. There's loads of very interesting stuff and a fair amount about Crass.

I must get this. [looking through book] City Fun – a Manchester zine. That was a bit full of itself, City Fun, and pseudo, I always felt.

HAMISH: In that book, one of the things that I noticed was it seems

that some of them can get a bit po-faced. Some of them have very strict rules about who they can include and who they can't. They'd get into these disputes, like, 'Okay, we're totally for freedom of speech, but if someone submits an ultra-right-wing article so we have to publish that?' And they have these sorts of debates among themselves. But it does seem a little bit too earnest for a fanzine, to me. You don't get the impression with *Untermensch* that you had to be addressing issues like that.

We did have huge ... it was, like, ever looking for the sell-out, you know? That's the discussion I have with my younger self, constantly, with everything I do. 'Would you have done that at 16 or 17?' It did spoil ... it was too weighty. 'Shall we do this? No ...' And it's such a small, poxy level, like anyone gave a damn!

I remember the *Rochdale Observer* did a piece on us. We did that to try and get more people involved. I don't know if I wrote it, but one of us did a piece about 'please don't accuse us of selling out'. Like anyone cares! But it did matter to us. And when you've got Crass ...

I got to know the members of Crass subsequently, and they did live it in those days. They said they did have two days of letter writing. I said 'How many letters would you write?' 'About fifty each.' And they always did that, that kind of bespoke approach. And I said, 'How did you get the vans? And where were you getting the gear? Did you not all get bad backs lugging all this gear?' 'Oh yeah, we did – and then we got a mate to lease an amp.' And then they go on about they broke down at three in the morning somewhere. They never once resorted to the conventional rock'n'roll way of being – 'We'll get someone else to do that, we'll hire a nice van with seats in it.' Cold, horrible, early eighties, up and down that motorway, to go and play to raise money for, I don't know, a rape crisis centre. Or they would have done one for someone's fanzine if they were having trouble. Playing scout huts, pubs where bands didn't normally play, so quite often there'd be fighting with skinheads and fascists, because that was another thing that was going on at the time. I think 'My God, they went through all that?' I couldn't have done it.

HAMISH: And when did they stop, because they didn't continue into the nineties, did they?

Another wonderful thing they did, they said, 'We will split up in 1984. Wherever we are at that point, this band ends. Because bands get boring after that, and that's the length of our mission.'

HAMISH: **Right. Never reformed?**

Penny [Rimbaud], the drummer, does like a jazz thing – he calls it Crass Agenda – but they've never done Crass, no. They've been true to their word. Talk about broad shoulders, I've been where they live, and you think, 'Well, they could do with a few bob.' If they reformed they could play the Shepherd's Bush Empire five nights running. Steve Ignorant, the singer, has done some old Crass songs in his set, but Crass have never reformed. They could tour America. It was massive over there. You know PM Press and things like that? They're a big anarchist network – *positive* anarchists, not blowing things up. They'd support that kind of a tour. They could play for a whole year and make such a lot of money, if they wanted. But that's not what they're into. They grow cauliflowers now!

GAVIN: **Do they still live on the commune?**

They still live there, yeah.

HAMISH: **Do you feel like your political ideas, because obviously you started when you were like fifteen, and I guess from your family and everything, that wouldn't lead you towards anarchism or communism, but do you feel you were learning things from Crass basically?**

Very much so. It felt like they just lifted the top off your head, stirred it all up, put it back on and said 'Right, what are you going to do with that now?'

HAMISH: **But you must have just agreed with it on a gut level. I mean, if they'd been ultra-right wing and done that you wouldn't have been as receptive.**

No, when I say . . . it was like I'd lifted the top off and said 'come in'. But it was a very dangerous enlightenment, because it taught you to fight the foe. A lot of people couldn't deal with it properly because it was so anti the family, it was anti . . . it was a very difficult message in some ways to discern, the lifestyle it was presenting. And it relied on you being intelligent enough to make sense of it and then adopt it or not.

What Crass was, although it came with punk, was a very proactive form of hippydom. They considered they'd learned the lessons from the passivity of hippydom. They were saying, 'No, you need to agitate, you need to do a bit more than that.' It didn't feel like dope-smoking culture and laid back – those shows were visceral. More so than the Dead Kennedys, the loudest, harshest gigs I ever went to were Crass gigs. You came out feeling bruised.

HAMISH: When I was doing my fanzine, which was starting in about 1989, the nearest equivalent I can think of would be Fugazi.

Very much like them.

HAMISH: You know, they thought everything out, their stance on everything, and they really stuck by it. Like, they didn't like stage-diving, and that would only entice people to try and do it, and that sort of thing. I think they were vegan, and they were against alcohol.

GAVIN: Yeah, they were straight edge.

HAMISH: I suspect they probably took a lot from Crass, without me knowing it at the time. I was just hearing Fugazi like it was brand new stuff, but everything comes from something else, doesn't it?

Yeah. My girlfriend makes radio programmes, and one of the ideas she had was albums that really did sound nothing like anything else. We came up with about five and I've got three thousand albums up there! Crass were one of those groups. They got called punk, but the bass player sounds like he's Gregory Isaac's bass player speeded up, there's a reggae thing going on. The drummer was military-trained, military drumming, so it's all this paradiddling all over the place. And then there's shouting . . . and then the girls are harmonising . . . Fucking hell!

GAVIN: And with fanzines, how long was it that you kept buying them?

Always kept buying them. I was thinking about this the other day, do you remember when John Peel seemed weird, that he was 40 and into all these bands? And he was the only person in the world like that. And I think he's kind of . . . he's generated a whole *movement* of people that have stuck with it now. We are all mini John Peels, aren't we? I go to Sheffield, to Record Collector, and I'll buy thirty CDs – you know them that he's got on for a pound each? And I bring them home in the hope of finding that thrill that you found at eighteen when Peel was playing English Subtitles, or Native Hipsters, or the Gynaecologists. All these household-name bands! That, in a small way, changed you.

So, in answer, I'll always buy a fanzine. And never stop doing. Because . . . I've written for *The Times* for thirty years, but . . . it's that fanzine people don't pretend to be what they're not. There's a purity, and an honesty, that I really, really enjoy.

When I first started playing guitar, I had no training. So I'm doing all sorts of weird stuff. I think in that kind of naivety, stumbling into it, there's a real . . . quality. And excitement. And I still see that in fanzines. And you think 'This lad, or this girl, will write really well one day, but this is . . . it's from the heart.' I know it sounds corny, but it's what they really want to say in the way they can say it at that point. And there's a beauty in it. In naivety. And, like I said to you before, I don't disown me being a kid. I can still read that [*Untermensch*], and I'll answer for it. It wasn't a different person.

GAVIN: **That's got to be the starting point, hasn't it, that kind of writing from the heart, and maybe in a slightly naive way . . . but you can't bypass that step, can you? If you're going to start doing something, it's got to be that.**

Yeah. And also – I go on about class too much, probably, but I think, if you've not had a lot of encouragement, and tutelage, once you stumble into this kind of thing at seventeen, eighteen, it does have a real purity. Where you're not emulating anybody else, because you've not had that much going in. We weren't self-aware at all. I think if we'd come from a different home, a more middle-class home, we might have learnt a little bit of cynicism here and there. And we didn't have any of that. There's a real purity in it. And I see that mainly in fanzines. It's important.

GAVIN: **One question I've not asked, before we finish: what makes a zine a zine?**

Naivety, purity ... Enthusiasm. Because when you do it, you must really want – like you're talking, Hamish, about your books – you *really* want to do it. And, in this world, people do fuck all. They just get by. And to actually make it happen – and *want* it to happen, and *force* it to happen – that should be supported. And it's such a fantastic quality. It's very very rare.

People just *moan*. And *do* nothing. And we were always against apathy, that was our big thing. Alright, there's no gig – so we put them on. And then they get smashed up. You can only have a lifespan of so much, but then each of us turned to something else. You know, we didn't just watch *Coronation Street* or go to Tiffs on a Friday night. It was realising you had to do it. Your dad weren't going to do it. You weren't in that environment where *anyone* did *anything*, generationally, before you. So you said, 'Well, why don't *we*?'

6

WILLIAM POTTER

interviewed by Gavin Hogg

It was Karren Ablaze who mentioned William Potter to me as a possible interviewee for this book. I thought he'd be an interesting subject, having produced his own zine, written a thesis on fanzines, designed several covers for *Ablaze!* (issues 4–6) and, as a member of the band Cud, been interviewed in other zines.

There were three A5 issues of *Groin* produced between 1985 and 1986, when William was an art student at Leeds Poly. They straddle the boundary between a fanzine and a comic. Alongside comic strips like 'Bastard Cock', the tale of a cockerel who agrees to be experimented on for money, there are articles such as an ambitious travel guide to Europe, as well as interviews with the likes of Sonic Youth and the Mighty Lemon Drops, Olympic swimmer Duncan Goodhew and fellow fanzine writer James Brown from *Attack on Bzag!* James recorded the interview to prevent being misquoted, so William deliberately kept in every 'er' and 'um'. Despite this, James later offered William the chance to write gig reviews for the *NME*. For many zine editors of this period, including several in this book, producing a fanzine was the first step to a career as a music writer. Unfortunately for William he wrote two reviews but failed the audition.

It all worked out though. Despite planning a fourth issue of *Groin* and even carrying out an interview with Brix Smith and Marcia Schofield from the Fall, the issue never came out as Cud had become a going concern. After releasing records on a couple of independent labels, they signed to A&M Records in 1991. They split up in 1995,

William Potter, Sheffield, October 2019.

after three top 40 singles, but reformed in 2006 and still tour. William now lives in Surrey, and is a writer and editor of books and comics (see williampotter.com). We met when William was in Sheffield in October 2019 for a Cud gig at the Leadmill. The interview took place in the bar of a nearby independent cinema, the Showroom.

Thanks for bringing an old issue of Groin along with you. I guess this is where it all started, right?

Yeah, that was the last issue, we only did three.

What started you on that path?

I went to Leeds Poly on an arts course as an aspiring band member rather than an artist. I was really into comics and I knew that Leeds had a reputation for being the place where bands formed. The kind of art that I did was more about media and getting out to people, not trying to get things into galleries. I started to work on fanzines and things like posters and badges for election campaigns. We'd get money from the Student Union. The unfortunate consequence was that I became social secretary for a year and actually had to do a job.

The fanzine was a good way of mixing my design ideas with my love for music. Also it helped me to meet lots of new people, especially bands, and to get into gigs for free.

Free records?

Not many, no. But I did some writing later for Leeds Student newspaper, when it was edited by Jay Rayner, so it did lead on to some freelance stuff. I saw Groin more as an arts statement than a serious music zine.

Did you see it mainly as a fanzine or a comic?

It's a mix of both. There are four pages of drawings and I think the people that bought it were more interested in the anarchic comic. It's got the formula of a magazine really, pieces on travel, on art, interviews with bands and zine writers, the comic section. I never saw it as a way of getting into writing for the music papers, though some people did.

I liked the aesthetic of it as well. A lot of the stuff I was doing at art college was getting access to a cheap photocopier and enlarging

Covers of all three issues of *Groin*, published in 1985–86.

or shrinking things. It was all about reproduction and the throwaway nature of the work I was doing. I wasn't interested in my art being permanent, I was interested in getting a reaction, making links and contacting people. It went pretty well; I'd sell it at gigs and the Student Union bar for 25p.

How many would you get printed?

I can't remember exactly but no more than 500.

Was there a direct inspiration? Were you buying many zines before you made this first one?

No, I wasn't buying many. What happens in the fanzine world is that you bump into other fanzine sellers, they see yours and you end up swapping with each other. You end up with a load of zines better or worse than yours and no money to pay the printing bills! It becomes a network of people swapping and reviewing each other's fanzines. This issue ended up being reviewed in *Melody Maker* and I got some orders from America as a result.

It was a social thing before social networks – 'I like these bands, please get in touch with me'. I gave a copy to Carl [Puttnam, singer with Cud] earlier on, he'd not seen a copy for years. He was saying that even now, with everything you can do with technology, there's still

this love of the aesthetic of cutting out pictures and text and sticking them down, taking headlines and adverts from tabloid newspapers, using poor reproductions. I love all that.

I noticed there was an article on Cud in this issue. Was this the first feature on the band?

Yes, an exclusive! Of course I was going to market us as well. It was before we'd done much, just a few demos.

Did you go on to do a Cud fanzine?

Well, I did a zine for the fans. When we became more established we set up a fan club and we even continued it when we were on a major label. I tried to make it a bit more professional looking than *Groin*. I'd interview the members of the band about their record collections, stuff about Cud's history, latest news, stuff like that. It makes me a bit sad to think that now I'd just put that kind of information on our Facebook page.

You might be the only person who was responsible for the fan club magazine, as well as being a band member.

I think it was because I enjoyed that side of it. In retrospect I should have concentrated more on the musical side of it. Mike, our guitarist was very musical and wrote most of the songs and Carl wrote most of the lyrics, whereas I handled other stuff like sleeve design, doing the zine, dealing with fans. I still do a lot of those roles now. Rather than contribute much musically, I'll work out the set lists. So, when it comes to royalties at the end of the day I don't get as much of them. I have a career in editing though so it all works out. You get those bands where one of them is a choreographer, or chooses the clothes – maybe I'm Cud's equivalent to Andrew Ridgeley!

I know you wrote a thesis about fanzines – what do you remember about it?

It was done as an extension of the work I was doing anyway – lots of photocopy work, drawing and then reproducing my drawings. It was a history of fanzines but I presented it like it was an issue of *Groin*, with two or three colours and cut out and pasted text. I went from *Sniffin' Glue* to *Groin* – which was clearly the pinnacle! Of course when the lecturers came to judge, they had no idea what it was really, I don't know if they actually read it. It wasn't about the history of art. It was about a subject they knew nothing of, the history of writers and bands and all done in a style they'd never seen. I think the presentation was a bit radical for them. I wish I could find it again. I did my research;

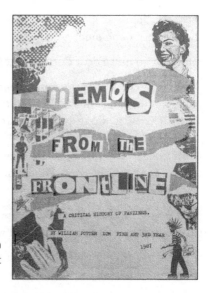

Cover of William's thesis, produced in the third year of his fine art course at Leeds Poly in 1987.

120

I looked in the Colindale newspaper library and I had my own collection of zines.

The main three at the time were *The Legend!*, *Attack on Bzag!* by James Brown and John Robb's *Rox*. That trio were known nationally, they were getting the best bands and had great design that I aspired to. I wanted my zine to be as cool as them but then the band started taking off and *Groin* got left by the wayside.

I still love the form. I sometimes do bits of design work on children's magazines and might try to twist things, put some bits of text at angles, drop in some factoids here and there, some random pictures.

What do you do on children's magazines?

When the band split up I went to London to become a comic artist. I ended up becoming a comic writer and editor for *Sonic the Comic*. Then I did some work for *Cindy*, *Winnie the Pooh*, *Shrek* and *SpongeBob SquarePants*. I did *Dick and Dom in da Bungalow*, that was the most punk title I did. Now I'm the website editor and manager for the company that produces *Star Trek* and *Doctor Who*. There's a lot of freedom with it, I can pretty much write what I want.

I write comics and children's books too so the experience of doing the fanzines was a useful one. I enjoyed the writing and the editorial as much as doing the pictures.

It was the seed for a lot of things that followed.

Yes it was, though I don't think many people in the office know that I had a magazine called *Groin*.

Why did you stop making it? Was it not having enough time or money?

Yes, I did put a lot of work into it. Actually producing the magazine was the least of it, most of the work was trying to sell it. If you were lucky you'd sell 10 at a gig and you'd end up giving a lot away or swapping them. It was a way of getting into a gig for free but very time-consuming.

I did a self-published comic called *Red Herring* and it was a similar story with that. I printed about 500 of them and a lot of work went into trying to sell it.

With *Groin* I spent a lot of time on National Express going to record shops like Probe in Liverpool or Piccadilly in Manchester. I put them in those shops and might have sold a few but I could never afford to go back and get the money or pick up unsold ones! It was just a way of distributing them or maybe getting a review in a paper that might lead to a few mail orders. I've given you one of my remaining copies but I recycled about 50 copies.

As a member of a band you must have been interviewed many times by fanzine writers?

Yeah, many times. I can see my cheeky younger self in them: 'Can I get on the guest list? Can I bring a friend?' Also the unprepared questions. I naively interviewed Sonic Youth without knowing anything about them. I said they sounded a bit like the Doors and asked if they liked them.

Do you still get interviewed by zines?

Not so much now. It tends to be people who've set up their own internet radio stations now. I do have piles and piles of old fanzines at home with Cud interviews and they're funny artefacts to have. I've become the main archivist for the band. I keep all that kind of stuff, scan it and put pieces on the website. Maybe one day I'll write the book, who knows?

What are Cud like as interviewees?

Well, we're never rude to people from zines, we know they're not professional interviewers. We're quite chatty so there's never any problem trying to get us to talk.

Didn't you do a comic book history of the band?

Yes, there were four issues of that. Shelly Bond was the editor of Vertigo Comics and she set up her own imprint called Black Crown. The idea was to mix music and comics. Her husband was Philip Bond, who'd worked on *Deadline*, which I'd written and drawn for.

I shared something on social media about one of her books. She noticed it, saw my Twitter name was @willcud and realised I was in the band that her husband had introduced her to. I pitched her the idea of a weird history of Cud, from the perspective of me and Carl being locked up in an old folk's home, trying to escape – which isn't far from the truth! It was an amazing thing to have out there. Philip drew it and it looked gorgeous. I don't think that any of the people who picked it up in the States would have had any idea what it was all about. I hope some of them did some research and realised that we actually existed. We never got invited to do a US tour off the back of it anyway.

What makes a fanzine a fanzine?

Essentially it's a magazine created by fans, to express an enthusiasm for an area – lesser-known bands, genre books, steam trains, whatever – that they feel is not being covered by magazines on the newsstands. But it goes beyond that – it's important that there's a strong DIY element. As the creator becomes a better writer and designer, the fanzine can take on the appearance of a professional magazine, as *Ablaze!* did, but as long as it retains its integrity and personality it can safely be called a fanzine. *Ablaze!* became so sleek that it could have been picked up and distributed by WHSmith's, yet it retained its character as it was filled with Karren's favourite bands. She chose the content, not record pluggers, advertisers or an editorial committee. It was produced for a love of music, not a career.

I think it has to be something created by fans, something that's cheap, a little bit crude, but with a lot of heart in it. There doesn't need to be any design knowledge, enthusiasm is enough. It's the same with fansites, they do the job of zines now. They're put together by people eager to share their enthusiasm and meet other people into the same stuff as them.

So it's all about the passion?

I think so. I can't say I was passionate about all the bands I wrote about, it was mostly about having fun with words. I just did it for a bit of cheek, I loved interviewing bands. I knew the drummer from the Mission and kept pestering him to be interviewed. I didn't like the band's music but he was a nice guy. I'd ask questions like 'Why do you wear black? You'll get too hot under the stage lights. Wear white, it reflects the light and you'll be cooler.'

You mentioned *Ablaze!*, which you did a bit of work on. How did you become involved?

Karren liked what I was doing style-wise so she asked if I could help out. I never worked on any of the editorial content but I did some cover and design work.

My one regret working with Karren was that I once spent a whole night designing one of her zines when I could have gone to see the Happy Mondays at the Warehouse in Leeds. Cud's manager had booked them for this gig and I had a free ticket. It was just before they got really big.

Do you buy zines anymore?

I don't see them around at gigs these days. The nearest I get is buying independent comics from conventions or little stores. If I like the look of them and the art, I'll pick up a copy. If I want to read about bands I look online. Back then, at the time when there were four music papers, they didn't report on the smaller, local bands, they wouldn't care about them. It was fanzines that knew more about those scenes and would have access to the bands. Hopefully the national music press would see that at some point and decide to report on them. Now all the bands are on social media themselves and there seems to be less of a need for someone with their finger on the pulse.

How is the experience of playing together again now?

It's good. We've got better relationships with the bands that were our rivals back then – 'Why did they get Single of the Week?', 'Why are they on the front of *Melody Maker*?', 'How come they're selling more than us?' That rivalry has dissipated. We see the same faces like Jim Bob, the Wedding Present and the Wonder Stuff around and we're all in the same boat. Well, they're still pulling more people to their gigs! It's good to chat to them, ask them about their kids. It's just a laugh now, we're not trying to compete with younger bands. We play a few gigs and go back to waiting outside the school gates.

7

PETE PAPHIDES

interviewed by Gavin Hogg

Pete Paphides's *Perturbed* was the first zine I ever bought: Ros, a mutual friend, sold me a copy at college in late 1987. It was a black-and-white, DIY, sweary version of *Smash Hits*. I didn't have a frame of reference for what I'd just bought, but Ros was very cool; she knew about all the obscure bands that I'd never heard of, so I was happy to own it and to feel part of an alternative, unknown universe. I lived in Solihull, not far from Pete in age or miles. He lived in Acocks Green, where he'd already printed a few issues of *Perturbed*. He made five issues between 1986 and 1988, putting together a final copy a few years later at the end of his second year of university.

Fanzines have played a pivotal role in Pete's professional and personal life. *Perturbed* issue 6 was noticed in the *Melody Maker* office and he was offered a job, which meant a move to London. After he finished working at King's Reach Tower Pete went on to write for a variety of publications including *Q*, *The Guardian*, *Time Out*, *The Word* and *Mojo*.

He first met his wife-to-be, Caitlin Moran, after encountering her while on an assignment for *Ablaze!* (see Chapter 9 for more on that zine). He'd just finished interviewing Levitation (Terry Bickers's post-House of Love band), and Caitlin was next in line to speak to them for *The Times*.

From 2005 he spent five years as the chief rock critic for *The Times*. Over the years he's made various music documentaries for Radio 4, and in 2011 BBC 6 Music broadcast his series *Vinyl Revival*, in which

Pete Paphides in Golders Green, March 2018, experiencing the mixture of pride and embarrassment that any editor feels on rereading their own zine.

he spoke to musicians such as Tom Jones, Florence Welch and Damon Albarn about their record collections.

In 2019 he set up his own record label, Needle Mythology, which reissues albums that weren't originally released on vinyl. A year later he published *Broken Greek* (Quercus), a memoir of his childhood and how pop music helped him to make sense of his life. It's a wonderful book for many reasons, but my personal highlight is the fact that, like me and my pal Simmo, he also chose 'A Taste of Aggro' by the Barron Knights as the first seven-inch single he should spend his precious pocket money on.

I interviewed Pete in March 2018 in Golders Green, at the sort of caff that might have featured in an early Dexys Midnight Runners video. We began by reminiscing about the period in the mid-eighties when the C86 movement ushered in a fresh wave of excellent zines, including titles such as *Juniper Beri-beri*, *Trout Fishing in Leytonstone*, *Slow Dazzle* and *Hungry Beat*, as well as *Perturbed*.

It's hard to explain to someone of my daughter's age what purpose fanzines served. There was a period when lots of zines popped up and they all seemed to have a similar aesthetic, and the people who wrote them looked similar, yet there was no internet. How did this moment of psychic mutual attunement happen?

How did it flourish and blossom?

How was it that you had editors in Edinburgh, the Malverns and Hastings alighting on the same aesthetic? It's not like everyone gathered together in a huddle and planned it. It's an interesting question, why did it happen? There has to be a reason. I have my own theories. Why do you think it happened?

Why did it all come together at that time? I've never really thought about what it was about the C86 scene that led to that. Up to that point there'd been zines about single artists . . . and I guess punk zines were the starting point for the indie zines . . . I don't know. What's your idea?

I think there's a sort of rejection of machismo and the codes of mainstream rock coming through in a post-Smiths world, where your cultural and political interests were merging. There would be a Socialist Worker presence at a lot of sixth form colleges. Even though you may not have been totally invested in that there was some kind of traffic between where you were politically and where you were personally as a young adult. You were defined as much by what you were rejecting and what seemed obsolete to you. It came partly from punk's rejection of the past and also a sense that rock was quite gauche. Although I wasn't articulating it to myself like this then, I was in my mid-teens and I was probably quite afraid of what it was to be a man and this all seemed to be a good stopping off point between childhood and maturity. It felt like a better way to be an adult. It was inclusive and respectful, unisex and more fun.

It's funny what you said about rejecting rock music. It was an insult for an indie band to be called 'rockist'; I remember the out-cry among Smiths fans when Johnny Marr did a guitar solo on 'Shoplifters of the World Unite'.

Oh really?

Yeah. I think because he liked to pack away the Jack Daniels then there was a concern that he was going down the Led Zeppelin route. No one would care about that stuff now.

Well, now we know that anyone who's in a band with Morrissey would be driven to distraction. Johnny's one of the most abstemious people there is. He doesn't even drink tea or coffee now.

He's a marathon-running vegan.

He is and it's interesting that most people don't know that; it's just a product of his joie de vivre. Morrissey's vegetarianism seems more about his dislike of humans I think.

At that time mainstream music felt commodified and looking for your own things in the margins was more interesting.

All drums sounded horrible in the eighties and in my naivety I thought 'Well, maybe this is the way all drums will have to sound from now on. Maybe they just *have* to be the loudest things on records now.'

I've heard the future and it sounds like this!

I thought that REM and the Smiths were the last groups who'd ever have normal-sounding drums on records. They just sounded better than the other stuff.

An amazingly lucky thing happened to me at about 16 or 17 when I befriended Joe Foster.

I remember his name. What was his record label?

Kaleidoscope Sound.

That's it. I had an I Ludicrous single that he put out.

He was brilliant, a really important figure to those of us in Birmingham at that time. I remember going to a club called the Sensateria with him and some mates of my own age. I heard this amazing record which sounded like the most beautiful noise I'd ever heard. I said 'What's this?' In a lovely, unpatronising way he told me it was the Byrds, I think it was one of the really well-known ones like 'Feel A Whole Lot Better'. He was just happy that I loved it. I thought 'I want all guitars on records to sound like this or "Driver 8" by REM'. There were so few things that sounded like that then so you'd have to content yourself with 'Mary's Prayer' by Danny Wilson and think that maybe that was as good as guitars were going to sound, notwithstanding the Smiths. Then you'd hear 'Get Out of My Dream' by the Clouds or 'Once More' by the Wedding Present and think 'How did they do that?'. In my naivety I thought there were six guitars all playing at once! Then I went to see them at the Barrel Organ in Birmingham to interview them for my zine and there were only two guitarists. It was done with gusto, youth and a disregard for hi-fidelity. I still love those records. Anyway we're getting ahead of ourselves . . .

Well, let's talk about your fanzine. How old were you when you started writing *Perturbed*?

I'd failed my O levels and had to go to FE college. I was 16, suddenly surrounded by older people and really had to learn how to carry myself. It was great because no one knew how unpopular or what a fucking idiot I'd been at school. I wasn't edgy at all. I'd been to Live Aid, I'd loved every band, thought it was the best day for pop music ever.

A few months later I went to college and I thought I was quite left-field, more than my old school-friends anyway. You're going to have to edit this to fuck by the way! I liked Echo and the Bunnymen, Lloyd Cole and the Commotions and Aztec Camera. In my mind these things made me a young man with good taste. So I was scoping my surroundings to see who I could be friends with while I was doing my sociology O level. There was a girl in my class who looked unbelievably cool and the idea that I could ever be friends with her was frightening. She had a floppy fringe, her hair was shaved at the sides and she wore radical makeup. Her name was Angela and she was clearly the most fashion-wise, edgy person in the class. I thought 'I'd love to be friends with her, but how will that ever happen?' I was wearing flared jeans because my mum still bought my clothes and I was too embarrassed to ask her to take them in. Anyway, we were given a project and put into groups of four to discuss what it means to seize the means of control or something. Angela had this folder with names of bands I'd never heard of written on it like the Soup Dragons, Primal Scream, Sonic Youth and the Wedding Present. I said 'What are these on here?'

She said, 'Oh, they're all my favourite bands.'

'Where can I hear them?'

'Well, you can listen to John Peel – but the show I really like is Andy Kershaw, 10 o'clock till midnight every Thursday.'

At the time that was the kind of music he was playing. He'd play a bit of African music too, which was great, but two-thirds of his show was noisy guitar stuff. I was a bit besotted with her but I never thought I stood a chance of going out with her – and quite rightly so, I never did. It was like that bit in *Gregory's Girl* where he just wants to stand near Dorothy.

And bask in the reflected glow from this magnificent person.

I just wanted to be near her. So I decided to listen to Andy Kershaw and do whatever it took to know who these bands were. I'd just got an Aiwa personal stereo so I got a cassette and taped as much as I could of a show onto a C90. In that one show he played 'Spring Rain' by the Go-Betweens, 'Rolling Moon' by the Chills, Iggy's 'Lust for Life', 'Once More' by the Wedding Present, 'Going Back' by the Byrds, 'The Backyard' by the Miracle Legion, 'Somewhere In China' by the Shop Assistants – still one of my all-time favourite tracks – some Ivor Cutler . . . it was just a complete education, I could go in all sorts of directions. I taped his show every week after that and dutifully reported back to Angela.

I knew that fanzines existed because my brother was at Manchester Polytechnic doing fine art. He would bring some back home some-times, like *Debris* by Dave Haslam and one called *Acrylic Daze* which I remember because they once had Paddy McAloon on the cover. As far as Angela was concerned we had similar tastes in music, but I had to keep the ball rolling. There was talk about starting a college magazine because there wasn't one at the time, so I said, 'Well, let's make it a fanzine and we can both write for it.'

It all started quite quickly after that. Angela used to follow the Housemartins around so she managed to get a little interview with them. By this time it was about February 1986 and I've gone from the position of knowing nothing to starting a fanzine. I'm listening to the Kershaw shows and buying more and more records. One Friday in May my brother called me from Manchester and said 'You like the Go-

Betweens, don't you?' I'd seen them supporting Aztec Camera and had the 'Part Company' single. He said he'd been to see them in Manchester and got talking to Lindy Morrison, their drummer, and told her about me and the fanzine. She said she wanted to meet me and that I should go to the Birmingham Triangle at Aston University at half past three just after their soundcheck. Their album *Liberty Belle and the Black Diamond Express* came out that day or the day before. I took it all very seriously indeed. On Saturday morning I went and bought the record and listened to it for a few hours, paralysed by nerves. It felt like it was the most important thing that was ever going to happen to me.

Like your whole life was leading up to this point?

Yeah. I was reading the lyrics and didn't know what a lot of it meant. I was thinking 'Oh God, how am I going to get through this?' Also, I wanted her to like me. I turned up and she was very kind. When I look back now I see someone being nice to a child. I was only 16. Every time I opened my mouth I could hear my voice shaking and that was making me even more nervous. Halfway through the interview in her dressing room, Robert Forster comes in. You know when you go to the zoo and you're just waiting for the giraffes to appear? They come out really slowly. He was like a glamorous giraffe, walked in and sat down cross-legged. He started joining in and they just took the interview over. I transcribed it all and put it in the fanzine. She was great.

So was that in the first issue?

Hardly anyone has ever seen the first issue because we had to go to Friends of the Earth to get it printed. They had one of those old-school printing presses which were really smelly.

A Banda machine?

Yeah, so I did them all manually. You could barely read it, the quality was so bad that I recycled half of the things in the first issue and put them in the second one – so the interview with Lindy and Robert was in both. By that time Angela wasn't so involved, it was mainly me and a friend called Richard who'd been my best friend since primary school. He was good at writing really funny things, fake interviews and stuff. There was a made-up interview with Matt Johnson and a thing called the Mike Nolan column. That was a tabloid-style pop column where the joke was that because he'd had that coach crash it all degenerated into nonsense with him getting all the details mixed up. It was awful really but it's what teenagers do.

Meanwhile, I started to get a bit more confident at college. What I really loved was Smash Hits, which was really funny. I thought we could do a parody of the song lyrics which were just piss-takes. We had a common room at college and I showed them to my new friends, and if they thought they were funny then I knew I could put them in. The Jesus and Mary Chain had just done 'Some Candy Talking', so I did a song called 'My Girlfriend Heroin' or something. We did a Cocteau Twins one which was thirty vowels and a New Order one too which was like a poem a five-year-old would write, based on 'State of the Nation.'

I'd phone venues and ask to speak to the tour manager, and they'd just put me through. When they heard that I was young they found it quite charming. If I did it now as a 48-year-old man it would be weird. In a short space of time I spoke to Bobby Gillespie and Pop Will Eat Itself on the same night, on another night I spoke to Edwyn Collins and Dennis Bovell, who was in his band at the time.

The other one we did, which was just bizarre, was Geoffrey Hayes off the TV show Rainbow. I lied to the Thames press officer, saying I was the editor of a Birmingham arts magazine and we were doing a piece on children's TV. He said it was odd because he'd worked there since the mid-seventies and no one had asked to interview him before. 'I'll call him and if he's up for it then he'll come down.' So we were taken out for a three-course meal, paid for by Thames, me and a friend who was posing as a photographer, just there having dinner with Geoffrey Hayes from Rainbow. It backfired a bit because when we ran the interview, no one believed it was him.

How many copies did you get printed of each one?

Up to a thousand. We'd sell them at gigs. I'd just go down the line, people were very nice.

I took a load to Reading '91 and was too shy to ask people to buy it!

Basically I did one more issue of my fanzine.

How many did you do altogether?

There were six issues – there had been a two-and-a-half-year gap before the last one. I'd enjoyed doing it, I was in my teens and had built up some momentum then I sacked it all off. I was at university, I'd split up with my girlfriend and I thought I should do one more at the end of my second year. It was a way of clawing back something positive. I did that one, sent it off to the Melody Maker, the NME and all the usual places and went off to see my parents in Cyprus for the summer holidays. I came back late in August, arrived home at one in the morning, tried to open the front door and could feel there was loads of post. I thought it was bills and stuff, but when I looked everything was addressed to me. In my absence it had been reviewed in NME, Record Collector, Melody Maker and Select. Q had printed an excerpt of it on their letters page because I'd done a Van Morrison lyric pastiche which they thought was funny. Q never did zine reviews so that was amazing. I just thought 'fucking hell', scooped them up, took them into the front room, started opening the envelopes up and getting all these 50 pence pieces sellotaped to card. There was one envelope without a coin in, from Jim Irvin, the lead singer of Furniture.

They're one of my all-time favourite bands.

Me too. I'd written him a fan letter when 'Brilliant Mind' had been a hit and the band had let me interview them for an earlier edition of Perturbed. By this point he was writing for Melody Maker under the name Jim Arundel and this letter said 'When your fanzine came in I recognised your name but before I could get my hands on it, it was getting passed round the office. People seemed to think it was pretty good. I mentioned to the reviews editor Andrew Mueller that I knew you and he wants you to try doing some test reviews.' So I tried my hand at that and he ran them. Then I thought 'That's it, the moment I finish my degree I'll move to London, there's nothing else I can do, I'm literally talentless.' This is the final issue [produces it from bag].

A lot of this . . . I can't read it back, I was like a kid really. The only interview in there was with Lilac Time. I'd written everything else and sent a letter to Stephen Duffy asking for an interview. I had different things prepared for the middle pages so if he got in touch at the last minute I could print off a thousand copies and insert them. He rang me at my parents on a Sunday night and said he was ready for an interview. He's so nice but it was like Lindy Morrison all over again, I couldn't handle it. He still is my songwriting hero.

I had to write this during the night to get it done in time. I haven't read it again since I wrote it, God knows what it's like. I think he was quite pleased when I got to work at the *Melody Maker* because there was someone in the music press batting for him. Most of the press hated him. He called me up a few months after I moved to London and said that now I'd moved down he'd show me a few things. He took me on a rock sight-seeing tour, showing me things like the back of the Savoy where Dylan filmed the 'Subterranean Homesick Blues' thing. He's a really good friend still but the first five times I met him all I could think was 'Why are you bothering with me? I'm just pathetically nervous in your company.'

He called me in the summer of 1993. Do you remember his album *Music in Colours* with Nigel Kennedy? It was great, modern psychedelic baroque pop album, but really out of step with the times, and he knew he probably wouldn't get a chance to make another. The best he could hope for was an advance from Parlophone. He called me up at *Melody Maker* and said 'Look, they've called me in for a meeting. I think they're

Covers of *Perturbed* issues 5 (1988) and 6 (1991).

going to drop me. Depending how it goes, do you want to meet up later?' I asked what the plan was. 'Well, I'm going to tell them the idea for the next album and try to get some money out of them.' He called about five hours later and said they'd just given him twenty thousand pounds. 'Do you want to go for sushi? Meet me at my flat.' He had a place in Covent Garden, a single-room flat. I went round and he had a bed that went into the wall. I didn't know they were real, I thought they were just in comics! I'd never had sushi before, I didn't know how to use chopsticks and had to harpoon things when he was looking the other way.

It must have been exciting to suddenly be part of this world.

Yeah, what it felt like was that my life had been a conceit like a late-seventies sit-com. That was how I made sense of my life. I'd gone to university, I was making the fanzine, doing some DJing and for the only time in my life I felt quite alpha. None of us ever wanted it to end.

Then I went to London and had to start again. I used to go to the offices at Melody Maker where no one would speak to me because I was hanging round too much. I was too needy and didn't know what the social protocols were. Suddenly I was a protagonist in another show, a spin-off from a very successful sit-com about the golden age of friends at university.

This was a bit darker and a bit more tragic.

I was the star of my own disappointing spin-off, probably called Making It On My Own. The opening credits would be me alighting at Blackfriars tube station, going over the bridge and the camera pans back with the credits going along the bottom. There would be a weedy Gerard Kenny-esque theme song where the chorus just explodes with drums. It would be pulled halfway through the run.

Dwindling audience figures after interest in the first episode.

No one would make it to the end of the first series and there would be no episodes on YouTube. Not even TV Cream would remember it . . . and that's what my first year at Melody Maker was like!

What were your favourite memories from your fanzine days?

I was really bad at picking up social cues. I remember trying really hard to get an interview with the Bangles just after 'Manic Monday' was a hit, being put through to their tour manager and thinking I could persuade him to let me meet the band. I'd get told to fuck off and ten minutes later I'd ring again and say 'No, this will be really good, I promise'. I'm kind of amazed how pushy I was. It's a very important part of being young. I try to impart some of this to my kids – you might have a planned endpoint, where you hope some of this might lead to, but it doesn't really matter if you don't know how's it's going to happen. It's kind of like rock climbing, you just need to know where the next few ledges are. The rest will kind of happen.

You just need to make a start and you'll find a way.

Doing nothing isn't going to result in anything. I remember it was usually me and my mate Richard doing the interviews and we pinched a lot of our questions from Smash Hits because we loved it. [Looks through old fanzine] This Les Dawson picture with a caption saying 'My wife is dead'. It's just awful.

I had this when I was 17 and I thought it was hilarious.

Well yeah, we did at the time. We thought it was the funniest thing ever! It's only funny when teenagers do it. If I did it now, it would just be trolling. Iconoclasm is only suited to the young, it's when you're sifting through the world that your parents' generation has created for you and deciding what you need or don't need. Poor old Les Dawson, he was brilliant – I was just being stupid. I remember we interviewed Peter and Chris Coyne from the Godfathers in Wolverhampton Poly. We turned up with a copy of this issue, they turned to the picture and said 'What's funny about this? This is sick.'

They were being serious?

Yeah, they were like the indie Two Rons. We had to do an interview on the back of that, they hated us. It was awful. We didn't know any better, we were just terrible teenagers.

Lots of bands were nice though. Pop Will Eat Itself were great to us, that was very early on, as was Bobby Gillespie, who we interviewed the same night in the toilets of Burberries. There was Julian Cope too. For the third issue my guileless technique of just calling the venue and hoping for the best struck lucky. He was playing the Digbeth Irish

Centre, 'World Shut Your Mouth' had just been a hit and I was going to the gig anyway. I called the venue and a sweet little Irish lady answered the phone.

'Could I speak to Julian Cope's tour manager please?'

'Julian who?'

'Julian Cope, the artist who's playing tonight.'

'Just a minute dear.'

I hear the call being redirected then a voice. 'Hello?'

I said 'Hello, who's that?'

'This is Julian.'

'Hi Julian, my name's Pete. I do a fanzine called Perturbed, I wanted to see if I could do an interview with you.'

'Yeah, that sounds cool. Come to the venue tonight. Ask for my tour manager Cally, he'll know about it and we'll find a place to do it.'

I quickly rang my friend Carl who was the biggest Cope fan I knew. I told him he had to come along, we got the bus and hotfooted it down to the venue. I found Cally and said 'I'm here to interview Julian.'

'I don't think you are.'

'Honestly, I spoke to him on the phone, he said it was fine.'

'How on earth did you speak to him on the phone?' So I told him the story even though he clearly didn't want us to be there. He went and conferred with Julian and came back and said 'You need to be at the Albany hotel at half past six. You can do the interview there.'

Like Lindy Morrison, he could see I was a kid and he took the interview over, just talked and talked. I don't even have a copy of that issue; even if I did I would be too scared to read it now.

At that age it's really important to get some validation from an adult that means something to you. It means a lot doesn't it?

Absolutely. After the interview I was walking on air. He was a proper pop star who'd been on Top of the Pops. In the space of a year I'd gone from being at secondary school with no mates and no real direction and suddenly all these exciting things were happening.

What were some of the fanzines you remember fondly? You mentioned Ablaze! earlier.

Ablaze! was great, Karren's voice was really ahead of its time. It prefigured the riot grrrl thing. I liked Kvatch, which was by Clare Wadd, the co-founder of Sarah Records. I bought a copy at Warwick University when I'd been to see the Go-Betweens and there was a Ewan MacColl interview. I liked the density of it, I read it all the way home. *Are You Scared To Get Happy?* [by Matt Haynes, the other half of Sarah Records] was another one. At the time I tried to affect an aloofness from it. In fact I was a bit jealous, I didn't really feel a part of that world, there wasn't a lot going on in Birmingham. I loved all the bands that were featured in those zines. I took the piss out of *Debris* a lot, I saw it as quite funny because it was all about music and there was a kind of northern austerity about it. I was just silly, I wanted everything to be like *Smash Hits*.

I was the same. I think if you liked *Smash Hits*, its spirit infected you and had to come out.

That's well put. Now that I understand what Dave Haslam's about I have so much respect for him but at the time I just thought it was miserable. That grim, white bread world, which I guess is why so much brilliant music has come from Manchester. Again, I was jealous of all that stuff, of older people who seemed to have it sorted out. I was scared of my future. I thought I was going to fail on a massive level so I was scared and jealous of anyone who was part of a gang who seemed to be having more fun than me.

Jealous and scared . . . I remember that feeling!

You take the piss out of something if you think they're never going to like you.

Do you still listen to many of the bands you wrote about then?

Yeah, I do. I did a C86 DJ night about three years ago and a series of live one-hour mixes which I uploaded. I feel very defensive of that music – there were a lot of criticisms of that scene, that it was fey, in denial of adulthood, but everything was actually quite deliberate. If you try to describe a song like 'Truck Train Tractor' by the Pastels it probably sounds a bit weedy, but play it and it sounds fucking great, really driving. Even something like the song 'Talulah Gosh', 'Therese' by the Bodines or a single called 'Lucibelle Green' by Friends of the Family, an early version of Pram. It's an extraordinary piece of psyche-delic lo-fi guitar music.

Sometimes when I go on the running machine in the gym I listen to the mixes I did. It's not dissimilar to listening to something like Can – quite reductive, constant forward motion that builds and builds. I love 'Almost Prayed' by the Weather Prophets. It's really charming, it's clearly written by someone who's just learnt how to write good songs. I love the confidence of thinking 'I'm going to write a song about how these things happened to me and it almost made me pray.' It's like a Brill Building idea. You don't get hung up on whether these things sound authentic or not, these people were just writing their first songs. It's a false argument to say it all sounds lily-livered because firstly it doesn't and secondly it was made by a musician in direct opposition to that 'rock' aesthetic – that's why so many people were disappointed by Primal Scream when they became a rock group, it's like they didn't understand what was so good about their early incarnation. The song 'Gentle Tuesday' sounds great, it's fizzing with the stuff of life. I keep thinking of more, 'Ballad of the Band' and 'I Will Die with My Head in Flames' by Felt or 'Ten Miles' by Phil Wilson. Creation records had a seamless run between their releases CRE 28 and CRE 42.

Was it all worth the effort you put into it?

My best friend at university at the time of the last issue was called Andrew. At the end of my second year I had nothing to do for months at a time. I was in a market town in west Wales and I thought I'd just give it another go. I was sharing a kitchen with some other people on the same corridor at the halls of residence. I hated all of them apart from Andrew, who was a theology undergraduate. We got on really well, but he didn't know why he liked me; he was very sporty, popular and pretty mainstream. All the zine pages were done on separate bits of paper and I'd pin each one up onto a notice board so I could see my progress. He didn't understand fanzines or the world they came from, he'd be nice about it but he thought they were a loser's folly. He'd often come down to the corridor with his mates from the football team. On one of these drunken nights, when I was typing away on my electric typewriter, he banged on my door so hard it just opened and they all ended up in my room. They started passing round the pages and laughing and it was the first time I thought to myself 'This might actually be okay'. They liked the lyrics and Paul Buchanan's problem page seemed to be going down quite well. Andrew was so drunk and shocked at seeing so many people in my room that he sank to his knees and started crying – the logic of the drunken mind I guess. What was the question again?

Whether it was all worth the effort.

Oh yeah. Well, it was, because it got me my first work at the *Melody Maker*. Even though I was a terrible writer for the first couple of years, they didn't sack me – so that was good. There was no parent figure there, no moral guidance. A lot of us younger writers wrote things we shouldn't have written because we were just trying to impress the older kids. We were kind of encouraged to do that, to try to be cool. A lot of us just had to learn to try to become better people over time. I don't look upon my time there too fondly.

When is a fanzine a fanzine?

I think a fanzine has to exist physically, otherwise it's a blog, and it almost has to be something that no one has asked for.

Something no one knows they want?

Yeah, something initiated by one person or a small group of people. I guess it becomes a magazine when it becomes subject to the criteria you have to fulfil to be stocked in WHSmith's, something that comes out on a regular basis, with a barcode.

8

MARK TAYLOR

interviewed by Hamish Ironside

The Wikipedia page for 'Fanzine' mentions in its preamble: 'The term fanzine is sometimes confused with "fan magazine", but the latter term most often refers to commercially produced publications for (rather than by) fans.' Yet there is (or at least was) a large subgenre of zines both by and for fans: these are the zines devoted entirely to a single artist.

In fact, if you arrived at the world of zines from a certain perspective – such as having spent a lot of time in your bedroom reading *Record Collector*, line by line, and not going out much – there's a fair chance that the only zines you would have been aware of were the likes of *T'Mershi Duween* (about Frank Zappa), *Zilch* (about the Monkees) and *Black Rose* (about Thin Lizzy). My own collection of zines even includes a fanzine devoted to children's TV presenter Janet Ellis, entitled *The Janet Ellis Fanzine*. It consists almost entirely of photographs of Janet, without comment.

For me, the paradigmatic example of the single-artist fanzine would be *Smiths Indeed*, edited by Mark Taylor. Like the band to whom it was devoted, it enjoyed a short but very productive lifespan, and was highly successful. A total of twelve issues were published at regular intervals between summer 1986 and November 1989. By comparison, the Smiths formed in 1982, had their first hit in 1983, and split up in 1987. The band's split therefore came around halfway through the run of *Smiths Indeed*, and the drama of the split and its ramifications become one of the main topics of debate in the later issues.

Original issues of *Smiths Indeed* are highly collectable now, but the entire run has recently been republished as a limited edition box set, under Mark's guidance, and is available for £100 plus shipping at the time this book was published (search '*Smiths Indeed* box set' on eBay).

Perhaps no band has ever meant more to its fans than the Smiths did during those years. This is one of the things that is apparent from the many contributions squeezed into the pages of *Smiths Indeed*, and it is one of the things that made the zine so readable at the time, and no less so now. The other main factor in the zine's success is Mark's natural aptitude for editing, which is equally apparent from a cursory look at any of the twelve issues. The care taken over the design and editorial work is hugely impressive, and it is no surprise that, while *Smiths Indeed* began as a labour of love, the skills Mark developed in the course of its production have led to a successful journalistic career.

I met Mark in his hometown of Bristol in September 2021, having reread several issues of *Smiths Indeed* during the train journey from London. The final issue includes an interview with Mark himself by John McMahon, one of his readers, of which Mark says in his editorial: 'I decided it was such an absurd idea to publish an interview with myself in my own fanzine, that I just couldn't refuse.' One of the things mentioned in the interview is that Mark bought his first fanzine when he was just eleven years old. I began by asking him about that.

━━━━━━━━━━━━━━━━━━━━━━━━━━━━━━

I was born in 1969, so I'd have been ten or eleven in 1980. And I would imagine the first fanzine I saw was SFX, which was a Sheffield fanzine. It would have covered bands like Pulp, Clock DVA . . . and I would have picked it up in a Bristol comic shop, I guess. There was a shop called Forever People in Bristol, which always had loads of fanzines, loads of second-hand music papers. So you'd just go in there on a Saturday afternoon and buy whatever you saw. And I would never have seen fanzines until then, and I probably wouldn't even have known what they were. Because I wouldn't have seen *Sniffin' Glue*, you know – I'd probably heard of *Sniffin' Glue*, because obviously by then it was pretty legendary. So I knew it was an alternative to the mainstream music

Mark Taylor at Bristol's sunny harbourside in September 2021, sitting in front of Gavin Hogg's cherished collection of all twelve issues of *Smiths Indeed*.

press. And an alternative to . . . getting a job with a mainstream music paper, or something.

Eleven is very young. I mean, I was just getting into music when I was probably about ten, I definitely wouldn't have been buying fanzines until I was about sixteen. Or even encountering them.

No, I mean I did – I got into music very young. The first band I was really into was Tubeway Army and Gary Numan, back in '79, and I was only ten then. I suppose part of it is that I went to a pretty rough school, and nobody really liked that kind of music at all, so I guess it was some sort of rebellious streak in me that wanted to do things differently, and maybe like different bands to what the mainstream liked. I liked some of the Two-Tone stuff as well, round about the same time. It was always slightly – it wasn't the chart stuff, it wasn't the mainstream pop stuff that I was into.

And when you were reading zines, were you gradually percolating the idea of doing one yourself?

Yeah. I just found them fascinating. I found the writing really refreshing and exciting. I liked the idea of people creating their own – I suppose, the DIY, punk ethic of creating your own product. And I suppose, because I had no idea how to break into any kind of 'proper' journalism at that point, or writing for anybody, I suppose I probably saw it as an open door for getting your own story across and writing about the things you love. *Smiths Indeed* came a bit later, but I was buying fanzines probably from about '81 to '85 period. I remember *Debris* very well, from Manchester, by Dave Haslam, before he was a DJ. That was a big influence on me.

So most of these fanzines are, like, not specific to one band?

General fanzines. Covering indie stuff. And covering other stuff – *Debris* covered all sorts of things. They would do greasy spoon cafe reviews, and articles on Mancunian workhouses . . . they were filled with whatever they could find, I guess. Whatever they felt like publishing.

So were you thinking about maybe doing that sort of a fanzine yourself?

Maybe thinking of a general one. I think I did one at school, round about '83, I did one called *Volume*, which was photocopied on my dad's work photocopier. All the pictures were cut out of the music papers, you know? So, yeah, even '82, '83, I was producing my own fanzines. To about ten copies, sold to my family and perhaps two friends at school.

Have you kept all those?

Yeah, I have, actually.

So you were getting some practice in, doing that?

Definitely. Absolutely. And I was quite good at art at school – I was quite interested in art and English, and that was about it really, so . . . what more can you do? Music, art and English.

So the Smiths obviously started around '82, '83, and I guess you'd have first heard them around –

'83. They formed in '82, they were doing a couple of gigs in '82, but they didn't get onto my radar until a John Peel session in May '83, I guess. And then of course 'Hand in Glove' came out. So, yeah, from that moment, that was it. They were the band for me.

Yeah, so they immediately became your favourite band.

Oh yeah, I'd never heard anything like it. They just had something about them which I just . . . just loved, and felt strongly about. That was really before even *seeing* Morrissey, I'd probably heard them without even seeing them. Like you would, on a session, because you couldn't really – unless they'd been in the NME that week, you wouldn't know what they looked like, you wouldn't know much about them, what they represented. So yeah, I heard them, bought the record the minute it came out, and then, I didn't do the fanzine until '86 . . . so that was three years later.

Exactly, so that was what I was thinking: there's quite a long period when the Smiths are getting bigger, and you're thinking – I assume there's no fanzine for them yet –

Well, I had to get *serious*, and do things like O levels and try and find work. So those things got in the way.

But it is quite surprising there wasn't someone else doing one first.

Absolutely.

Especially given how many there were after Smiths Indeed started.

Yeah, and also, um ... they didn't have a fan club either. They were very much anti-fan club. I think. And yeah, it didn't really happen until '86. Probably early '86 I started thinking, you know ... I would imagine that would have been when I'd left school by then. And I was just thinking, 'What shall I do in between the boredom of my day job?' Which was working in insurance for about a year.

Oh, okay. This is what I was wondering, what you were doing – so you'd left school –

I left school at sixteen. No university or anything. I went straight into work.

You didn't fancy it, or ...

My family didn't come from any kind of background of university education. It wasn't even on the table. I regret that now, I really wish they had ... pushed me into a certain direction ... but it was never offered. Kids at our school didn't go to university. Most went to prison! I don't remember anybody actually talking about university at school.

No. It was sort of the opposite for me, because I went to university, just because it was sort of expected, but I didn't have any kind of idea this would lead on to something. I never used it for anything. I did maths and philosophy, and it didn't lead to anything. It was just sort of three years ... not *wasted* exactly, but ...

It would have been nice to have the option. It would have been nice for somebody to actually say in a careers lesson, you know, 'Go to university! You might do quite well.' I suppose that was my antidote to going to university, was doing my own fanzine. And *meeting* people. Although that was all postal – I rarely met people face to face, apart from at gigs, and later on ... it was just to meet people, I guess, and meet like-minded people. That was the obvious way to do it. I was very lucky that John Peel and Janice Long gave me some nice mentions.

Yeah. So you were sixteen, seventeen, when you started up *Smiths Indeed* . . . I'm just wondering – hard data about print runs and sales, do you remember much about that?

I don't remember much about print runs. I think the first issue was definitely quite a high print run. Mainly because I was selling it on the tour. So *The Queen is Dead* tour, October '86, is when I timed the first issue.

Ah! And you were selling at the actual gigs?

Yeah, absolutely.

Did you manage to go to every gig on the tour?

Yeah.

Wow!

Just under my own steam, and on the train. And so, I was basically reprinting it during the tour because it was selling so quickly. So I started with probably 1,000, I guess. Which is quite ambitious. And it probably cost me a fortune at the time. And I had all the tickets for gigs, and all the B&Bs booked. And I would just rock up at every gig with as many as I could carry. I probably reprinted them as I went along . . . I was often coming back from various venues, back to Bristol, to collect more. Because I didn't drive, so I was on the train. So I would take another two bags – you know, holdalls – say, 200 copies each time – and sell them on the stall.

And these would have been 50p, were they?

I think they were, yeah.

Should I tell you how that came about? Selling on the tour? Because it was quite a significant thing, really, for me. The first date of that tour was probably either the end of September '86, or even October, so it was already out at that point. But I was selling them – when people were waiting for the band to arrive, before the sound-check, I'd sold a couple of copies before they turned up, just saying 'Do you want to buy a fanzine?' And people were buying them, quite . . . vigorously.

I'm not surprised.

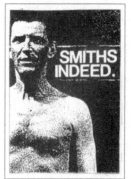

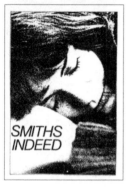

This page: *Smiths Indeed* issues 1–3 (top row) and 4–6. Opposite page: issues 7–9 (top row) and 10–12. Fun quiz: try naming all twelve cover stars. Answers at end of chapter . . .

Because they'd never seen anything like it. And I think it was something like – it wasn't Wolverhampton, it was something like – it may have been Wolverhampton, actually – it might have been Wolverhampton . . . a lot of people were hanging around then, backstage, you know, by the stage door. And as the band came in to the stage door, a guy called Grant Showbiz, he was the sound man on that tour. He was the Fall's producer, but he was also doing a bit with the Smiths. And he saw a copy, he kind of grabbed a copy, took it in. And then I saw him later on, he was saying 'Oh, this is amazing! The band love it!' You know? 'Do you want to sell it on the stall, next to the merch?'

Oh, really?

Yeah. So I was like: 'My God, I can't believe this! This is just . . . unbelievable.' You know?

That's brilliant.

Within about an hour I was given a backstage pass. I was told to go and set up on the end of the stall where they were selling the merch. Just put them out. And I remember, it was a terrifying experience! Because obviously I'd never done anything like that before. I'd suddenly just seen – because it was a standing venue – and people had been queuing for hours to get to the front – you could just see thousands of people, through the glass of the door, all waiting for the doors to open. To rush to the front. But they all rushed to the merchandise stall as well, to buy their stuff. So I'd probably sold out in about ten minutes.

I'm sure, yeah. That's amazing. So were you able to, sort of – you were knocking around with the band, backstage?

Well – I'd met them a few times, you know, I'd met them a few times on that tour; I wasn't hanging out with them, but they approved of it, otherwise I wouldn't have been on the merchandise stall.

But could you have done an interview for the fanzine?

I didn't even ask to do it. I was just too stuck in the headlights of trying to sell them all, going back to my B&B, next morning going back to Bristol, and then going – probably doing *twice* the journey, to get more fanzines – up to Nottingham, back to Bristol . . . up to Dundee . . . you know? Hopefully try and get back to somewhere else to get some more copies . . .

Living with your parents at this time?

Yeah, living with my parents and my sister.

And what did they make of it all?

Well, I think they were quite pleased I was doing something useful with my time. My sister was a little bit rebellious, and she was probably quite approving of it anyway. Because she was into bands anyway, so she probably thought it was quite cool. She used to help me collate them, when they used to come back from the printers, on the dining room table. We'd have to kind of walk round, pick each page up and staple them.

I'm glad you brought up the collation, because I like to find out about the production side of it. Just to get back to print runs and sales – you think you did a thousand of the first issue, and obviously in time you sold through all of those –

It was also helped by a John Peel mention, and a Janice Long mention, on Radio 1. Obviously that helps. So there were times I would literally wake up to a post van arriving with just literally a sack of mail.

Was that happening pretty quickly from issues 2 and 3?

It happened during issue 1, and it would have carried on. Peel and Janice Long were very generous to mention me whenever I sent them a copy. *Record Mirror* did as well, the music papers did, Q magazine did a whole page about me.

But I guess Smiths fans are the sort . . . literary types, really, so they're the sort who would pick one up at a gig and would then subscribe?

Yeah, we didn't do subscriptions, really. It was just literally –

Oh, really? I assumed most of them were subscriptions.

No, there were no subscriptions. No, I never even thought about that at the time. It was literally, they would wait – and I would be pretty good on the deadlines – I would say 'This next issue's going to be out on this particular week', and hit that deadline. So I was quite good on that.

So selling through shops and at gigs as well?

Record shops, local record shops, gigs, and most of it mail order.

But then if the Smiths weren't touring, it was just through . . .

Through mail order. Yeah, so literally *sackloads*; most days there would be two or three sacks of mail. People sending fifty pences stuck to bits of folded cereal packets . . .

Yeah, which must be what I did . . .

Postal orders, you know . . . Americans sending just *cash* . . . There was no business model there, it was all very much . . . you know . . . I winged it, basically. But it seemed to work. And it became my main job. I wasn't working then, you know?

Yeah – you said you had an insurance job for a year?

I had a pretty boring insurance job, and then I kind of gave it up. I think during the time of about, probably, issue 4 or 5, I picked up a part-time production job for a newspaper. Putting the paper together physically, proper old school. And of course I was doing stuff like that anyway for the fanzine, so I picked it up really quickly. And then I learnt from that as well how to do other processes. And I could also use their cameras for screening all the pictures, which was quite useful. Quite cost-efficient as well, because it's quite expensive to do all that stuff, you know?

So around that sort of time – issue 5 – that was becoming a very eventful time in the Smiths' career. I've got a little note: issue 5, *Strangeways* came out; issue 6, the Smiths split was confirmed; issue 7 I've just written 'readership over a thousand'! But then issue 8, *Viva*

Hate is reviewed. So there was an awful lot happening in that time, and it also, I guess, was beginning to make you question, 'Do I just carry on after the Smiths have split up?'

Yeah, I mean, I supposed I could have realised that most of the fans were going to go to the Morrissey side rather than the Marr side, maybe –

But you could cover them both, couldn't you?

Well, I could, and I did cover them both, and then, you know – and I was in neither camp, I was a Smiths fan – but there was still a lot to talk about the Smiths, there were still things happening around the Smiths, and I think it would have been very odd to leave it hanging as soon as they split. It got increasingly difficult to fill pages, I think.

That wasn't my impression, though, because when you're reading those later issues, they're densely packed with text, there's an incredible amount of contributions.

Yeah, the quality of the contributions was definitely improving, as far as – the quality, the writing . . . People were kind of seeking me out. I wasn't paying anybody, I couldn't afford to pay anybody. People like Siân Pattenden – I mean, she wrote for me. Katharine Viner, who's now editor of *The Guardian*, she wrote her first piece for me.

It looks like the text is mainly done on a manual typewriter –

Which I've still got. Yeah.

You must have spent an awful lot of time – and also, the little bits of other text that's in other fonts, is that Letraset?

Letraset, yeah. I spent most of my money on Letraset and typewriter ribbon. And Tippex.

And you must have spent an awful lot of time –

Typing?

Yes, typing! It's very impressive, there are very few mistakes. And, as I say, in the later issues, there's an incredible amount of text in there, the word count's very very high.

Yeah, it was. I was working on it all day every day, and into the night.

I didn't really get more than about five or six hours' sleep. Because I would still have to do all the admin, as in sending stuff out. So most of my day was spent visiting the local post office with bags of fanzines to send off. I knew the people in the post office more than I knew my family!

But in terms of the amount of time you were putting in, it's like a full-time job, but somewhere in one issue you say you were really only just covering your costs – which I could understand, because for most fanzines, that's how it is –

Well, Letraset was really expensive . . . all the printing was very expensive – very expensive . . . and, you know, all the travelling to gigs and all the rest of it . . .

So was part of the factor of giving it up, was it just that you wanted to be making some money?

Yeah, I probably got to the point where I just thought 'I need to have a proper job now.' A lot of people would probably say I don't have a proper job now!

By the time you got to issue 12, what sort of print runs would you have been doing then?

Because it was getting bigger – the actual physical fanzine – and it was being printed, not photocopied – it was actually coming down a bit, because the cost was so prohibitive. So if you look at issue 12 compared with issue 1, the original issue 1 was all done on a photocopier, but by the time we got to the last issue, that was being printed and it was very expensive. And I wasn't charging that much more, I probably charged a pound by the end of it. So, yeah, it was hardly making any money.

Yeah. Would you have printed less than a thousand?

No, never less than a thousand, but it would have been probably back to a thousand by the end. Although I think the last issue I probably had a few more than a thousand, probably had fifteen hundred? Maybe more. I mean, I never took notes, I never kept any sort of information about the actual business side of it. Which probably explains a lot!

In the last couple there's other people credited with artwork and

layout, and things like that –

Yeah, that was all me! It's all me.

Oh, is it?

Yeah, with different names. I got so bored of doing it [under my own name].

Oh, is that right? Lawrence Weston, and –

That's an area of Bristol! And sometimes they were *Carry On* characters.

I did wonder about James Bedsop . . .

Yeah . . . it would have been from a film, probably. Probably a *Carry On* film.

It just sounded like a classic Smiths fan name, actually.

No, I mean, I did everything.

And that was just for fun? Was it to make it look a bit more like it was –

No, no, just that I got so tired of having to say that I did everything. And I was probably slightly embarrassed . . . and probably just thought I'll make a few names up, you know? It was a bit of an in-joke with a friend of mine as well, a girl called Lucette, who's appeared in a Smiths video, or a Morrissey video. It was just a funny thing we used to have between us, making up names, you know?

And so, after the final issue, did you carry on doing any Smiths-related stuff, contribute to other fanzines, or were you sort of relieved to be done with them?

I didn't write for anybody else, but I did one more fanzine called *Sounds Like Morrissey*, which was an A4 fanzine. Which was round about . . . I'll have to check the dates. Probably his first British tour, I think. Or post that. I did that tour, followed that tour round, and took some amazing photos, and did a whole diary of the whole tour. And I did that very much in the same style as *Smiths Indeed*, but on a bigger format, A4. Gave a bit more space. And I quite enjoyed doing it on A4 rather than A5, actually. But, again, very very text-heavy. Lot of typing. Lot of Let-raset. But the photos were very good, and I'd taken them all myself . . .

And did you still have a sort of semi-official status, like were you able to sell on the merch stand?

I didn't sell on the merch stand, because this was historic to the tour, so the tour had already happened. But I'm sure I could have done that. But I didn't pursue that. You know, I never kind of . . . I never pushed it. On the Smiths or on Morrissey. You know, I came quite close to Morrissey, certainly with the filming of that video, when all the readers were the stars of the video . . . do you know about that?

Yeah, because that's covered in one of them, isn't it?

Yeah. That was the 'I Started Something I Couldn't Finish' video. I got a phone call out of the blue from one of Morrissey's people, they just said 'We're doing this video, we want some Morrissey lookalikes and fans for the video. You obviously know everybody, so can you just send us a few ideas and contact a few people you think might be up for it?' Because I'd met some of them, or seen them at gigs, I kind of knew that they'd be appropriate, or looked like Morrissey, or dressed like Morrissey. So I sent them letters, and they all replied, and then I had to send them to Morrissey's people. And then we spent the whole day in Manchester, filming the video around different landmarks of the Smiths. Which was . . . an incredible day, actually. . . Really good day. This is when I was talking to Morrissey a lot, and he offered me a lift back to Bath, and all the rest of it.

Did he?

Yeah. Which I didn't take, because I'd already arranged to do something that day.

It almost seems like you're spurning all these fantastic opportunities!

It is, actually, in hindsight! Perhaps because – I don't know! Maybe I was . . . I didn't want to get too close. I wanted some distance, maybe. 'Don't meet your heroes' type of thing.

Was it, like, a kind of awe?

Yeah, I wasn't scared of them at all but I didn't want to be too close to them in case the magic could have disappeared. I was thinking about this the other day, because I've met most of my heroes – musical heroes – apart from Nick Cave, who I saw in Poole the other night. And I was thinking, I could have easily hung around, got him to sign something. But I thought, no, he's one of the few people who still has that kind of aura. Perhaps it is shattering that aura, when you meet someone.

So you've met Gary Numan, for example?

Yeah, absolutely.

And did that shatter the aura at all?

I think I was probably starting to go off him by then anyway. You know, but Nick Cave was someone I've never met, but I still find him fascinating to watch. In concert, I think he's a fascinating performer. And I don't *want* to meet him, you know?

So one of the things I wanted to get on to was how you look back at not just the Smiths but also Morrissey and his subsequent career.

I don't follow it too closely, to be honest.

Did you stop liking the music, you just felt that wasn't anything like as good as the Smiths?

Well, I think I would have probably said that from the start anyway because I was such a Smiths fan, nothing would have compared to the Smiths. I did like some of the early Morrissey solo stuff, and I did see him quite a few times on tour, did quite a few tours.

Yeah. Did you like *Strangeways*, by the way? Because I really felt that they were going off when that came out.

Yeah, I think it's a very *sad* record. It sounds like a kind of . . . *deflated* record. Compared to *The Queen Is Dead*, for example.

I always think of it as like a Morrissey solo record. It's that much worse than the rest of the Smiths.

And the weird thing is, of course, they never toured with it. They'd split up by then.

Yeah, well, like I say, I couldn't believe how quickly it was all happening.

It happened *really* quickly. Like a pack of cards, wasn't it?

And it's a fantastic way to read it, in the pages of *Smiths Indeed*.

It is. It did feel like you were breaking stories at the same time, even though it was perhaps not like you would nowadays on a website or something. It was as close as you could in that kind of time frame of a fanzine. Because obviously fanzines take a long time to produce. It did feel like you were in the middle of it, a bit of a maelstrom at the time.

One of the quite troubling things I found reading the later issues was mention of several fans' suicides because of the Smiths – either because of them splitting up or just because of Morrissey's almost glamourising suicide. Do you feel that was quite an ethically difficult thing to present?

It *was* tough, and I did have to think about whether I was going to publish some of that stuff. But it was definitely happening, you know? You couldn't really hide away from it. That's what people were feeling; they felt so strongly about it, and that was probably just the tip of the iceberg. The people that were actually prepared to say that in print. And there must be a lot of people who probably did do that, after that, and Morrissey probably knows that.

That's what I was wondering – I didn't know if Morrissey had ever been asked about that.

Well, he's always been a little bit trite when he talks about these things. He has been trite on a lot of issues, you know. He brushes it off – he always says things like, 'People can do what they like with their lives', which I don't think is very helpful to the cause.

So does that put you off him a bit, and by extension make you look at the Smiths stuff in a slightly less enthusiastic way?

I can separate the two, I can separate the music and the band from Morrissey and the comments he's made about certain things. And that probably extends to the things he's claimed to have said in recent years as well. For me, the Smiths is in a box here, all the rest of it is in a separate box, and I don't necessarily have to dip into those boxes. But I can see why people have turned against him. Including most record labels. It must be very hard to be Morrissey these days.

Do you think he regrets it at all? Or does he almost like that position?

I think he likes it. He's a bit of an antagonist, isn't he? He likes to ruffle feathers, and for what cause I don't know. But it seems to be getting worse.

In the last year or so you've made the entire run of Smiths Indeed available again as a limited edition box set. Could you tell me a bit about that?

A guy I know who's a printer, he didn't print the original copies, but he used to buy them. But he's now got his own printing business, and he's very, kind of – I think, to be honest, it was probably something to do with the pandemic, and he didn't have any work, and he just thought 'What can I do to bring some work in?' And we'd just met, and he said 'Why don't you do a box set? Because everybody still wants copies, and they're going for good money on eBay.' So I said, 'Well, yeah, okay, if you want to do all the work! I can sign some postcards . . . you just do it and I'll pay for it.'

So they're actual facsimiles?

Well, no, a lot of them are straight from the original artwork, because I still have the original artwork for most of them – certainly for issues 6 to 12. I still had them. Although a lot of them had stuck together because there was a lot of use of Spray Mount, and I hadn't separated them with any kind of acetate. When I got them out of these envelopes they were starting to stick together, and headlines were coming off. So I had to kind of restore them for him to print. That was the first time I'd looked at them for . . . fifteen years, maybe?

Was that a pleasurable experience? Were you sort of thinking, 'These are . . . these are pretty good!'

Yeah! [laughs] It's always a pleasurable experience to see – yeah, because it just brings back a lot of memories. And good times. They were good times. And it was very exciting to be involved with it. To be seen as the official 'voice of the Smiths'. Because they were fairly untouchable. Because you couldn't write to them, really – they wouldn't write back. You couldn't really meet them very often. They had no fan club. Deliberately. Probably the only band at the time not to have a fan club. So I'm quite proud, really. It was a proud period.

Yeah. I mean, my impression, even at the time, when Smiths Indeed was one of hundreds of fanzines I was looking at, was that it was one of the really professionally run ones, you know?

That's very kind.

Which is not to say . . . I mean in a way some people would say fanzines are meant to be amateurish – so I'm not decrying it when I say 'professional'. I'm just saying you seem like you were a natural editor. And this is why I'm wondering whether it was a springboard for going on to do other things as more of a professional thing?

Oh, absolutely. I've been a journalist ever since, so it was my education into journalism, and to editing, and I've been an editor since, and a features editor, for newspapers and magazines, so . . . yeah, it was definitely my university, to get into print, and now digital. And I still write every day, and edit stuff for people every day.

And so you're basically a freelance journalist, but did you do any other actual publications that you were editing as your own project?

Well, there's Fork. Fork was a food magazine which lasted for about three years. It was successful as well, did very well within the business. Again, it was a bit of a trailblazer, because nobody had done one before – a kind of non-celebrity food magazine.

And that's still going?

No, it kind of stopped about four or five years ago. It got a bit messy with the guys I was involved with, who were designing it. They wanted to buy it off me, I didn't want to sell it, and it just disappeared into the ether. Like a lot of these things do, because there's no contract or anything like that. But people still talk about it, and it did get me a lot of work subsequently in the food press. It opened a lot of doors for me that way.

And was that because you were getting more into food than you had been into music?

Well, I've been a features writer since the mid-nineties, for newspapers, and in that first kind of period I was the first to bring in restaurant reviews to the paper – *Bristol Post* – which it didn't have before, so since then I've been a food writer more than a music writer. Although general features as well.

But, yeah, food is the new rock'n'roll! But the magazines like *Delicious* and *Olive* – they're a bit too glossy, a bit too celebrity-driven. So that's why I did *Fork* – it's more about producers and artisans, and interviewing those guys, rather than celebrity chefs.

But do you feel that's something you could start up again?

Ah, well, as you get older, and you've got mortgages and school fees, you want a bit more of a regular income.

Yeah, I know, I understand that.

I think I probably lost money on a lot of things like *Fork* and *Smiths Indeed*, ultimately. I'm not a business person.

Yeah. Same with me and Boatwhistle!

I did it for a long time. I did it, and I kept my head above water. Doing something I loved. But, you know, I'm fifty-two now, so you've got to be realistic sometimes, when you've got people to feed and clothe. All the obvious boring old things. You don't take too many risks . . . everything I've done in self-publishing has been a risk. Obviously *Smiths Indeed* paid off, and it was successful, and people still talk about it now. Which is lovely.

Exactly, I mean, it benefits you in ways other than financially.

If I hadn't done that, I probably wouldn't be doing the journalism I'm doing now. No, absolutely, it was a springboard for a lot of things. I'm proud that it was the first and the only fanzine for the Smiths at the time. And then around the world probably fifty or more came out soon afterwards. Mostly by people that I knew, that had bought *Smiths Indeed*. And they all looked like *Smiths Indeed*! In different languages. But they didn't really have the – a lot of the stuff in the background, all this stuff [pointing to images behind the text in one of the issues] was carefully sourced. I used to collect film magazines, old film magazines, and music magazines. So I'd have these blown up to certain sizes. And I had to . . . all the copy is actually different sizes, if you look at it carefully.

I know, that's one of the things I was wondering, and you were doing it mostly on a photocopier?

So I had to work out the percentages of the reduction on the type to fit in with the pictures. So it was quite technical. Which I taught myself through my job at the newspaper. Because I was kind of sizing pictures for editors.

See, I think a lot of people would look at it and just think, 'Oh, that's cut and paste, just a classic fanzine thing', but actually it's done incredibly precisely.

So this here, for example, this would have been a map, which I then put another kind of grey tint on, to make it look slightly different. And all of these would have been enlarged to a certain percentage, to get everything in.

Bits of Letraset here . . .

Yeah, exactly! And if you see the originals of these, these are all borders – in those days you could buy these little rolls of clear tape, like really thin Sellotape, but quite thick plastic, with different lines on. It's what we used to use in newspapers – I used to nick them from the newspaper! And then you'd use a scalpel to kind of cut them to the right length.

You could buy Letraset tint. A whole sheet of grey dots, which you just cut and – so everything was done with a scalpel. And I've still got the scalpel, and the green cutting mat as well, the original one. And I think [looking at the issue] I just ran out of time, so it's handwritten – there's a lot of handwritten stuff in there as well. It took ages. Each issue took a long time.

I can imagine you hating having to do that little handwritten bit, at the last moment!

Yeah, it was really depressing! You've ruined the whole issue! The whole look of it, you know?

As for Fork, I guess that was all done in InDesign, or something like that?

It is, yeah. Or was. Absolutely.

It's amazing how the technology has changed over the years. I guess you've kept up with it through your job.

I have, through newspapers. I was a sub-editor as well, so that was my job: to create pages on InDesign, and QuarkXPress originally. But at the end of the day, it's all about words, and all about stories. That's what I care about, mostly.

Smiths Indeed cover stars quiz answers: issue 1, Cicely Courtneidge; issue 2, Tom Bell; issue 3, Liz Frazer; issue 4, unknown (we thought this was Rita Tushingham but Mark says it's not!); issue 5, the lost boy in the 1961 British Transport Film documentary *Terminus*; issue 6, Carol White; issue 7, Rachel Roberts; issue 8, Dandy Nichols; issue 9, Hattie Jacques; issue 10, Albert Finney; issue 11, Tom Bell again; issue 12, Charles Hawtrey.

9

KARREN ABLAZE

interviewed by Gavin Hogg

Of all the fanzines of the late eighties and early nineties, *Ablaze!* retains a larger place than most in people's memories and affections. It had a clear identity and was opinionated, full of passion for the music it loved and scathing about anything else. There were spats with Morrissey and Sonic Youth, and they went on tour with Pavement – the kind of thing that might happen in the proper music papers.

Ablaze! was the well-drilled and ambitious team of mavericks that got into the Champions League every year, while the rest of us were shuffling about in the lower reaches of the amateur leagues. A positive mention in the *Melody Maker* or by John Peel equated to a good cup run, but Karren – the editor and main writer – always had her sights set higher. *Ablaze!* kept getting bigger, even in a literal sense: the first three issues were in A5 format, while subsequent issues expanded to A4, and issues 6–10 came with a free flexidisc.

Karren's first attempt at a zine was *The Value of Defiance*, written around 1984 in Manchester. It was never completed, but two years later she made a few copies of *Karrenoia '86: I Hate Punks* to give to friends at college. They read it from cover to cover, and this positive reaction was the impetus to get more serious.

Made in Manchester, a celebration of Manchester's burgeoning music scene (featuring a tape with interviews and tracks by Inca Babies, the Stone Roses and the Railway Children), came out in the summer of 1987, and later that year *Ablaze!* was born. After issue 1, Karren moved from Manchester to Leeds, where the next nine issues were written. Later editions had the support of team members and contributors, including Gavin Bradbury and Chris Trout.

The roll-call of bands interviewed in *Ablaze!* reads like an index of significant and cult alternative and independent artists of the era: Nirvana, Mercury Rev, Huggy Bear, Throwing Muses, Henry Rollins, the Pastels, Pavement, the Shamen and the Nation of Ulysses, to name a fraction. There were also comprehensive album, demo tape and zine review sections. What *Ablaze!* seemed to do so well was to ally the independence and passion of zine culture with the organisation and ambition of more mainstream publications.

The main run of *Ablaze!* ended with publication of issue 10 in 1993, when Karren got a job with Southern Records in London, and once she returned to Leeds 'things just changed'. The aforementioned row with Sonic Youth was the concomitant to her college friends' enthusiasm half a decade earlier, and the impetus had ebbed away. A spell of play-ing in bands followed, among other activities. Then, after a gap of over twenty years, *Ablaze!* issue 11 came out in 2015. If you're interested in reading the ten back issues as well as fragments from other zines, they were compiled in a book, *The City Is Ablaze!*, published as a limited run in 2012 and reprinted the following year for Record Store Day.

Karren has now turned her hand to fiction writing, and her first novel, *Revolution on the Rock*, will be out soon. She describes it as 'Pussy Riot meet Erin Brockovich on a post-punk-powered Mediterra-nean odyssey', in which a sound engineer from Leeds gets stranded without her passport in Gibraltar and ends up initiating a protest movement. Read more at Mittens On Publishing (www.mittenson. co.uk).

I met Karren in October 2018. I'd slowly travelled back to Shef-field from London that day via several buses after a train cancellation, before haring over to Leeds without having time to eat. None of this was the ideal preparation for an interview. We met in Kadampa Meditation Centre Leeds, talking quietly while unseen people in near-by rooms meditated. Karren kindly fixed me up some food and herbal tea, and we began.

Karren Ablaze, Leeds, October 2018.

What was your musical awakening?

I guess everyone gets into music when they're a little kid, don't they?

I was about 9 or 10 really before I started investigating music.

I depends what you mean. Kids used to get records given to them for birthdays. I'm embarrassed to tell you the first record I bought: 'Don't Give Up on Us' by David Soul, I loved that. Then I got into Kate Bush. I was in hospital with pneumonia and I heard 'Wuthering Heights' on hospital radio. I just thought 'Wooaah!' I got all her albums and then started getting into new wave and post-punk in the early eighties.

In terms of fanzines, when did you first start becoming aware of them?

I was at school – it was possibly through listening to John Peel mentioning them. It was a great culture. You'd hear him talk about one, quickly write the address down, send your SAE and a little letter. You might end up writing lots of letters from that first interaction. I think *Grim Humour* was one I bought after hearing about it on Peel. There was also one called *Kvatch* from York that was run by Clare Wadd who went on to run Sarah Records. I had a correspondence with her when I was at school. I got in touch with her recently and was disappointed because she didn't remember me; it had meant a lot to me writing to this cool fanzine writer girl. I made friends with Mark Williams, a fanzine writer in Wales, and we wrote to each other with soap or sellotape on the stamps so we could reuse them. Every day I'd be getting a letter or he'd be getting a letter – sometimes two. It was really full-on!

You were about 14 or 15 then?

Something like that, yeah. I started my own first zine around then. I heard a local radio show about fanzines with some enthusiastic young people saying 'It's easy, it's cheap, do it!' That was my wake-up call, changing me from being a consumer to thinking 'Oh . . . I could do that . . . oh, right.' I'd not immediately thought I could make a zine myself – you'd see these things and think they're cool but that's that. You just need someone to say 'And you can do it'. Because then you think 'I could type something and cut it out and get pictures and stick them down. I could do all those things and take it to a photocopier.'

The last part was too big a hurdle – I was at a convent school and the administration was too scary. The nuns were disapproving of me, they didn't appreciate my creative spirit and post-punk ways and they wouldn't have helped me. I was too scared to ask if they could photocopy it and I didn't think of going anywhere else. I half-made this fanzine called *The Value of Defiance*, named after a Scritti Politti lyric, which ended up in the bottom of a wardrobe. It included that Morrissey letter which made it into the *Ablaze!* book. That was totally mental.

What had you done to upset him? I can't remember.

I'd gone to see the Smiths at the Free Trade Hall in 1984 and it was the night that all the seats got smashed up. The venue didn't have any security because they didn't usually put gigs on – they were only used to nice old people. They didn't stop any of the people coming down from the circles into the stalls. There was a crush and someone broke a leg. I was hanging around the T-shirt stall writing a letter to Morrissey asking for an interview. I didn't realise that the way I'd phrased it sounded really bratty. I wrote 'When you're in Manchester, remember Manchester.' He wrote this angry reply saying how Manchester had never helped the Smiths and how he hated everyone there. It was a massive self-pitying rant, it was spectacular. My friend Justine added to the letter, telling him he should have stopped the concert when the chairs were being broken. That didn't go down too well either. He replied that he didn't care about the chairs at the Free Trade Hall. It was a pretty interesting piece of mail to get on your way to school in the morning!

'Ooh, a letter from Morrissey . . . and he hates me!'

He wasn't too happy.

Were you living around Manchester then?

Yes, in south Manchester, very much in Smiths territory.

So you had that unfinished first issue that ended up in the wardrobe. What happened next?

Then I went to a further education college, where I gained more confidence. I'd gone to one college, dropped out and then sat around on the dole all summer. I made a zine then called *Karrenoia '86: I Hate Punks* and photocopied five of them. It was quite a courageous act, to dare to do it. That was a turning point for me. I took them into the refectory at college and handed them to people I knew. They did this amazing thing [mimes slowly reading, cover to cover]. It was the most notice that anyone had ever taken of me and what I had to say in my life. I thought 'Someone's listening to me, they won't listen to me when I speak but if I write it down and type it up they think it's important.' It was like a drug; I was addicted for the next seven years, trying to make it on a bigger scale every time, daring too big. Print more, make it bigger.

That was the thing I remember about *Ablaze!* My first one I got was probably around issue 4 and it felt like each one got bigger, more spectacular, more ambitious. What was the size of the print run?

The last one I printed was 5,000. There were a few boxes left at the end but I sold most of them.

That's incredible. My zines had a print run of 100 – and I still had loads left!

Every stage of that process there was an element of encouragement when one person would say something positive and that would move it forward. Or I'd meet someone like William Potter who did the logo and showed me how to improve the design in exciting ways. There was always something to encourage me and by the end there was a lot of positive feedback from the readers who would write to me with their life stories. I'd get some letters that were eight A4 pages long, telling me what they had to tell me.

That must have been a powerful thing. Did it feel good?

I guess by that time I got used to it. Sometimes the post would come in a sack, filled with letters and records, it was like Christmas. By that time there were a few of us working on it. We got spoilt by how great it was I think.

A lot of the fanzine writers around that time went on to become music journalists for the weeklies. Was that ever an ambition of yours?

It was. I feel that there was a pathway from zines to music journalism, but it was pretty much only open to guys. I don't think I was an amazing writer – so that wouldn't have helped – but it was quite noticeable that a lot of guys did a zine, got a call from the NME or the *Melody Maker*, got into journalism and then books and an academic career. I don't think that route was open to women in the same way. That's my feeling anyway, when I look back on it. Also, I wasn't a very confident person. I was building up my confidence doing what I was doing, but I don't know if I'd have survived very well in the male-dominated environment of the music press. It was very sexist. It was essentially the NME that spawned *Loaded* and lad culture, which exacerbated rape culture to a huge degree. So it wasn't as progressive as it thought it was.

Did you ever get close to working for the mainstream music press?

I was invited to review a Nerve Rack gig for Everett True at *Melody Maker*. It was just rejected but no one ever came back to me and explained how I could improve it. I observed how the music press responded to riot grrrl – the NME were very destructive and negative, though *Melody Maker* did some good pieces at the beginning. I was also very confrontational towards those papers and I saw myself in competition with them. I was cynical about how the advertising led them, so we didn't have the most harmonious relationship.

You released flexidiscs with the zine too. What was that like? Was it complicated to do in terms of licensing the music and the logistics? You released tracks by some big bands like the Wedding Present and Pavement.

It was all pretty informal. I remember looking at that [licensing issues] and not doing anything about it. We used to get tracks on reel-to-reel tapes, or cassettes in Pavement's case, and send it to the flexi-pressing people in Tunbridge Wells. They're not there anymore.

Was it a good feeling to do that – like having your own record label?

Yeah, I guess I didn't think of it as a record label, but it was good fun making these flexis. My main memory is kneeling on the floor in my cellar. For a long time I'd be collating the zines myself or with friends. There'd be a pile of this page and that page, so you'd have to

Top to bottom:
Ablaze! issues 1, 2 and 3.

take them all, assemble them, fold them. I didn't bother with staples, I didn't have a big enough stapler! Then we'd get a bit of sellotape and tape the flexi to the back. People would help out and I'd give them pizza.

What were your favourite zines? You mentioned Grim Humour earlier.

The Rox was a big influence.

What that John Robb's?

Yeah. I really liked the energy of it. Do you remember it?

No, it was before my time.

It was very beautiful and chaotic. There were typed bits, handwritten bits and comments on what they'd written. There was lots of cartoon artwork too, which I think Sid from the Membranes did. I really adored that zine. My friend Simon Morris did one called *The Turnip Flag*, lots of collage artwork.

Why did you end Ablaze! when you did? Did you feel you'd just devoted enough time and energy to it?

I think I got distracted, I always was going to do *Ablaze!* 11 back then. I got a job in London with Southern Records to pay off my debts. I'm not sure how I ran them up – I'd borrow money to pay the printers, go to gigs and sell the zines. I'd go home with a pocketful of coins, which I'd spend on riding around in taxis, and I'd still owe the bank all this money. So I went and did that job for a bit and then things just changed.

You've probably seen the Sonic Youth controversy section in the book – that had an impact. I think that made me feel anxious about writing because it was such a weird personal attack. Obviously they felt it was a personal attack by me.

What was the issue – a review you'd written?

I'd done an interview in late '92 with Kim Gordon and I called what they did 'old people's music'. I went from adoring them so much to being bored with them. I'd have thought it was impossible for me to get fed up with Sonic Youth but I obviously did and I expressed that in the article. They interpreted what I said as being ageist. I had this thing where I called certain things 'old people's music' and I was only interested in things from '77 onwards, I had a real Year Zero approach. I wasn't open-minded musically. They interpreted it in a weird way, saying I was sexist because I was ageist and this whole string of things based on that. Thurston Moore wrote this fax that they sent to record labels and people all around the States like the Kill Rock Stars label and Kurt and Courtney. It felt like an attempt to shut me down and it kind of did, emotionally. We made up and that was okay, but I felt anxious about writing after that.

Were you always second-guessing yourself after that? Was it harder to write freely?

I had some critical American voices in my head – which was quite frightening. I still

Top to bottom:
Ablaze! issues 4, 5 and 6.

Top to bottom:
Ablaze! issues 7, 8 and 9.

wasn't very old, I was only 23. I understand now that you're still an adolescent at that age.

Yeah, it doesn't feel like it at the time – but when you look back you see you were still pretty much a kid. So was that a big point in terms of thinking it might be time to end it?

Well, I did other stuff too. I formed bands and played in them for a few years, and did a lot of work in the riot grrrl movement.

Also, I got physically ill. I was diagnosed with rheumatoid arthritis in '94, which is something I've been dealing with ever since. It was really strange: I was mugged in London on my birthday and they took my bag; all it had in it was the cassette of the Kim Gordon interview and my Young Person's Railcard. I got injured, which sparked off my illness, and that changed my life. Something was really pivotal about the Sonic Youth interview, everything turned on that.

That's weird, like it was some kind of sign. Were you becoming any less enthusiastic about the kind of music you were writing about then or did you still have the passion?

Yeah, it was just the same. There was still some great stuff coming out, like Polvo, and And You Will Know Us By the Trail of Dead.

Do you often listen now to the music that you wrote about then?

I don't like to listen to it very much, just

because I used to hear it a lot over a long period of time. I think everyone's relationship to music has changed. Having the internet and not having John Peel, those two things have been the main reasons.

Did Peel champion Ablaze! much?

Yeah, he liked it like any other fanzine.

He was kind to all the zines, wasn't he? He championed the spirit of doing something and used his platform for that. I wanted to ask about the gap between issues 10 and 11. How long was that?

Twenty and a half years!

So, what was it like doing it again after all that time?

It was different because I didn't used to have a PC back then, I couldn't afford one. I had a little word processor with a built-in printer. It had five different fonts – and we used them all! I kind of know how to do desktop publishing stuff but it doesn't come easily to me. While I was putting the book together [The City Is Ablaze!] I decided to do a cut-and-paste page for it, and that showed me why people don't it anymore. There was paper all over the floor, Pritt Stick in my eyes, Tippex all down my arms, the whole place was a total mess! The book came out in 2012 and issue 11 came out at the end of 2015. I worked with Edu Matto, a designer in Barcelona, so that was great, I could just feed the stuff to him. Because the technology was a lot easier to use, I could do it in a much shorter space of time

Ablaze! issue 10 (top), and issue 11 – consecutive issues published over 20 years apart! To the best of our knowledge, that is the longest gap between issues of any zine.

than I used to. I guess when you were typing things out and then try-ing to correct it after you had less creative freedom. We could do a lot online too, like the Kate Nash interview by email.

The biggest difference was selling it. I used to go to gigs with a bag full of zines and they'd sell like hot cakes. I could still do that at All Tomorrow's Parties; it would be slow because people wanted to talk to you, they'd be like 'A fanzine, sit down, have a drink!' It would take ages to get round the venue, but you could still sell them that way. Everywhere else, even at DIY Space in London – where you'd think people would be into DIY things – I'd approach trendy-looking people and they'd look at me like I was going to do something to them. 'Why's this person talking to me, they want something, I don't like it!' A lot of younger people don't know what a fanzine is, they don't know why you're doing it, they're suspicious of your motives, they want to know where the money is going, they want to know if it's officially sponsored by the event. So I'd walk up to people and say 'This is a fanzine. I've written it. All the money goes to me. Do you want one?'

And how did that go?

That worked better. They didn't mind, they just wanted to understand what kind of a thing it was – it's not natural to people now. That whole amazing 'going to gigs and buying a fanzine' thing … you'd make so many friends that way. That's doesn't exist so much now. Also the infra-structure of record shops is very different now, it's not so easy any-more. It's harder to sell and people don't want to pay for information.

How many books did you get printed up?

We did a limited version of 500 for Record Store Day and another 1500. We didn't sell all of them but we sold more than a thousand, which is pretty good by today's standards.

Looking back, what would you say was your most memorable moment? It sounds like that moment when the students in the refectory read your zine was very important.

Maybe the Pavement stuff. I was introduced to their music by my friend Justine who I used to live with. She was going out with Keith from the Wedding Present. They used to go over to the States and came back with this tape. They kept playing it and I'd say 'Who's this? It sounds like the Fall.' I kept asking them and they kept saying 'It's Pavement.' I'd go out of the room and two hours later I'd ask again 'Who's this? It sounds like the Fall.'

'It's Pavement.'

'Okay, I quite like this Pavement.'

So I got in touch with them. I sent a cassette with the interview questions on. My flatmate Barry had a keyboard with a fanfare sound on it, so we'd press that button and ask a question. It must have captured their imagination because they sent back this amazing tape, it was a real work of art. I wish I knew where it was now. The tape of their answers was set in a hospital, or at least they said it was in a hospital. I couldn't tell what was real. They were pretending there were doctors there.

Was it like a strange radio play where you didn't know what was going on?

Yeah, it was magical. They played a song and Stephen Malkmus had a poem called 'Karren's Secret Darts'. It went:

Karren's secret darts
Karren's secret darts
I heard the one about the Fall
But that was just the start.

There was a two track version of 'Secret Knowledge of Back Roads' on the tape and when we asked for something for a flexi they sent 'My First Mine', which ended up on the compilation LP they did – *Westing (By Musket and Sextant)*. The flexi was the first Pavement release in the UK. When they toured over here we went along with them and sold our zines and their T-shirts. That was one of the highs.

Was that a relationship that never went sour? No Sonic Youth-style meltdowns?

They probably got a bit fed up with me on tour sometimes but we never came to blows!

10

DAVE THOMAS

interviewed by Hamish Ironside

Like the science fiction zines examined in Chapter 1, football zines form a distinct subsection of the overall world of zinedom. The vast majority of football zines are devoted to a single club, and they tap into supporters' traditional diehard loyalty to that club. A music fan could easily be a devoted fan of both the Smiths and Nick Drake, say, and therefore a keen reader of both *Smiths Indeed* and *Pynk Moon*, as well as any of the countless more general zines about music. But most readers of football zines will probably only ever look at a zine about their own club. Also, while musical tastes may change over the years, loyalty to a club is lifelong, and to the true fan it persists regardless of the fluctuations of results on the pitch.

Perhaps as a result of this, whereas other zines typically last for fewer than ten issues, a good football zine can still be going strong after a hundred or more issues. As noted in Chapter 13, *Fly Me to the Moon* has produced an almost incredible 625 issues – the most of any zine I am aware of. Other examples of long-running football zines include *The Gooner* (an Arsenal zine), with 293 issues at time of writing, and *Red All Over the Land* (a Liverpool zine), still going strong after 282 issues. Another notable title with a long history is the subject of this chapter: *A Kick Up the R's*, a zine devoted to Queens Park Rangers.

A Kick Up the R's was one of the earliest football zines, with its first issue appearing in 1987. By April 2022 it had published 366 issues, and every one of those issues has been edited by Dave Thomas. I encountered the zine in a roundabout way. I had heard that Pete Doherty (one

Dave Thomas in the Tavern Fayre, Bolton, in February 2022.

of my favourite musicians) had produced his own QPR fanzine in his teens, and I wrote to Dave on the offchance that he knew something about Pete's zine, which was called *All Quiet on the Western Avenue*. I discovered that Dave himself had actually helped Pete get his zine off the ground. Although I've still not seen a copy of *All Quiet on the Western Avenue*, that disappointment has been more than compensated by discovering *A Kick Up the R's*.

The zine is A5 (148.5 × 210 mm), usually 64 pages, printed on weighty, glossy paper, with a colour cover and at least some colour content inside as well. Dave writes a lot of the regular articles himself, including his editorial, match reports, 'All for the Love of QPR' (Dave's personal diary of QPR-related events), 'Ed-lines' (a sort of bonus editorial), as well as quizzes and puzzles, all done with consummate skill. Like other football zines, though, he also benefits from contributions from readers, which is a sure sign of a thriving zine. One example is 'Our Dear Watson' by John O'Mahony, an impressively well-researched and well-written two-part biography of 'the quiet and unassuming, but always reliable, Ian Watson'. This long article about one of the least remarkable players of a side from over 50 years ago is captivating, even if you are not a QPR fan.

A Kick Up the R's is even supported by ads, including a regular back-page slot for W. Sherry & Sons, 'independent family funeral directors since 1850', with the tag line 'Rangers 'til I die'. The overall impression is of a high-quality product – indeed, in the interview that follows I find myself describing it as 'professional'. Yet, given that a large part of what I like about fanzines is their amateurism (not quite the same thing as amateurishness), isn't it faint praise, if not an insult, to say a fanzine looks professional? I think what I want to say is that it seems both professional and amateur in different ways, and in the right ways: amateur in its spirit, professional in its production.

When I asked Dave if I could interview him, I was partly thinking that it would be quite convenient for us to meet, since I am only ten miles or so from QPR's ground in Shepherd's Bush. Then I discovered that Dave actually lives in Bolton. Nothing daunted, I set out in my trusty Ford Ka in February 2022 and met Dave at the Tavern Fayre on the edge of Bolton. At this point most Covid restrictions had been relaxed, and there was a sense that everything really was getting 'back to normal' at last. Dave began by telling me how the Covid disruptions had affected *A Kick Up the R's*.

We took almost an eighteen-month sabbatical, shall we say, while Covid was doing its worst. Obviously we couldn't print, because it was just uneconomic. Because . . . we've slightly moved on from the days of Letraset, and copy and paste.

Absolutely. QuarkXpress now!

Well – yes, it has been for a good number of years. In fact even that's considered to be a little bit outdated. But, like everything else, fella came up to me at the game the other day and said, 'Do you really do all this on QuarkXpress?', and I said, 'Well, *yeah* . . .' And he said, 'Cor, bit old-fashioned!' I'm thinking, 'Mate, it works for me.' It's what I know; I haven't got time to start learning new software; it does it perfectly. It's not about fancy design – it's never going to win any design awards. The cover's always done professionally, and the cover is always something that we . . . you know, it's our sort of trademark, if you like. But inside – I wouldn't say it's as basic as it comes – it's probably a couple of notches up from absolutely basic . . .

Well, I'm going to have to disagree with you, because compared with other fanzines I think it looks really, really professional. It's really polished, I would say.

Yeah. Well, one thing I've learnt over the years is how to be a good editor. If nothing else, I've taught myself – I suppose I must always have had those inherent skills, but in terms of journalistic quality – and in terms of having the commas in the right places, and the proper use of semi-colons, and Oxford commas, things like that – it's as professional and polished as any. Yes, typos still get in, of course they do, but that's usually due to the lack of time to be able to proofread it as diligently as I like. I mean, you know yourself that copy flow on a magazine or a newspaper or a book can go round maybe six or seven times with somebody else and you always spot something that somebody else has missed, whereas I have to do it all myself. And sometimes when the printers are shouting for it, saying 'It should have been here twenty minutes ago', you haven't got time to say 'Oh, I just want to do a quick proof of it.' Because you can't.

Well, like I say, it seems really polished to me. Shall we go back to the beginning? Because you started off in 1987 . . .

Certainly did. One of the very first of what was to become an explosion in football fanzines.

Yeah, yeah. Can I ask, what sort of age were you at that time, and what were your circumstances?

Okay. I was . . . I was 31 at the time when I started it. And it came out of the failed merger between QPR and Fulham. Earlier in the year, about six months previously, we'd woken up, as QPR fans, to newspaper headlines that said QPR and Fulham were going to merge, and the new club would be called Fulham Park Rangers, and everything was great . . . except it *wasn't*, because both sets of fans railed against it. Up until that point, I'd never been involved in any protests. I just kind of bowled through life not caring, really, basically. But this was different: this was my football team. I mean, they say, 'Cometh the hour, cometh the man' – I'm sort of loth to even say that, but it's what people have said about me. I took up the reins – I took up the cudgels, shall we say. And I somehow found myself as a sort of figurehead at the QPR side of things, really. And we successfully fought off the merger.

So what was your role in that? Was it actually starting the magazine or was it some other campaign?

Well, I was leading some of the protests – there was a pitch invasion, and things like that – I wasn't part of it, I was the one negotiating with the police and the club, and everything else like that. Once the merger was finished, and the whole idea of Fulham Park Rangers was dead in the water, those that had been involved in it felt that we needed to continue to protect the long-term interests of QPR. The bottom line is, we decided that we wanted to . . . we *needed* to protect the future of QPR, because to suddenly have your football club taken away from you in that way . . . it's *huge*. It's momentous. And we thought, 'Well, if it can happen once, it can certainly happen again.' So there were two sort of offshoots that came out of it that have been lasting. The first one was an independent supporters' association. Now, pretty much every club has an independent supporters' association, and the QPR one – which is called the LSA, the Loyal Supporters' Association – was really the first in the country. Now, at the time, I was in the throes of moving from London – which is not where I'm from originally, I'm from the Isle of Wight originally – but I lived in London for a number of years and was looking to move on. At that time, with my then wife, we were looking to move up north. And we moved to Shropshire, actually, in 1988, so the fanzine had only been going for about six months when I was upping roots and moving to a different part of the country. In the subsequent years I've moved from Shropshire to Cheshire, and then into Manchester, and now into Lancashire, so I'm getting ever further north – I expect to be in Scotland in another few years!

Is there any reason for that? Is it work takes you up there?

Yes, it's work and relationships, and all sorts of things, really. Yeah, it's as simple as that. But we live in a very transient country, where people move around. Now, I'd already started the fanzine, and I never expected it to last more than six months, a year at the most, really. And so to still be going now, 35 years later, is incredible. So, of course, that immediately tells you that I'm probably the oldest fanzine editor in the country, I would imagine. I can't imagine there's anybody older than me.

And you didn't know of any fanzines before you set up?

Well, during the merger, we had a lot of help from two Birmingham-based people who did Off the Ball. Now, are you aware of Off the Ball? I'm guessing you must be?

Uhh . . . no.

Okay. Well, Off the Ball – you know about Foul?

Yes, I think I've heard of that, because – I'll tell you why, because I'm a Liverpool fan, and I read Red All Over the Land, which is the only surviving Liverpool fanzine.

That's right, I know John – John Pearman, isn't it?

John Pearman, that's right. He's quite good on . . . you know, he's

very supportive of other fanzines, and he's had the odd article covering football fanzine history. And I think *Foul* was mentioned in there, and *Off the Ball* may have been, I'm just going on memory. And they're sort of like . . . not to a particular club, but more about just football in general?

Well, *Foul* began in the early 1970s, but it was Oxbridge-produced, really, it was done by students at Cambridge University. And then somewhere around the mid-eighties there were a couple of club-based fanzines. One was *City Gent*, at Bradford City, which is still probably one of the longest. There was a magazine called *Terrace Talk*, which was York City, so it was like the York Nomads, as they called themselves – so that was like an independent publication. And there were two that emerged at the same time. One was called *Off the Ball*, which was produced in Birmingham by a Birmingham/West Brom group, a group of four. One of them was a guy called Steve Beauchamp, who you may have come across. Steve, unfortunately, died last year. But he went on to be involved with the FSA, which is the Football Supporters' Association, he was heavily involved in that, eventually. And the other guy who was involved that I got to know really well was a chap called Adrian Goldberg. Now, Adrian has gone on to be quite successful on television and radio, he used to do *Watchdog* and things like that. He also did *Off the Ball*. And at the same time, there was a music fanzine that was produced by a guy called Mike Ticher, who was a [coughs] Chelsea fan! He did a music fanzine, but he decided to do a little football piece in the middle. The football piece became more . . . he called that *When Saturday Comes*. Well, I don't need to tell you . . .

Oh, yeah . . .

But the guys from *Off the Ball* came down, and they really inspired me to want to put pen to paper, really. Because I loved *Off the Ball*, because it was so irreverent, and it was speaking the sort of language that the *Match* and the *Shoots* of this world never could. And it was hard-hitting.

So you were without any kind of experience of doing it?

None whatsoever.

Which I think is a good way to start a fanzine.

I'd only ever written out a betting slip. But I must have had something that I could do, because I guess, even at that age, I was still fairly
directionless in life, and so this gave me a purpose. But I never believed
it would last. I was driving a lorry at the time, actually, and I used to
call in at Birmingham and meet up with the lads there, and we'd throw
ideas around. You know, because at that time, when the football fanzine explosion happened in the late eighties, it was all about the titles.
You know, *Dial M for Merthyr* [Merthyr Town fanzine], things like that
– they're all really well-known names. I sometimes, to this day, I still
kind of regret *A Kick Up the R's* [as a title], because it's a bit . . . I mean,
the alternative was *Up the Queen's R's*, and all sorts of things, really. But
that wouldn't have lasted. And I still get – I had a couple of coppers the
other day say to me, 'Can I just ask, what is it you're shouting?' And I
still get comments: 'Yeah, that's what they need, mate!' Which sort of
lost its appeal after the first ten million times I heard it. But generally
speaking, it's a name that stands out, I guess, and it's all part of it. But
it's evolved over the years . . .

**Yeah, so when you started, was it, like, literally, you wrote it all,
and manual typewriter, cutting pictures out, or drawing pictures,
or something?**

Exactly, the tried and tested route to producing a publication. Folded,
and – I mean, my very first – I think it's about the first three or four
– I had typeset for me, by the people who actually printed it, funnily
enough. It started off with a company in London called Juma Print,
who are pretty well known. The guy who ran it, Martin Lacey, is a
Wealdstone fan. So he used to do lots of fanzines, I believe. But he was
also able to typeset it. Now, I have to say, the typesetting was very very
basic. It was also quite *costly* as well. Also, at the time we produced the
first one, it was priced at 40p, with no real thought about any profit
from it. Certainly didn't realise that we'd have to sell every single one
in order to even cover costs. So the first few issues just lost money
hand over fist, basically.

**So how many would you have printed of the first one? Did you have
an impression of how many you needed?**

Well, I'm slightly embarrassed to say, it was two thousand. And we used
to sell pretty much all of them, really. To be honest with you.

Yeah. So why be embarrassed?

Well, because nowadays two thousand would be . . . so much, you know. No, it's not embarrassing, that's probably the wrong word, really, but nowadays the print run's five or six hundred, at most.

Right, yeah. So you were doing two thousand, but you were selling them all – and just selling them outside the ground?

Yeah, that was it, really, and it just took off. At first we used to stand outside the ground on matchdays saying 'Would you like to buy a fanzine?' Stopping people as they walked past. Now they queue up for it, basically, so we don't really have to do that anymore. You know, returning after eighteen months away from the ground, everyone said, you know, 'It's so great to come back to QPR, and see you there. Because you're the fixture on a matchday.' We're part of people's matchday routines.

That's so brilliant.

Oh, it's fantastic. But it doesn't equate necessarily to sales, because obviously, as everyone knows, print media nowadays has gone . . . you know, it's suffering, really, because of the internet, and things like that.

That's what I was wondering, is it, like, people turn up, because they've got their smartphones, they don't feel like they need a fanzine?

Yeah, I think so. And most . . . I'd say our readership is predominantly older. Much older. Not exclusively, but predominantly. But we know people that have been with us for all of those 35 years. And it's an important . . . Well, I don't know what it is to people, really, all I know is that the feedback that we get – which doesn't come as fulsome and as readily as we'd like, sometimes – but when we do get feedback it's clear that it's a very important publication to people.

I nearly printed you off something, actually. Last Friday I got an email from somebody who said, 'You'll know my sister Jacqui', because she's one of my regular customers. And I've since written about it – about her – to say . . . I really don't know anything about her, I don't know what she likes, I don't know what her politics are, I don't know this, I don't know that, anything about her. But she was somebody I'd

A Kick Up the R's issue 1 (August/September 1987) and issue 100 (March 1998).

banter with – because you know all your customers now, really, you know who's going to walk straight past you and you know who's going to walk up and buy a copy. And she was somebody I've known for years and years and years, but don't really know anything about – like lots of my customers, really. I didn't know she had cancer. She died last week. The email said . . . I wish I'd printed it out now, because I wasn't going to touch on it, really. But basically, she said – even on her deathbed – this sounds so emotive, I know it does, but anyway . . . I'm not saying it was her last words, but her brother used to take copies in to her when she was in hospital, and it was always, like, it was so important to her. He said to pass on to me that no matter how much I get hassled by stewards, or this, that and the other, it's very very important to her, and that it's meant so much to her over the years. Because it's a real connection between – because we're really articulating . . . the fans' own thoughts, really, and their passions, and that support for the football club. And that's what people identify with. And you don't set out to do that, it's because it just comes across. I guess it's like writing a song that means something to somebody – you have no idea how it's going to be treated, and viewed, or consumed, if you like, when you write it – you just hope that what you've done touches somebody somewhere. And I don't necessarily know or appreciate the extent of that. I just

A Kick Up the R's issue 200 (December 2006) and issue 300 (February 2015).

know from what I've picked up over the years that the magazine itself is very very important to people.

That's the best reward for doing it, isn't it?

Well, anybody who writes anything to be consumed wants that kind of feedback. Yeah, absolutely.

So that justifies all the work, really.

Absolutely, yeah. I mean, I have to say that I think over the years it's developed in terms of style, content . . . you know, just professionalism, but at the end of the day, it's really just about sharing that passion for a football club. I mean, I've had people say to me, 'Why don't you do one for other clubs?' Well, I don't know about other clubs, I don't *care* about other clubs! And, as I say, I thought it was going to last for six months, a year maybe, and then I'd lose interest, or whatever. But here we are, 35 years later, still going.

Well, looking at an issue now, you've obviously got such a solid group of collaborators. You've got people writing columns, people doing the different aspects – like, you've got people doing the sales with you, haven't you?

A Kick Up the R's issue 338 (April 2018) and issue 364 (January 2022).

Yes, I have, and again, that's very ... I mean, somebody who helps me sell them is my ex, who, despite the fact that we no longer have that relationship, the relationship with the magazine is still as strong as ever. She's a really important part of that. People know her at the ground, and it gives her something – she's actually a very shy person, really, but she's quite happy to stand outside the ground shouting 'Here you are, *A Kick Up the R's*, brand new issue!' And of course, people know her, and in a way it kind of strengthens her bond with the football club. I mean, she's been in Cornwall, where she goes frequently, been walking along one day and somebody shouts out, 'Hi, Julie! *Kick Up the R's!*' So we're kind of well known in that respect. We're part of the matchday experience. That doesn't reflect in massive sales, because we still struggle to ... I mean, we charge five pounds for an edition, which is quite ... quite expensive. But that's just simply the economics of it.

Probably about the same as a programme, isn't it?

Probably a bit more, really. The programme is – I don't even know how much it is at QPR, I think it's £3.50, for a programme. But in order to justify its continuation, the fanzine has to make a profit of sorts. It has to cover its costs at the very minimum.

Is your aim to break even? I mean, taking into account *all* the costs, like the print cost, plus whatever –

Travel . . . Yeah, it's the many hours of work. It's hours and hours spent slaving over a hot typewriter, burning the midnight oil, setting the alarm for 3 a.m. so that you can hit the deadline six hours later, things like that. We're on issue 366 now, and it's like running 366 marathons. It's a mental battle, each one, really. It's the product of hard work, and all hard work has to eventually be rewarded, otherwise there's no point in doing it. Unfortunately, I still have to do a full-time . . . well, a full-time part-time job, if that makes sense! I certainly don't make enough from the magazine. It covers its costs comfortably, these days.

That's great in itself, because that's quite rare for a fanzine, I think.

Yeah. Well, it wouldn't exist otherwise, because I can't – I've not got a bottomless pit – we still have to go out . . . we work in entertainment, myself and my partner. That's our main source of income. When I say 'partner' I'm talking about business partner – but we are very close, and we've worked together for a long long time, really. I'm sort of like part of her family now. She works at Man City, actually, she's a tour guide there, so that's her part-time work, whereas the fanzine is really mine. So the magazine has become like a full-time hobby, if that makes sense.

Yeah, I can understand that. So is it two days a week, something like that it equates to? Or even more?

I think it's . . . put it to bed, then concentrate on which games you're selling it at, getting it to, transporting it around . . . don't think about it for two weeks . . . and then start all over again. You sort of try and cram it all in, really. I'm not disciplined enough to say, 'Right, Monday and Tuesday, I'm going to be working . . .' And also it depends on what we're doing in terms of our work, because as I say, we work in entertainment. She's a singer, and I'm her manager stroke . . . roadie, chauffeur, sound engineer, you name it, basically, that's what we do. So there's no real set pattern to what we do. There's always something to do on the magazine. I try and have rests in between.

Getting back to selling around the grounds, you sell at away games as well, do you?

Yeah.

And they're always alright with that, are they, the other clubs?

No, not necessarily. You get the jobsworths. Over the years there's been less hassle, but I'm quite cute towards it now. You sort of get to know where you can and where you can't sell. Derby, for example, is a place where, if you stand there before the game, as people are going in, the stewards – because they've got nothing better to do, and they're bored– they move you on. West Brom's another one.

I've heard this from *Red All Over the Land* as well – there's some grounds where they're fine with it and there's some where they are, like you say, jobsworths.

I wouldn't say it's dependent on the result, but the result helps, obviously. But generally speaking, you get your sales at the end of the games, when people are filing out. Very often, like at Barnsley on Saturday, I walk around at half-time, and you get sales like that as well. People just spot you. But normally, when people are coming out, you've got the entire away support – especially at a club like QPR – the entire away support will at some point walk past you. So you do all your business in just a few minutes at the end of the game. Although, conversely, at Barnsley I did stand there before the game for an hour. But that's not always the case. The stewards never bother you at the end of the game, so you can afford to be a bit more lippy, because they're not going to stop you coming in.

The only place I've ever had any real trouble was at Sheffield Wednesday. It was our promotion game – if we won we were promoted. We took 8,000 to Sheffield Wednesday. The Sheffield Wednesday fans were unhappy, they were protesting as well. So it was quite a tense day all round, with 8,000 QPR fans turning up. When I was going in, one of the security guys wouldn't let me take me bag in. And again, that's very unusual. Now, I have to say, I usually carry a rucksack with copies in – sometimes I can take 20, sometimes I can take 50, because I know my market, basically. But on this day I had a bag, and the guy said to me, 'You're not coming in with that.' And I said to him, 'Well, what am I supposed to do?' And he said, 'Well, I don't know, dump them.' I said, 'Well, this is my livelihood, mate.' And I actually walked down to Leppings Lane – I don't need to tell you the significance of that – and there was a bloke painting his fence, and I said, 'Can I ask you a favour? They won't let me come in with the bag there. Can I leave it with you and collect it later?' He said, 'Yeah, that's absolutely fine.' He was really good about it. When I walked back, there was a grinning steward, all pleased with himself, and I gave him my ticket, and he swiped it, and he said, 'Right, you ain't coming in. Fuck off.' And at that point – bearing in mind this is our biggest game of the season – I didn't get in. And I was really shocked by it as well. Now, we made representations to Sheffield Wednesday, as did QPR. The security firm which this steward was from – I think he was coked up, to be honest with you, because he looked aggressive – they got sacked. It made the headlines all over the place.

What year was that?

This was 2003. QPR, bless them, sent me a video of the game. They also invited me to travel on the team bus, when we did a promotion thing, which was really very very good of them. The irony of ironies is that I got held up in traffic, and I didn't get there before the parade started.

I didn't really want to be on the team bus. Because, to be honest with you, I don't think I had any right to be there. But I didn't mind travelling on the bus with all the staff and things like that, because I felt that was more appropriate, really. I didn't want reflected glory. But the fact that I was allowed on there as well was just a massive honour. It was supposed to take half an hour from the starting point to Hammersmith Town Hall, where there was going to be a celebration of promotion and things like that, and it took three and a half hours, there were so many people out on the streets. It was an incredible experience, one of the greatest experiences of my life, really. And that all stemmed from not getting in to the big game. It caused all sorts of ructions. And it's still mentioned to this day. But generally speaking, you don't really get any hassle at away games.

Do you ever get away fans buying it?

Occasionally. Very occasionally somebody will come down, and then they usually go, 'How much is it?' and you go 'A fiver'. Very often I might say, 'Just give us three quid', because it's not really for them, if that makes sense. But that's quite rare these days, to be honest.

And when you go to away games, are you seeing fanzines being sold for the home team? Are there many other fanzines being sold now?

No.

Because Liverpool's still got *Red All Over the Land*, and I've seen at Arsenal *The Gooner*, which is quite a glossy one.

Well, I know the guys who do *The Gooner*, and once upon a time, when fanzines first started, they went from absolutely nowhere to suddenly . . . they called it – and you may have heard this phrase – it was called the publishing success story of the eighties. Because suddenly, from nowhere, came hundreds of titles. And they were selling millions of copies, basically.

At first, fanzines would send their fanzine to other fanzines, and you'd kind of list other fanzines that were available. But eventually that kind of died out, and everyone went their own way then. I very rarely see fanzines on sale at other grounds these days. And when I do, it's usually some nineteen-year-old standing there rather apologetically, clutching a handful of these magazines, and people just walking past, ignoring them. Whereas if you come to QPR you can't miss us, because we are right in people's faces, if you like. On the street, before the game, we're in our regular places, and people know where we are. They look out for us.

People still walk past, don't get me wrong. I mean, it's very hard to go into the figures, because they do tend to vary. Sky mess us around. Sky affect our sales *massively*. Because it reduces crowds – the kick-offs are all the wrong time. The only decent sales we've had all this season are the games that have taken place at 3 o'clock, Saturday afternoon. It's a theme that I bang on about all the time. It's really, really important that games take place at the traditional 3 o'clock. I think a lot of our sales go to people who want to read something on the train home. Back to the south coast, or back to Somerset, or Devon. Or Northampton. Or . . . whatever. QPR draw a lot of our support from outside the home counties. And also from all parts of around London, you know, Essex, Kent, Surrey, Sussex . . . I would say that those people form the bulk of our readership. It's when a game is moved by Sky to a Monday night – we know straight away that we're going to lose maybe a hundred sales, and that hundred is vital to the economics of the magazine. Once or twice you can live with it. This season it's been relentless. We didn't have a Saturday 3 o'clock home game between the beginning of October and January the 15th.

So for a Saturday 3 o'clock home game, how many would you expect to sell? Couple of hundred?

Well, again, it's come down massively over the years. A couple of years ago it dipped to the point where we didn't even know if we could continue, really. But I think nowadays it's usually round about 250, perhaps. And although we might think that's really modest – it is modest – but when the crowd's only 12,000, and there's usually a good away following . . . so even if we're selling to, maybe, one in forty of the people who are going to the game, that's actually quite good, really, if you think of it in those terms.

Oh yeah, I think so.

Because it's only me involved in the costs and the finances, I don't answer to anybody on it: it's my publication, I'm the editor, the publisher, the accountant, the everything else, really. We charge five pounds for it because it's quality, and also because, as a London club, we can stand it. I'm not sure you'd get away with charging five quid for a Crewe fanzine, for example.

Yeah, well, Red All Over the Land, I think it's two pounds now. And it's really good value for that.

Yes it is.

But yours is full colour, glossy . . .

We're not even full colour, to be honest with you, it's only a section in it that's full colour, really. But the regular readers just take it for what it says more than anything, really. And we've got no . . . I guess when we first started there was this idea that we were standing up for supporters. There was no political angle to it as such, apart from our politics being the best interests of Queens Park Rangers Football Club, which is at the very crux of it. But we don't batter people with our own politics. We don't need to take up causes or rattle sabres and things like that. We have a very good relationship with the club, actually, they're very tolerant of us.

So basically, since that mooted merger with Fulham, there hasn't been any sort of controversy to rally behind?

Well, the very first issue that we ever did, I was asked to go to the club, and I met the managing director and a marketing guy called Brian Rowe, and Brian really tried to kill us at birth, basically. I think he saw it as a threat. Because nobody had ever done anything that was independent, and he wasn't very happy. He wasn't happy about some of the criticism made about the then club secretary getting behind the proposed merger, and things like that. So it caused a lot of rifts, as you can imagine. Many years later, Brian and his family, the Rowe family – they live in Solihull, massive QPR fans, heavily involved – and they're some of my best customers now. So it just goes to show, what goes around comes around. It's gone full circle, really. We take part in the fans' forums, things like that, and we're represented in meetings with the club. Over the years, we've taken a leading role, we've taken a back seat, we've taken all sorts of things. We're no longer that campaigning publication that we wanted to be when we started out. Because the club is run much better now.

Just to finish off with, what got me in touch with you in the first place was that I was interested in Pete Doherty's fanzine, and I found out when I contacted you that you were basically mentoring him when he started it off. So how did that come about?

I remember being contacted, back in the day – long before email – by letter, from a fourteen-year-old Pete Doherty, who was living in Nuneaton at the time. His dad was in the army, I believe, so they moved around quite a lot. And Pete, basically, was asking me for tips and pointers, because he wanted to start up his own fanzine. I think he would probably say that I was quite encouraging. I just wrote to him and gave him some tips. I mean, I'd hate now to see that letter because it probably said, 'Yeah, you need Letraset, you need a pair of scissors and some glue', things like that! And that's really how his fanzine begun, from that, with a little bit of support and encouragement from myself. But that was as far as it went really. He is a creative man anyway, so everything that went into it was entirely him. It was so far removed from A Kick Up the R's that it was great, because it was two different publications.

In what way did it differ? Did he write everything?

Yeah, he did. Whereas I had contributors, and we were a little bit more mainstream, his was really very . . . I wouldn't call it surreal, I wouldn't call it flights of fancy, but he was . . . he was far more creative in his writing. I can't even give an example of that – you just sort of know from reading it that there was a sort of melody to it, if you like. So his had that touch of whatever it is – creative genius, shall we say – that really kind of worked. And it became very very popular.

Now, over the years, because Pete lived in Nuneaton – I know I lived even further north than he did – I'd just see him at games, basically. I don't think he displayed any particular musical bent, when I knew him as a youngster, but I guess over the years he went off on a different career path. *All Quiet on the Western Avenue* – which is a brilliant title, I wish I'd come up with that – I don't know how many editions he did, I can't imagine it was more than a dozen, probably less.

Did you see him around the ground selling his? Did he do all that himself, just a one-man act?

Absolutely. Just a one-man band, exactly. And then over the years we discovered that we had a mutual appreciation of Tony Hancock. And Pete was a member of the Tony Hancock Appreciation Society, which is still going strong to this day. We used to quote Hancock to each other at the game. It sounds ridiculous now. There's a famous *Hancock's Half Hour* called 'The Reunion', and there's a famous line in it – out of context it won't even seem remotely funny – but he opens the door and he says, 'Stone the crows, Dopey Kent!'. So for years, and perhaps even to this day – although I haven't seen him for a number of years now – I'd always go, 'Stone the crows, Dopey Kent!'

But he used to prank call me, and it was at a point where I was going through quite a rough time in my life, and I didn't really take very kindly to that. I can have a joke the same as everybody else, but at the time I got a little bit . . . because I knew it was him – and there was nothing malicious in it – but it was a bit juvenile, and it didn't really go down very well with me.

Would that be after you'd known him for a couple of years or something, so he'd be about sixteen or so?

ALL QUIET ON THE WESTERN AVENUE
Issue one. £1-00. August 1994.

ALL QUIET ON THE WESTERN AVENUE
ISSUE 3. £1.00. FEBRUARY 1995.

ALL QUIET ON THE WESTERN AVENUE.
ISSUE FOUR. £1.00. AUGUST/SEPTEMBER 1995

All Quiet On The Western Avenue.
Issue Five £1

Covers of four of the five issues of Peter Doherty's *All Quiet on the Western Avenue* zine. Huge thanks to Liam Duggan for photographing his copies for us. Liam recalls Pete as 'a Rangers obsessive' who 'knew the history very well and had good relationships with long-standing supporters. The fan culture at Rangers meant a lot to him. Also, his writing was excellent. Funny and offbeat.'

Since our interview with Dave, Pete's memoir, *A Likely Lad*, has been published, in which he recalls Dave as 'a great old Rangers faithful character, always in denim with a Stan Bowles haircut. Dave was like a folk hero to me.'

196

Yeah, yeah. I don't want to make a big thing about it, because it isn't a big thing, but I still think to this day . . . I was talking a friend the other day – QPR fan, he goes everywhere – and he bumped into Pete in Holland or something like that. I can't remember the circumstances. But he said, 'Oh, Pete sends his regards.' And he told me that Pete said, 'I don't think Dave Thomas likes me that much.' And I said, 'No, that's not it at all, really.' Because every time I've ever seen him – I remember bumping into him outside Crystal Palace one day, just outside Selhurst Park – and Pete was there, and we did the old, 'Hello mate, how are you?' But I don't see him these days at all, really.

No, well he lives in France, so he probably doesn't get to a lot of games.

I'd like to get across to him that I don't hold a grudge. And it probably only happened half a dozen times, maybe. It just wasn't the right time for me. I lost my sense of humour a little bit, really. And although there was no falling out as such – because I've seen him in the years since, and it's never even mentioned – but I've got a feeling that's where it probably stems from. It's like when somebody comes up and says, 'Oh, you and him don't get on, do you?' 'Yeah, we do – what gives you that impression?' It was like completely news to me, I had no concept that he felt like that.

Do you still have your copies of his fanzine?

No. No, listen, I don't even have a full run of my own. Because I'm not really a collector, to be honest with you. You'd imagine that I'd have the complete set of 365 issues – plus the various specials that we've done – all on a bookshelf somewhere . . . nah! I haven't got it.

But do you not regret that? Do you not think, 'I'd love to see that issue 1 again'?

Not really. I'm not that bothered, really, to be honest. I don't collect anything – I don't collect programmes, I don't collect . . . I kind of move on. If you walked in my house you wouldn't really know I supported QPR, to be honest, because I don't have framed shirts on the wall and things like that.

I've got Liverpool stuff all over the place. Liverpool mugs . . .

I'm not that sort of person. Once it's put to bed, and it's gone, it's for-gotten about and finished. I very rarely look at them when they come back, because I don't want to see all the mistakes! I mean, apart from handling them to sell at the game, once it's put to bed, that's it.

I suppose I'm proud of the achievement, and how it's lasted, and where it's gone, and what it is to people. Something that crops up is a phrase you may have heard, and it may mean the same to you as well: relationships come and go, but your football club is the one con-stant thread that goes throughout your life. Your football club is always there. And in a way, A Kick Up the R's is that same thread. You know, supporting your team – supporting the fanzine – is exactly the same. Generally speaking, the readers are a regular, loyal bunch for whom it's very important. Because it's their thread through their life as well. It complements the support of the club. It was certainly important to Jacqui, in a way that I had no idea. To be told how important it is . . . it's very humbling really, because it means I've touched her life in some way. And that's an amazing thing, really, to be made aware of. Because I had no idea.

11

RHODRI MARSDEN

interviewed by Gavin Hogg

Rhodri Marsden was the first person I spoke to at the start of this project. I'd chosen him because I knew that he'd ended up meeting John Peel through his zine, *Glottal Stop*. I remember how I felt when I heard John Peel reading the name of my zine live on Radio One in 1991, and giving the address for potential buyers to contact me. It was a highlight of my teenage years. I wanted to know from Rhodri how he'd ended up meeting Peel and what effect it had had on him.

I was also curious about Rhodri's many other activities. He has played with several bands, including the Keatons (thrown off the support slot on Blur's first UK tour for unprofessional conduct), Frank Sidebottom's Oh Blimey Big Band, Dream Themes (a TV theme tribute band), Microdisney and Scritti Politti. As Article 54 he's released disco albums dealing with pressing twenty-first-century issues. His response to Brexit was *The Hustle*, with songs such as 'Canada Plus' and 'Let's Go WTO', and the Covid-19 pandemic inspired *Stayin' Alive*. His work has been published in many newspapers and magazines, including *Time Out*, *New Statesman*, *Radio Times*, *The Word* and he wrote the regular Guitarist Wanted column in *The Observer*, in which he went undercover to audition for bands he had no intention of joining.

He has a large Twitter following, and every Christmas he invites adults to send photos of the unusual Yuletide sleeping arrangements their family have organised for them – beds constructed under ironing boards, garish childhood duvet and pillow sets that should have been cut up for rags many years earlier, and creepy dolls placed in rooms

Rhodri Marsden in the cafe of the British Library, March 2018.

by well-meaning mothers. Rhodri's book *A Very British Christmas* (HQ, 2017) expanded on the theme. It garnered many positive reviews, though one American reader wasn't impressed: 'If you're looking for something funny, light and Christmassy - this is NOT your book. A depressing look at the secularism and emptiness of Christmas without Christ.'

Rhodri's career as a zine editor was comparatively brief. He produced two issues of *Glottal Stop* in A5 format between 1988 and 1989, which focused on spiky, uncommercial bands like Bogshed, Death By Milkfloat and Big Flame. He had not even finished writing issue 1 when he wrote a speculative letter to Peel about it, but Peel's response encouraged him to carry on, and Rhodri's dad lent him the money to print up 300 copies. The rest is history!

I arrived to meet Rhodri at the British Library in March 2018, suffering slightly after a thoroughgoing debauch with my co-author Hamish the night before.

How old were you when you wrote your first issue?

Probably sixteen. It all stemmed from . . . it's weird how things pan out isn't it? If you took it right back to the beginning, there's a cool kid at school called Jason who likes odd music and he's got an older brother who has a load of records. So, I'm pals with him and go round to his house and he's playing Die Toten Hosen or Bogshed and I suddenly became aware of this other area of music that I was hitherto ignorant of. So I start wondering, hang on, how does this work? Why aren't I aware of this stuff? How are these bands even making records? Quite elementary questions really.

So it was a perfect storm?

Well, at that point I had to ask him, 'How do you know about this?' and he told me to listen to John Peel. I started listening to Peel and went weirder than he did. I became a bit fascinated by how obscure you could get, really pursuing the very dark underbelly of all this, finding bands that only ever put out one demo tape. There's that moment as a kid when you recognise that critical acceptance and popularity doesn't equal quality and also that everyone is putting the same amount of effort into it. I was buying obscure seven-inch singles and sending off for cassettes I'd read about.

Then I went to my first gig which was the Dog Faced Hermans and Bastard Kestrel in Bedford. I really wanted to go but it was twenty miles away so my dad agreed to take me. Now that thought makes me squirm with embarrassment, the idea that he would take me to that gig. I'd be worried about him being bored or watching it and thinking 'What on earth is my son doing?' At the time I thought it was great. He's 6 foot 7 and he was standing at the back of the room with his arms folded and his hand on his chin in a suit and tie while I was down at the front. Everett True was there for some reason, flailing around.

What year would that have been?

About 1987/88 . . . this is a long preamble . . . at the gig there were some people selling fanzines. I wasn't really aware of them but someone said '50p for a fanzine' and so I handed over my money, not knowing what I'd get in return and got this forty-eight-page zine called *Rabid Turtle*. It was A5, black and white and stapled in the middle. I got it home and that was the moment. Being musical and being in a shitty town like Dunstable, struggling to find the people to form a band, there was no way of expressing that feeling of 'Fuuuuck'. I must have looked at it and thought 'Well, this is what I'll do, how I'll channel this enthusiasm I have.' I contacted James, the editor, who was my age and living in Retford. I wrote him a letter and he replied saying it was simple, just do your pages on A4 and send them to the printers. 'The printers?!?' He told me about this vegan printer called Hamish who lived in Shropshire [a different Hamish than the co-author of this book], who'd do three hundred copies for £60 or something. That was it. I just did it page by page.

So it happened pretty quickly after buying your first zine?

Yeah, I started the following week I think.

And do you remember what was in the first issue? Did you interview any bands for it?

Yeah, Alan Brown's band, The Great Leap Forward. He'd been in Big Flame, who were my favourite band when I was sixteen. They only released seven-inch, three-track singles and had decided they would only exist for three years. They had all that perfect manifesto style stuff which I loved. I was obsessed with them.

I spent my last two years at my parents' house just being on the phone when I should have been revising for A levels. I was just ringing up bands and chatting about stuff. Again it was about connecting with other people who felt the same about music. My dad had to put a lock on it because I was running up huge bills, so then I spent all my time at a phone box round the corner.

Just feeding the 10p pieces into the slot?

Exactly. I must have spent so much money just ringing bands. It's quite embarrassing to look at the fanzine now.

You mean the style of writing?

Yeah.

I think everyone probably feels like that about the stuff they wrote when they were younger.

Probably, yeah.

At 16, 17, 18 you write with such enthusiasm – which is good – but you look back and think 'Jesus' . . . I guess it's just about starting the process, getting used to writing about something and that feeling of wanting to create.

Maybe, yeah. I never had an interest in writing then, I didn't like English lessons. In a rather male way I read non-fiction but I wasn't interested in stories.

The zine was more about connecting and plugging into that world and doing what you could to get a slice of it for yourself.

Yeah, it was an expression of unbelievable enthusiasm, in the sense of 'I've found my thing' – then creating something and selling it.

How many copies of the first one did you get printed?

Three hundred. I didn't have £60 so my dad lent it to me. By this time I was going to London to see bands so I'd go to gigs and sell it there. I remember there was a plastic screw-top jar in the living room and

Dad said 'Just put the money in there as you sell them' so I paid him back that way.

Were you good at selling them? I was too shy.

I was pretty good actually, I was quite proud of it. My friend Sarah knitted me a bag which said Big Flame on it and I took them to gigs in this woollen bag. Very indie isn't it? I remember when people used to go to gigs and take their seven-inch singles, so I felt I was cooler than that – but not much.

One of the things that happened I was in this connecting mode was that someone gave me John Peel's home address and I sent him a letter. Quite a bold thing to do isn't it? Just send a note to his house.

It's the kind of thing you do at that age though, isn't it? You're so full of enthusiasm, you don't really know what the rules are.

Exactly. What could go wrong? I don't remember what I wrote, probably just gushing a bit and telling him I was working on a fanzine. I hadn't even finished it then, I was only halfway through it. About three or four days later I got a letter back from him saying 'Hi, thank you for the letter, do you want to come on the show in a few weeks and talk about your fanzine?' He did a local radio show on Sunday nights that was broadcast across East Anglia, Bedfordshire and Cambridgeshire. He gave me his home phone number so we could arrange it. I cannot tell you how thrilling it was, I couldn't believe it was happening.

My dad (once again) drove me to the studio a few weeks later. Now, as someone who's more used to being on the radio, I'd have done some preparation. 'What are they most likely to ask?' and think of some things to say. It didn't even occur to me then. I was mumbling and terrible. I still have the cassette of it but I can't bear to listen to it. He was ridiculously nice. At the end of the interview Peel said something like 'Thank you so much for coming on the show and thank you to your dad for bringing you up here. If you ever want to get in touch for any reason whatsoever, just drop me a line or give me a call.' And he said that on air.

And that's John Peel!

Exactly – but regardless of the fact that's he's nationally famous and actually instigated love for this music amongst thousands of people, it was tremendously selfless.

He treated you as a fellow human.

Yeah. I mean I've been on the radio with Robert Elms, they just ship a guest in, ship 'em out and he doesn't look up once. This meant I was allowed to pester people, it was like having my enthusiasm rubber-stamped. There's a pattern that still happens to a certain extent; someone recognising in me an enthusiasm for a thing. The zines I did weren't very good but there was a feeling of being nurtured by grownups. Someone would say 'I really like it, are you going to do another one?' Or you'd meet people at gigs and they were happy to meet you.

By the time I was on the programme I think the first issue was just back from the printers. He'd read out my address so I started getting orders through the post, 50p sellotaped to a bit of card.

So your dad made his money back?

I'm not sure, he certainly made some of it back. I think there was a point where I just started giving them away. I'm still in touch with some of the people like Jer Reid who either bought the fanzine or appeared in it.

30 years later.

Jer was in a band called Dawson, from Glasgow. They were in the first issue.

How many issues did you produce altogether?

Just the two, both done while I was at sixth form college, in the eighteen months between that first gig and me leaving home. I did a flexi disc with the second issue.

Who was on that?

Er ... fucking hell, let me think ... there were three short songs from three bands: a band from Birmingham called Dog Food, one from Brixton called Headbirth and Those Naughty Corinthians from Wigan.

I don't remember any of them.

Well, that was kind of the point. It wasn't 'What can I put on this in order to make people buy it?', it was 'What are the three things I can put on this that no one will know or no one will like?' It was a wilful obscurity. I've just remembered going to pick up the flexis from the pressing plant in southeast London. I was already at university then so it must have been 1989.

Why did you stop doing it?

I was in a band by that point.

So you were too busy?

It wasn't that I was too busy; as soon as I started playing in bands I thought I was so much better at that than writing. It's ironic as I now earn more of my living writing than being a musician. All of that momentum went into being in the Keatons, we were doing so many gigs, 90 to 100 a year. I had no ambition to be a writer, I just wanted to enthuse. I didn't want to be a famous musician either, I wasn't in the Keatons hoping we would be in the *NME*.

Is it a celebration of the underdog, is that what all of this is about?

Both issues of *Glottal Stop*, published in 1988 and 1989 respectively..

I don't know, I've never sat and thought about it. I'm not ambitious, not in any way. I'm just interested in the next thing, whether it's fun or any good.

When did the writing become a bigger part of your life again?

After university in 1992 I didn't know what I was going to do and ended up working for Nick Hobbs. He was the manager of Pere Ubu and Laibach, he'd been an agent at Rough Trade for many years, he'd set up Recommended Records with Chris Cutler and organised pioneering tours of eastern Europe taking people like Billy Bragg and Microdisney over there. I knew him as the singer with the Shrubs, a C86 band who I'd been to see. I was round his house for gig contacts in eastern Europe for the Keatons when he asked if I wanted a job as his assistant, doing logistics. It was another time when someone recognised that I was enthusiastic and reasonably conscientious. He was hugely influential for me in that he was making a living, albeit a chaotic one, out of doing stuff that he thought was important. All of his decisions were motivated by enthusiasm, rather than financial gain; if he needed to buy a thing he would do and worry about it later. He was really good at creating work and making it happen. He was a completely self-contained unit of creativity.

He sounds like a fascinating character.

Absolutely, I still see him occasionally. He lives in Istanbul now, doing the same kind of work. He's a real eccentric and we clashed a lot.

Another thing I got from him was that he was an absolute stickler for clarity of communication – whether we were dealing with what the Red Hot Chili Peppers' rider would be for their show in the Ukraine or communicating with Pere Ubu's record label. He would write these beautiful, concise letters. He drilled into me that there was no room in this business for omitting detail or not communicating exactly how things are. He was funny, he wasn't a writer but he made me good at organising my thoughts and organising them in a coherent way and that made me think that I could do this. He was on the internet very early, starting to communicate with people. I remember someone asking me if I'd considered writing for a living. I hadn't – but then I got to a point with Nick where the job was too stressful. It was taking up weekends and I was getting calls from angry people on the other side of the world at 3 a.m. I quit on Christmas Day in 2000. My idea was that I was leaving the job and I was going to write but I didn't have a strategy. I decided to give it six months and early on I got a job on a BBC series called *Attachments*. Then I started to get to know people and pitched a feature for *Time Out*. I was probably lucky timing-wise, I sneaked in under the wire.

How did you first get involved in doing some work for *The Word* magazine?

I can't quite remember ... I don't know how David [Hepworth] and Mark [Ellen] became aware I existed. I think it was because I was friends with Michèle Noach, the artist, who used to be married to Robyn Hitchcock. Robyn and Michelle were part of the Chiswick scene with Peter Blake and others. Mark Ellen was central to all that so I'd met him a few times through that.

I suppose by that time I had a lot of Twitter followers so David might have been aware of me through that. I had a column in the *Observer Music Monthly* for a while which was called 'Guitarist Wanted'. The idea was that a writer goes to audition for bands and then writes about it. It only had a limited shelf life and sometimes it was edited horribly, but anyway ... The editor and deputy editor took me for lunch and I thought 'This seems good'. They then told me they weren't going to do the column anymore but they asked if I wanted to review some records instead. I didn't really want to but I thought I should show willing. They sent me to review *You Are the Quarry* by Morrissey. I had to go to an office and sit with the album for an hour and a half and I wrote something which could be summed up as 'Well, I think it's kind of alright but who cares what I think about it?' And that was the only time I reviewed a record for a paid publication.

I think David would have got in touch with me for a similar reason as I like writing about the making of music, rather than the music itself. I think the first thing I wrote for them was about the art of songwriting. It was looking at how a song emerges, where do you go mentally, what do you do, do you sit down with a guitar?

And you went on to write some other pieces for them?

I think the main one, which ended up being a three-parter, was about the noises that made pop music. It was looking at the building blocks of pop, things like the Beach Boys' theremin, a backwards distorted guitar, a tambourine sound . . .

The cowbell?

Exactly, like 'Don't Fear the Reaper'. More cowbell! Also the 808 cowbell on 'Dance With Somebody'. *The Word* came back to me twice asking for more, it became quite a sizeable thing. I remember there was some interest from Radio 2 about doing a documentary but it never happened. I went on a *Word* podcast to talk about it.

Were they fun to do?

I think I ended up doing two. Green and I did some Scritti songs in the broom cupboard at the office.

Were you a fan of the magazine?

Yes, mainly because I really liked the people that made it. Mark Ellen is such an extraordinary force of nature. I know him quite well now through Michèle. She does these festivals in the Arctic, in a small town in Norway called Vaso. She invites some of her favourite musicians to go up and we make a show over the course of a week and then perform it. It was me, Terry Edwards, half of REM, John Paul Jones of Led Zeppelin, Alexis Taylor from Hot Chip – a very improbable collection. Mark came on the first one and he's just great. I don't know anyone as enthusiastic as him. When you enter a room and see him there you just think 'Brilliant, Mark's here!'

You mentioned *Rabid Turtle* earlier. Do you remember any favourite fanzines from back then?

Ablaze!, written by Karren. She was only a little bit older than me but she was putting out A4 zines with glossy covers.

What else? *Plane Truth* by Andrew in Preston. We knew him, he wrote in a studious way about things. He was really thinking about things; while I was just hurling myself around at Stretchheads or Dandelion Adventure gigs, he was as well but then he'd consider what it all meant. I used to like reading his stuff.

There must have been some Scottish things, Glasgow was such a hub for all that kind of scratchy stuff. Bands like Dawson, Stretchheads, Whirling Pig Dervish, Badgewearer. Latterly there was Yummy

Fur, Franz Ferdinand, Lung Leg. The Keatons played a lot in Scotland. There were pockets of enthusiastic people, like there'd be some kid in Kilmarnock who'd done a fanzine and he'd bring some bands together. You'd go up there and play for 30 people. These pockets of enthusiasm were often dotted around in improbable places like Blyth. There would just be a couple of people who wanted to make something happen.

Do you still listen to any of the bands that you used to write about?

I don't really listen to much music at all which is something I feel terribly guilty about. I feel like I should be across stuff and aware of more things. In answer to your question, I do quite often dig out things by Bogshed, Big Flame and Death By Milkfloat and listen to them. They have a strong association with a time that was utterly thrilling. There are other things that I associate with thrilling times later in life but this stuff has a very particular colour. Trying to explain it to someone else . . . well, I wouldn't even try. 'You see the thing you need to understand about Death By Milkfloat is . . .'

'The particular oeuvre of Bastard Kestrel was . . .'

Exactly, we've spent the last 30 years of our lives thinking about that in a subconscious way. The amount of meaning we ascribe to that kind of stuff is beyond what it is in reality. The things we can construct around bands is amazing – especially when you start music yourself and you see the reality is a bunch of people who don't particularly get on that well and are just trying to force out a thing, an expression of something. It's all it is, it's all quite accidental. When we're young we ascribe so much meaning to everything and think a lot of thought has gone into it.

Like there's a hidden truth in there that we need to find.

Yeah.

Looking back to your fanzine days, was it worth the amount of energy you put into it? I'm guessing yes.

Oh, God, absolutely. Writing a fanzine was the first emergence of me wanting to make shit happen.

It fed your enthusiasm for music.

And just stuff. I still get to write about things that aren't music-related at all. I've always just wanted to know how things work, to understand and write about them. There was no pain involved in writing the zine, so yes, it was worth it.

Nothing but fun.

It wasn't difficult, there wasn't anyone else asking you to change anything.

No one to say you were over the word count. You could just make your handwriting smaller or add another page.

It's just incredible to be able to make a thing that's yours and just present it to the world.

Is there a particular favourite memory from your *Glottal Stop* days? Was it the Peel episode?

That's a slightly traumatic memory. I'd love to be able to play it back and enjoy it or even to play it to someone else. I have played some bits to other people where I'm not really talking much just to prove that it did actually happen.

For me, when you first get that delivery from the printers . . .

That's exactly what I was about to say! It wasn't collated or anything, you had to pay Hamish extra to do that so there were stacks of these things. I remember just looking at it. It was half the size of what you sent, which was quite odd, you don't have a conception of what it's going to look like. There was the smell of it, opening it and the freshly printed paper. I remember exactly where I was and I can actually remember doing it, that memory sticks with me. I'd like to come up with something more profound than that . . . it was such a long time ago.

12

SIÂN PATTENDEN

interviewed by Gavin Hogg

One of my favourite podcasts is *Culture Bunker* (formerly known as *Bigmouth*). Andrew Harrison, one of the show's creators, once described the aim of the podcast as 'to make Radio Four's *Front Row* but not be boring'. A few years back I heard regular co-presenter Siân Pattenden mention that she'd scanned her old zines and was selling them as PDFs via her online shop. The title, *How to Win Friends and Influence People*, sounded familiar – and when I saw the digital versions I realised I'd bought a copy of the second of the three issues when it was first published in 1989.

How to Win Friends and Influence People was an A5 fanzine that ran from 1988 to 1990, created by Siân and her pal Nicky Stewart, born from a love of the pop magazine *Smash Hits* and the world of television. In the zine they would ask TV personalities like elderly actor Jill Summers (who played Phyllis Pearce in *Coronation Street*) if she liked 'Belgian New-Beat band Front 242', or request that comedian and writer Victoria Wood send them her favourite sandwich recipe. I'm not sure you could replicate this now; there's so much entertainment content swirling around in the ether that the pool of shared knowledge has virtually dried up. We all seem to have curated our own personal lists of celebrities that the vast majority of the population won't be aware of.

Nicky and Siân were brought together initially via the Penpals Wanted section of *Smiths Indeed* (the subject of Chapter 8 of this book), and their friendship and shared sense of humour are evident

213

when reading the zines. Speaking to Siân at the British Library in July 2019, thirty years after they were originally published, I was delighted to know that she and Nicky are still friends, and that they had as much fun writing them as I'd imagined. Nicky is now working as a knitting designer in the Scottish Highlands.

Although there were only three issues, *How to Win Friends and Influence People* helped Siân get a job at *Smash Hits*. She sent a couple of issues in and got hired on the basis that they made the editor laugh. Since then she's worked for a host of publications such as the *NME*, *The Face* and *The Guardian*, and contributed a chapter to *Excavate!* (Faber & Faber, 2021), Tessa Norton and Bob Stanley's all-angle exploration of the Fall. She also sells her artistic creations at Raw Art (https://raw-art.co.uk) and has written six children's books.

What was the story of the fanzine, how did you and Nicky get together?

It was all very 1980s, maybe we were pre-dating the internet by a billion years. You'd buy a fanzine, look at people who wanted pen-pals and start writing. You'd find the like-minded souls – which you would now do on a forum. I got a few zines, including Smiths Indeed, and I think she'd put something in the same issue that I had. We were teenagers. It sounds a bit sad but I was from Twickenham and she was from Guildford – there was no 'scene' in either place.

I grew up in Solihull so I understand.

It was quicker for me to go to London and see a gig in Hammersmith. But I was a bit young and scared of going to gigs – it was the days when there were riots at Jesus and Mary Chain gigs. You don't necessarily have a posse of people who share your taste in music. At my school it was just me, so I'd write to people. I wrote to her and immediately we wrote each other very silly letters. We created different characters and had running jokes. We became really good friends and met up in London in the summer holidays. We just spent the hours laughing, making up jokes about Alan Bennett because I was obsessed with him which she found really strange. We'd do things like getting on a bus without

Siân Pattenden at home in July 2022, three years after our interview. Siân took this photo herself on her trusty Ricoh camera, having seen our photos from the British Library and decided she could do better . . . she was right!

knowing where it was going, giggling on the top deck. Silly teenage stuff. I'd made a good friend, curiously through this fanzine.

I sent an article and some letters to Smiths Indeed. I had various awful ideas which I would annoy Mark, the editor, with. I was doing that and buying zines like Trout Fishing in Leytonstone and those other ones that liked Sarah Records. There was a network, you'd look in the back and see other zines reviewed. There's a chain of similar people doing similar things. I used to go to Beggar's Banquet shop and persuade them to take it as sale or return and people would do the same for you around the country. I had a penpal in Glasgow who did that for us.

We also had a thing which was almost a competition, to never have to pay for a stamp. We'd sellotape over it and keep reusing it.

Or a bit of soap.

Oh, I never knew that.

You'd rub soap on it and at the other end you could use a drop of water and the postmark would wipe off.

The postman obviously knew what was going on but it was a way of having free conversations with the one stamp. We were all sitting in our bedrooms writing to each other instead of going out and getting drunk. We'd have conversations about what adverts would be in-between Brookside because they were different in various parts of the country.

As your friendship with Nicky developed, at what point did you think 'We could do this'?

It was probably me being bossy. I was very anti the 'twee' movement. We used to have running jokes about certain bands that were too fey – not all bands on Sarah Records were like that, I'm not dissing the label. I said I really wanted us to do a fanzine together and it should be about telly because there wasn't one.

There was a flexi in one of them by the Candy Thieves, who went on to become Adorable.

I sold that very flexi on Discogs for about £15 a few months ago – someone in New York bought it off me.

You're joking! Oh, my mum has a load of them somewhere – though

she might have thrown them away. So we did that one and then someone else contacted us and asked if we could put their flexi with another
issue. We had a nod to the music scene and invented a very strange
character called Dave, our pop critic. It was a concession to music so
that we would be stocked in record shops but really we wanted to write
to TV people.

I had this book called *Who's Who on TV* which just listed everyone's management. I don't know what the audience was and I can't
remember how I got hold of a copy. You could find Dickie Davies's
management and write to them – so we did. It was an insight that we
could just contact these people. We liked books and music, but we also
were very fond of people like Jim Bowen. I was doing A levels at first
and Nicky was a year older than me, at university. There was a lot of
daytime telly to watch.

I had an electric typewriter, the ink was very expensive but it
looked professional. At first, I sent loads of questions off typed up,
looking neat, but never got any back. People from Brookside wouldn't
know what a fanzine was. But if you did a handwritten letter instead,
saying the interview was for a student magazine and only a few people
would see it, you'd get more replies. The more amateur it looked, the
better. Sometimes they didn't understand the questions but that made
it funnier.

Did you put in a stamped addressed envelope in with it?

Yes, if the envelope was all dog-eared I think they'd feel sorry for us
and reply.

Dickie Davies wrote his answers without saying what the questions
were – so we just printed them as he'd sent them to us. It comes across
like he's the most narcissistic sports presenter ever. 'My favourite
sport is athletics to watch and horse riding to do. My least favourite is
wrestling. I am not a keen gardener but I love to be in a beautiful
garden.'

For some reason we had this mission to destroy Howard Stableford.
He fancied himself as a bit of a rock'n'roll/*Top of the Pops* presenter.
Instead of just sending us one promo pic, he sent us five which we
thought was hilarious. That's why there are lots of pictures of him in
that issue.

Looking through it now, I can really see the *Smash Hits* influence on it, which I wasn't aware of at the time.

Were you an avid reader?

My sister got it so I used to read hers, and I would just not stop laughing when I read it. At that time I was about 15 or 16 and felt I shouldn't be reading it anymore, so I used to get the NME. Our fanzine helped me to join *Smash Hits* later. There was definitely something in that world that we wanted to use – a tone of irreverence.

There's something in that. *Smash Hits* was so influential. A lot of us who were teenagers in the mid- to late eighties used to use that kind of language that came from it.

[Flicking through the zine] I like this bit. This is my cat Felix who we gave an agony aunt page to. We gave him a catalogue number, like the cat at Factory Records. Felix was Groove Inc. 191. We also gave Anthony Wilson his own Groove Inc. number too. We were trying to take the piss out of people being cool.

It was your own take on Factory?

Yes, kind of. We just thought it was funny.

The cat turns up in your questionnaire with Claire Rayner where you ask her what she thinks about a cat called Felix being an agony aunt. That was the one question she refused to answer.

I met her once, though, and she was very nice.

Once you'd worked out the best way to maximise getting a response, did any celebrities refuse to be interviewed?

We never sent the fanzine to show an example of what we did. Some people would reply that they wanted to think about it first. I think Valerie Singleton did that. Pattie Cauldwell, the consumer rights presenter, replied that it looked like fun but no thanks. Maybe she thought we were going to stitch her up. Our method was rather random and scattergun and sometimes we sent out questionnaires only about central heating. They probably didn't read *Smash Hits* and may have been confused by these questions but some people were fine.

How to Win Friends and Influence People issue 1, published in 1988.

In terms of the two of you putting the fanzine together, was that ever difficult? Did you have different ideas?

No, we wanted to do the same things really. Nicky was in Guildford and then went to university for the second and third issues. We used to collect everything and then spend a day or two cutting it out and putting it all together.

The first one was done in my house in Twickenham. My mum still remembers the sound of us laughing from my bedroom. We would just spend twelve hours laughing. Then we'd take a break and go to Gateways supermarket, which later became Somerfields. We would buy a big bottle of cherryade and a load of Tunnock's Tea Cakes. We wouldn't eat any proper food, we basically just ate sugar for hours.

We'd work on our own pages, I don't think we ever argued about anything. One of the things we both did was to buy old books of helpful tips from charity shops and cut out some of the advice and fill any spaces with them. It's a designer's nightmare, every single millimetre of the page is filled with something.

The readers were getting their money's worth.

[Flicking through the zine] We've got this handwritten snack recipe from Gordon Jackson. We wasted it, we should have made a three-page spread, he was acting royalty! We weren't the consumers that we are now, we didn't maximise or 'monetise' things. There's none of that language that's used now.

I've just remembered where the money came from to print the first one. My grandma died and she'd left me £200, which in the middle of the eighties seemed like a lot of money. I used half of it to print the first one and we broke even. The price went down too – the first one was 65p, then down to 50p.

How many did you print of each one?

I can't quite remember, at least a hundred and maybe two hundred for the next two? There aren't many copies left. I don't know where they all went and I think my mum probably threw the originals out when she was clearing out the loft. That's why I scanned them, in case I lost these last ones.

How to Win Friends and Influence People issue 2, published in 1989.

I used to do a zine at the same time. There were interviews with bands in it but I also did articles on how to fill up your salad bowl on Pizza Hut. There were even diagrams on how to position lettuce for maximum salad capacity.

Things like that stay with me. I think there was something in *Trout Fishing in Leytonstone* where someone in an indie band was asked 'What advice would you give to anyone?' and his answer was 'Never buy economy washing-up liquid.' You never forget things like that, they always stick in my mind. No one's really interested in reading more serious interviews, there were millions of zines doing that.

What was the main way of selling them? You mentioned the Beggars Banquet shop before. Was it mainly shops or did you sell at gigs at all?

Oh God, no, I'd have been too shy. I gave a few to someone else take to a record shop but I wouldn't have had the confidence to go up to London and ask shops to sell them. There was a record shop in Twickenham which had been opened by a man who owned a wine bar. I think he liked MOR so he wouldn't have stocked it.

It was mainly an informal network, swapping them, posting them out with an SAE and reviewing each other's zines.

Which zines did you like reading yourself?

That's something I can't remember very well. Nicky read some but I don't think she bought them as much as me. She really loved Victor Lewis-Smith, she shared tapes of his stuff with me and got him to do a questionnaire for us.

You'd have regulars, people I still keep in touch with now who I got to know through the zine. People who wanted to write an article about hair or TV. You were too young to have a posse so it was a way of finding a nationwide gang. There was a girl called Kate who did a few articles for us and she desperately needed to get in touch with people who liked the same kind of music. She'd make Roky Erickson compilations that she'd taped over her mum's easy-listening cassettes. I think the DIY idea from punk fanzines, which we would have been too young to read, fed into what *Smash Hits* was doing, odd as that sounds.

When did you last buy a zine? Have you bought one recently?

How to Win Friends and Influence People issue 3, published in 1990.

No. What's around?

There's a lot of different ones, Etsy is a good place to look. Doing this book has been a bit of a journey for me, seeing how the world of zines has changed. They aren't often about music anymore, they tend to be personal stories.

My friend in Glasgow does one, that was the last one I bought. She does them about gender politics, sexual identity and fan-fiction-based things. The idea that you can speak to someone directly and interview them doesn't seem to be something that's needed anymore. This is more about your point of view and getting your voice heard. Our zine was a dramatisation of what we were. We called ourselves a name – Siân and Nicky Groove. We were taking on a persona. There's a real difference between the times – it was playing a role, which now contrasts with being 'genuine' and finding your identity.

That's interesting what you said about personalities. Maybe people can present a different personality on social media now and so a zine is a place to be more personal and intimate. It's likely that only the people that actually bought a copy will see it, it's offline.

There was a comment you made at the beginning of the first issue. 'The word fanzine implies humility and inferiority.'

Oh God, yes, that weird editorial. It was trying to be tongue-in-cheek.

It didn't come across like that.

I was very annoyed by the 'mop top and lollipop' zines. As a teenager I think I was annoyed by the asexualisation of things. Also they were reverent and we didn't like that, we wanted to poke fun. That's why this issue was about central heating, we so wanted to be off, into another world.

[Flicking through the zine] You can tell when I got a computer, look. I was working at *Smash Hits* at that point and I had the money for a tiny word processor.

What makes a zine a zine?

Good question. Independence, isn't it? It's about *doing what you do*. A fanzine wouldn't be published by a publishing house. A magazine is paid for by advertising, fundamentally. I think the essence of zines is not having any outside influence – because you're fed up with everything on the outside. Whether your vision is serious sexual politics or talking about Jim Bowen . . .

Ah, the twin poles of fanzines – the point they meet at would be the perfect fanzine.

It was the era when tours weren't sponsored by companies, unless they were big pop acts. They didn't have any associations. Marketing ruined rock'n'roll. The NME and their VO5 shampoo covers. I remember seeing the guy from Get Cape. Wear Cape. Fly doing an advert for trainers and just thought that the fun we'd had was gone. It was a different world then, advertising just wasn't allowed, your favourite bands wouldn't do it, it was selling out.

There was an ideological consideration, wasn't there?

Yes, people thought bands were selling out if they were on *Top of the Pops*. Some bands *wouldn't* do *Top of the Pops*. It's a populist culture now, but the point for us wasn't to sell thousands of copies, we just wanted to break even. Actually, we did make a bit of money on one of them. We got about sixty quid so Nicky and I went to Blackpool and slept in the back of this small van I had. We got really bored round Blackpool and went to the bingo every night. It wasn't the greatest holiday.

Tell me how you ended up getting a job with *Smash Hits*.

I sent them a copy of the first two fanzines.

Had a job been advertised?

No, I just sent them on spec. I'd just finished my A levels and was waiting for the results. Someone said, 'You like music and you like writing, why don't you write about music?' It took someone else to say that to me.

I sent the zines and quickly reviewed some singles too. A few weeks later the editor rang me and said he thought the reviews were trying too hard, they were too self-conscious – but that he'd really liked the fanzines, that they'd made him laugh in his office. So I went in on trial that August doing a couple of days a week. I wrote the competitions and did silly jokes and found myself in an office sitting next to Sylvia Patterson, Tom Doyle and Mike Soutar. These gods. I was still reading my sister's copy of the magazine so I knew the names of the writers and their writing styles so well, you pore over things at that age. They paid me thirty pounds a day, which they deeply apologised for, but I was living at home so I could afford to give a bit to my mum and use the rest for travel and food. The work built up.

So the fanzines really led to everything that came afterwards.

Definitely. I do feel for Nicky in a way because she was still at university. I hope she'd never felt that I trod on her toes.

Well, you're still friends now aren't you?

Yeah.

I have to digress a moment to talk to you about Ivor Cutler. You mentioned in an email that you would sometimes see him around?

He famously advertised for a room near Hampstead Heath and got one where he lived for many years. I must have lived near him because I used to see him about. I was a big fan and had some of his signed little poetry books. He often refused to write his signature because he said it was too egotistical, he'd do a little picture instead.

I saw him on the C11 bus once, a single-decker bus. I was sitting across from him and he was there with his hat on. A lanky schoolboy got on with his big bag and said 'Excuse me, is there room for me?' Ivor moved along so he could sit down. The schoolboy didn't know who he was and said, 'Sorry, I've got very long legs.' Ivor turned to him and said 'It's alright, I've got a very small brain.' That was so lovely, it will stay with me forever. It was great seeing him around, he was like a shaman in corduroy blessing everyone and making sure everything would be okay.

You said earlier you were obsessed with Alan Bennett.

When I lived in Camden I found out where he lived, somewhere round the corner from the Good Mixer. It was around the time of *Talking Heads*. This is his imperial phase – and because I was studying drama at school and was writing plays, he was a hero because of the way he wrote dialogue. I've since sent him some of my children's books and plays to look at. He sent a nice postcard back.

We wrote to him via his publishers and he was so sweet. He said we should have written to someone younger, Cliff Richard perhaps. He didn't realise how much we genuinely liked him. We asked everyone we interviewed what they thought about him and compiled them as a feature.

We had Victoria Wood in that issue too. I don't remember seeing people like that interviewed very much outside the *Radio Times*. It was a case then that you were a comedian or a writer or whatever and they weren't massive 'celebrities'. There was no 'reality TV'. And I don't think they realised how much we loved them.

What are your favourite memories of editing the zines? Mainly the laughs with Nicky?

Yeah. For issue 2 I went up to Manchester and we didn't get any sleep at all, we stayed up listening to The The and laughing. It was really easy to win prizes on Gary Crowley's Radio London show so I'd win things I knew she'd hate, like the latest Transvision Vamp LP, and get it sent to her. Suddenly she'd get these prizes she didn't want that she knew nothing about. I kept it going when I joined *Smash Hits*. Nicky has a piece of paper signed by all of En Vogue saying things like 'Thanks for all your support Nicky, I'm so glad to hear you're our number one fan.'

Those are the things I remember, our friendship was all bound up in doing it. Sadly it can't be replicated, everything I've done since is a way of trying to replicate making our fanzine in some way. The art stuff and the writing I do are both ways of being able to create your own world and be in your own bubble. I think Nicky has the same the same thing with the knitting she produces. It's something she can control, her own world she can orchestrate, I think it's something that's stuck with us. Maybe we should do another fanzine.

Would you do consider doing that?

Well, I hadn't thought about it until this very moment . . .

But now you're really thinking about it.

It would be nice. Also, it would be an excuse for us to sit down and laugh for a bit.

I think you should do it.

We could send questions off and say it's for a student magazine.

I like the fact that it's a paper thing that's fragile and decays. I've said to people who've bought it online that they should print it out and staple it together, that's how it's meant to be.

13

ROBERT NICHOLS

interviewed by Gavin Hogg

As a fresh student at Teesside Polytechnic in 1988, I first heard of Robert Nichols, or Bobby Shrug as he was generally known, from another student in our shared house. 'This band I saw were weird, they did this song about bingo and the lead singer was mad.' Aidy was mainly into Stock, Aitken and Waterman records, Depeche Mode, Erasure and the Pet Shop Boys, so Shrug's blend of ramshackle post punk with twin drummers, wonky keyboards and Robert's unusual songs which drew on history, pop culture and northeast oddness were never really going to win him over.

Over the next few years I saw the group on countless occasions. Middlesbrough was often missed by touring bands, playing gigs in Newcastle or Sunderland instead, but I considered myself lucky that Shrug were our local heroes and you would never be more than a few days away from one of their shows. Robert wove himself into the cultural life of the town through various DIY projects like putting together the A4 listings zine *Ket*, being part of the Middlesbrough Music Collective and organising gigs at the Empire pub on Monday nights. Like many other people, it took me a while to realise that the rather shy and softly spoken guy taking the 50ps on the door was the same person I'd seen a week before, singing about egg and chips or the van with square wheels. On stage he was a showman, wearing a range of unusual wigs, hats and shirts, and acting out songs without restraint.

Shrug were the first band I ever interviewed. Around 1989 I wanted to get involved with fanzines but had no idea how to go about it. I thought I should find some people who were in a group. As Shrug were the only group I vaguely knew, it seemed like a reasonably sensible first step to approach them – and they kindly agreed. I went round to Robert's house with my tape recorder and my interview with him and Richard, the guitarist, was published in my co-author Hamish's fanzine, *Saudade*. Suddenly I had become a writer.

Shrug continued to play gigs (and were the first Western band to play in the former East Berlin after the wall came down), while Robert became increasingly involved with the Middlesbrough FC zine *Fly Me to the Moon*, which Andy Smelt had started in 1988 with his pals Robbie Boal and Tony Pierre. Nigel Downing became a co-editor with Andy a year later. Around 1992 Robert began co-editing with Nigel, and he eventually bought the title from Andy in 1994. Nigel left the zine the

Robert Nichols at the *Fly Me to the Moon* thirtieth anniversary exhibition in Middlesbrough, November 2018.

following year to become an art teacher. As of January 2022 there have been 622 issues, all A5 in size bar the very occasional exception.

In November 2018, pretty much three decades to the day since I first became aware of Robert, I went back to Middlesbrough to see an exhibition at Boro Bookworm & Sacred Alien Comix celebrating thirty years of *Fly Me to the Moon*. I also took the opportunity to talk to Robert about his experiences as editor of the zine.

How did you start with fanzines? You did some before you were involved with Fly Me to the Moon didn't you?

We used to do zines ourselves and sell them at gigs. There was one called *Ket* which was a free listings zine, but we often missed the start of the month so it was out of date! We had adverts in it so we could give it away. Another one we did was called *A Mile of Bad Road* which we did a few issues of. We'd try and sell them at gigs, but it was hard because there weren't many people there and they'd want to have a drink and stuff.

Was that interviews with bands?

Yeah, exactly. Me and a couple of members of Shrug would write for that. Sarah [keyboards] did a long interview with David Gedge [singer with the Wedding Present] over the phone.

As a lead singer, you must have been interviewed yourself by quite a few zines.

Yeah, we did quite a lot, people would catch you at gigs or interview you over the phone. More often it was through the post with written questions – or emails. You didn't always meet the person doing the interview but if you did bump into them at gigs it was always good. We did a comeback album earlier this year and I was hoping to get interviewed by some fanzines – I was waiting for it but it didn't happen! It was part of my excitement for doing it because I really enjoyed it. I remember from doing zines and being interviewed by them that it would link you up with bands and other people too. There was a young girl that used to write to Sarah for advice on things.

You mean lifestyle stuff?

Absolutely. She felt Sarah could help and wrote her all these hand-written letters. When Shrug had been going for 25 years we did a pop-up exhibition. The two lads from the band Avalanche Party came along and were looking round thinking 'We couldn't do this. We'd just have to print out loads of emails and tweets.' I've got files of physical letters and photos. It's a period now where people have loads of photos on their phone or on Facebook but they might lose them, they might never have them to look back on. It was a very different era and I think that's why there's a lot of nostalgia for it. A lot of people like to have something tangible, an actual picture, something that's written down. It's still disposable to an extent but you can keep it. All the blogs are supposed to be there forever but they're not necessarily. You could wake up one day and they could be gone. Also it's lost in a sea of online content.

There's so much stuff out there that people don't know where to look. If someone has made the effort of actually printing something it almost demands attention.

I remember being interviewed by quite a few fanzines. Some of them were really inventive in putting out flexidiscs or compilation tapes. Of course cassettes have come back. I'm not a fan, they were pretty poor.

The cassette revival has passed me by. I like the fact that flexis still exist but I've got no love for tapes.

We put out some flexis with zines. We did one with Archbishop Kebab, the Scottish band. It's funny, I've just come away from a festival in Stockton called Songs from Northern Britain with half the bands from Scotland and half from the northeast of England. Vic Galloway [from Radio Scotland] is coming down. There are really strong bonds now between bands from the two areas as there was in the late eighties.

Which zines inspired you to start producing your own ones?

I remember *Ablaze!* fondly. Also, Michael Sanderson was a drummer with Shrug for a while and he did a zine called *Idea* which started out on paper and became a video zine, that was quite innovative.

I remember that. He used to film gigs at the Empire [Middlesbrough

pub where Robert organised DIY gigs], didn't he?

Yeah, he would travel round the country filming bands he liked. There were several zines from the Luton area too, like Clod – that was a surreal fanzine. They were all connected to the band Thrilled Skinny. I became friends with lots of people through those zines. I guess it was chronicled by John Robb in his book [Death to Trad Rock: The Post-Punk Scene 1982–87] about the end of new wave and punk rock.

So tell me about the history of football zines, I don't know much about them. I'm guessing they started in the eighties?

Yeah, the late eighties. You'd find a lot of people that had come from music zines because they'd discovered that it was potentially a lot easier to sell to twenty thousand football fans than twenty people at a gig – though you can't take that for granted as you only have one chance to do it. With music zines people could try to sell it in lots of places.

I didn't start Fly Me to the Moon but it was typical in that it was quickly put together as a simple A5 photocopied zine without staples and it was snapped up. Only a handful were done for the first issue to see how it worked and people went absolutely mad for it. They were printing two thousand for each home match within a very short time, it was that quick. There was a revolution happening; in the 1986/87 season there were a handful of zines and by 1988/89 if you'd bought When Saturday Comes [football fanzine that became a nationally distributed magazine] there was a list of all the clubs' fanzines and there were hardly any of the ninety-two professional clubs that didn't have one – and many had several. It was a massive upsurge and it came at the same time as the fans' movement. There were the disasters at Bradford City and Hillsborough and Thatcher was trying to bring in identity cards for fans. A lot of it was a reaction to that, the political side to it. They felt that supporters were being lumped together, being treated like the enemy within, and there was a lot of anger. Also, people used to buy a match programme because it was traditional and had a team sheet on the back; nine out of ten times it was out of date, totally wrong. So the football zines came from the music world where people had thought, 'We can write to other music fans without journalists.' It was the same with football fans, thinking they could cut out the middle man. It was by the fans, for the fans. I'm not meaning to have a go at journalists,

A selection of *Fly Me to the Moon* covers, beginning with issue 150, from January 1996. The couple on the cover of that issue are reading the very first issue of the zine, published for the match against Sheffield Wednesday on 26 November 1988. The other covers are issues 273 (August 2001), 536 (November 2013), 606 (July 2020), 609 (November 2020) and 622 (January 2022).

---

it's just that the zine writers were saying what football fans were thinking. A lot of the programmes in that period were very poor and there was little in them. Looking back I think a lot of the clubs were struggling financially before 1990 when more money came into the game. The programmes were pared back as a result. The football zines were snapped up everywhere and Middlesbrough was the same.

Was Fly Me to the Moon part of the first tranche?

Yeah, there's some dispute about the first one but it's probably *City Gent* for Bradford City. That's still going now and still a quality production. I used to write articles for loads of fanzines, no idea where they printed them! I just decided to think of something to do with Oxford or

I'd write to another team's fanzine about the last time Middlesbrough played them. I sent off to loads of them before I wrote anything for *Fly Me to the Moon.*

The sales of football zines blossomed very quickly but what's the current situation?

When I said earlier that sales were two thousand, that was when they were typed up on a typewriter. When it got past that point and you couldn't photocopy it anymore, it had to be printed. You had to find a way of typing it so the quality was good enough to be printed. We were lucky to find a designer who came on board and helped with the covers. People just pitched in together, that was one of the great things about it. We managed to get access to some of the first PCs in the area. I had a typewriter where you could take the ribbon out of it and type directly onto fax roll, and that was good enough to be printed off. I used that for music and football zines, it was just finding ways of getting round things. Technology was moving fast at that point. We did an issue every home match, by accident really. You have two weeks to produce a new one so if you're relying on handwritten letters coming in, that's pretty much full-time because our typing skills were rubbish.

Emails revolutionised the process. By the mid-nineties more or less everyone had a PC in their bedroom, before that you'd have to find someone with a typewriter. That period coincided with the team moving from Ayresome Park to the Riverside. We peaked at around two thousand at the end of the eighties and then it went down because it wasn't novel anymore. When we got Bryan Robson as manager, moved to the Riverside and bought Juninho, the circulation went up again. That period also brought loads of challenges because lots of matches were being rearranged. We were more successful and were in lots of trophies, so we had to do things really quickly. There was one week, and it's the only time I've done it, when I had to choose to work twenty-four hours, sleep the next night, work twenty-four hours and sleep the next night to hit the deadlines – we were driven!

You've only got that one chance to sell it really, that match.

Yeah, but I don't know why we didn't just miss some of the games! We had enough stuff to put together. I probably wrote more myself in those days, but there were lots of other contributors too. It gradually tailed off in this century, to the point where, a few seasons ago, I thought it was time to jack it in – but then lots of people came up to me at the last match of the season saying 'Don't stop, don't stop!' I've cut back to every month since then and it's mostly kept going through subscriptions. It never was before; we only had a handful of subscribers.

It was mostly sales outside the ground?

Yes, we only sell a couple of hundred or less now at matches, compared to the two thousand it had been. Last season we had two hundred subscribers and that's enough to keep it going. It's not as many this season so we'll have to see. You can't be sure if year on year of austerity is starting to kick in, even for something that doesn't cost that much. The great thing about doing it monthly is that it's much cheaper for subscribers, you're not asking for £40 up front.

I don't sell many digital-copy subscriptions, even abroad. There's a guy in America who subscribes to the printed version, even though it costs him a lot in postage. That tends to happen when people move, they want the actual fanzine.

I guess they're after the connection.

Absolutely, it is a connection, isn't it?

What's your relationship with the club like? You have a conjoined relationship but you want to have some independence. Have you been in bother with the club at all?

Stoke City's *Oatcake* overtook *Fly Me to the Moon* and got to three hundred issues first. We weren't the first to start but because we did them for every home match we had lots of back issues. They made a big thing out of it actually. I wound the editor up as he'd calculated when it was going to be. I pretended I was going to do one for a reserve game; I just put the announcement online somewhere I knew he'd see it! I mention him because the reason we overtook it is he had a massive problem with Stoke City at one point, there were legal cases and it knocked him out for a season. I was there a few weeks ago and the programme seller was also selling the *Oatcake* fanzine – I've never seen that anywhere else. I don't know how that came about!

There have been a lot of fanzines that have fallen out with clubs, particularly in the early days. There was Mission Impossible at Darlington and the editor got sued by the club. He called it a day when George Reynolds took over; his tactic was to go round to someone's house and stand there all night! For me, I remember trying to sell some at Grimsby Town and one of their guys came over and said I couldn't sell them right outside. It was a street of houses that the club didn't own. This bloke marched me to the end of the street and said I could sell from there, it was absolutely preposterous! There were a few clubs where you could have problems. Blackburn Rovers did buy the whole area around the ground so again you had to stand quite a way from the ground. I was only trying to sell a few at away games.

I had problems at Middlesbrough FC for a short time, not through anything in the fanzine but from interviews with the press. They liked to speak to a zine editor because it's something they can put after your name instead of vox pop.

It gives you a kind of semi-official status.

Yeah, I got misquoted in the Evening Standard, who I'd never done an interview with. They'd taken something I'd said to someone else and chopped it around. There was another time I was misquoted on BBC Radio 5 Live which was when BT Cellnet had changed to O_2, which meant the Riverside [Middlesbrough's ground] was going to change to the O_2 Riverside. A journalist had used me to say that Middlesbrough were already 2–0 down – it was a funny line but I hadn't said it! He rung me up and asked me if I agreed. I was told later by a friend who's a journalist that you should always say no or they'll use one of their lines as a quote. I actually said no but he still used it! I spoke on 5 Live, had a chance to put things right and that journalist got banned from the club.

I'm part of a fans' forum now and we meet with the club every month and discuss issues affecting fans. The government have, amazingly, said that all football clubs have to speak to fans and there's a structure in place. There has to be a liaison officer who has to meet with supporters a certain amount of times per season, it's called structured engagement.

Is it easier to write about the team when things are going really

badly or does it not matter how things are going on the pitch? I imagine that using gallows humour when your team is having a poor season offers some respite.

People often used to say that, that they liked the gallows humour, but I always took the opposite view. I don't think I could do it year after year if things were going that badly – it would depress me. I remember going to sell fanzines at Burnley once and a policeman came over and said 'So, who's your fanzine against then?' I said, 'What do you mean "against"?' He said, 'Well, we have a fanzine at Burnley that's against Blackburn Rovers.' The fanzine was just jokes and stuff about Blackburn, I didn't understand how they could keep doing that. There was a Leeds one, *Square Ball* I think, where a lot of the pages were anti-Manchester United. I think we sell a lot more and get a lot more people writing when the team's doing well.

How many writers are involved? Do you have a lot of random submissions?

Most people want to write for a season as a challenge. When I was doing it every two weeks I would try to balance it up with different people. You hope to have new writers coming in because you don't want people to think it's cliquey in any way. I don't know many of the people that submit stuff, though a lot of my friends have come through the fanzine.

For me, it's been an end in itself, I didn't have ambitions to do anything else. Other people, like Bob Fischer, who's now at BBC Tees, started by writing for the zine. There are lots of journalists too that began with us. There's a guy at the *Evening Gazette*, Andrew Glover, who's a sports reporter, and Joe Nicholson. He asked to interview me in a local cafe when he was a sixth-form student to see if I was suitable for his articles – he was really confident! He wrote for the zine and he had his own blog. He would interview himself before and after games on his iPhone and he ended up doing work experience with Sky and all sorts of stuff. He's a published journalist. There's been a few writers too. Daniel Gray from Edinburgh started writing for every issue of the fanzine and he's had several books published. He writes about travel and history, he even did one about the Spanish Civil War in Scotland. The first place he was regularly published was *Fly Me to the Moon*.

It's the first opportunity for people isn't it? To try things out and see how they get on.

Yes, maybe the discipline too, writing to a word count.

It's writing for a deadline and a specific audience too.

It's all those things. When it comes down to it, it's more difficult to be concise.

As well as the writers, the guy that did cartoons and caricatures went on to do some things for different companies and some semi-official stuff for one of the World Cup tournaments.

Have you got any other favourite football zines?

There were some really inventive ones early on. There was a brilliant one from Gillingham in the eighties called *Brian Moore's Head Looks Uncannily Like London Planetarium*. There was *Terrace Talk* from York, an early one that was good, *The Oatcake* was always interesting and *A Love Supreme* from Sunderland is still going strong. It looks quite plush, it's been in colour for years.

It's interesting that you'd mention Sunderland. Is there any solidarity between zine editors, even if it's teams where there'd normally be some animosity? Do you know them?

I did used to. I knew Martin from Sunderland, Mark who did *The Mag* in Newcastle and Michael who did another Newcastle zine. So I knew some of the local ones.

Did you have a good relationship with them?

Yeah, we'd sometimes get invited to TV or radio things, they were always decent. I guess that Sunderland and Newcastle don't really see Middlesbrough as their rivals! I knew a lot of the local ones but not many from the rest of the country. There aren't as many around now.

Why do think there aren't as many? Is it too many things competing for money and time?

You can imagine the early people probably jacked it in, no one thought of it as a career. There'd be groups of friends doing fanzines and then it would just come to an end. Also, as with all print, a lot of titles have gone completely or publish less often. This season, for the first time, clubs don't have to produce programmes – for some clubs it was costing them more than they were bringing in. Even Middlesbrough have reduced the size and price this season, trying to find a new way to do it. That's the reality now. The zines disappeared because there was a buzz about it and a buzz doesn't last forever. Some new fanzines have come up and there's even a new local music one. The editor interviewed me about Fly Me to the Moon and I gave him some tips. He does it as a hobby and pays for it for himself. He gives it away – I don't know how much it costs him to do it but he's done quite a few issues.

Are you aware of other sports that have a culture of fanzines? I guess cricket probably does.

Yeah, there were some. Steve, who did Mission Impossible, did a speedway one for a while, for Middlesbrough Tigers. They're the Redcar Bears now. Sticky Wicket, a cricket one, was pretty funny and lasted for a time. They're the only ones I know. I've got a lot of friends from Bergen and they don't get the humour in Fly Me to the Moon, they can't understand the jokes. That's the thing with other fanzines, you might not get the point that's being made, you've got to know a bit about the sport. There's a lad who writes for Fly Me to the Moon and he does a blog on darts – he says the best thing about it is that all the top darts players are really accessible. You just write to them and they get back and answer his questions.

Talking about accessibility, do you interview players much?

Not for a while but I used to. They used to do a lot of stuff in the community and I'd cover those events and interview the manager or players too. I go to press conferences with Tony Pulis* and sometimes ask him questions. He's quite an interesting character. Fly Me to the Moon started under Bruce Rioch and it's almost a full circle back to Tony Pulis, an old-school manager. Both of their teams were drilled in a disciplined way and were very knowledgeable about the game. Even as a player, Pulis used to spend all his spare time on coaching courses.

---

* Middlesbrough manager at time of this interview – he left at the end of 2018/19. Since then they have had three managers: Jonathan Woodgate, Neil Warnock and present incumbent Chris Wilder.

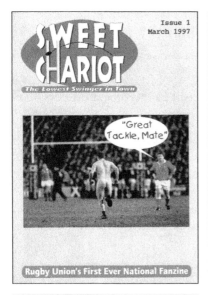

Behold the results of our best attempt at researching zines for sports other than football. Clockwise from top left: *Sweet Chariot* issue 1 (1997), a rugby union zine; *Not the Spin* issue 2 (June 2018), a cricket zine published by the Lancashire Action Group (https://lancsactiongroup.com); *Unlimited* issue 63 (1994), a zine about banger racing at the Smallfield Raceway in Surrey; and *British Wrestlers* issue 1 (c.2020), a magnificently old school zine, dedicated to the golden age of British wrestling, before 'American canker' infiltrated our TV screens, which 'heralded the ruination of our traditional and superior matwrestling'. Well said sir!

He's good in press conferences too, he always stands up, he's a bit of a one-off.

So you've not had less access as football has become more corporate then?

Not really. The last player I interviewed was Stuart Downing, a long-time player for Middlesbrough. That was at the unveiling of some of Alastair Brownlee's* commentary when we beat Steaua Bucharest. It's now written as you come down to the stadium. He was the voice of the Boro for years and it's a memorial for him. He was speaking as a fan really, so it's a great thing that's been immortalised on the bricks on your way into the stadium.

What's your passion for continuing with the fanzine like now?

It was always season to season, in fact before subscribers it was match to match. You sold the zines, paid for the printing and that was that, there wasn't any debt or pressure. With subscriptions, when you start a season, you can't stop halfway through. You get to the end of the season and in the summer you think about doing it again. In the middle of the winter there were a few matches when it hoyed it down, we got drenched before the game. There was one match against Leeds where there was loads of snow, one of those 'Beast from the East' things. I hardly sold any copies and I thought, 'This is ridiculous, what am I doing here?' Then it gets warmer and near the end of the season everyone comes and buys the zine and they say, 'Hope you're going to be back next season!'

You can't let your public down!

Yeah, exactly! The last match we did was our thirtieth birthday one and it's nice to stand there and be a part of people's match-day tradition. You have a chat with people and someone will always come up and ask what I think the score will be. I always say 2–1. 'You always say that!' 'Yeah, it'll be 2–1 one of these days!'

I guess as long as people want to keep writing for it, we'll keep

---

* Described on Wikipedia as 'English radio broadcaster best known for his coverage of Middlesbrough FC on BBC Tees from 1982 onwards.' Not to be confused with Alistair Brownlee, the legendary triathlete.

going. There's no shortage at the moment. It's not all nostalgia, but with it being the thirtieth year people like looking back. It puts things in context as well because football's a thing where people get heated about things. Maybe there's a rumour about someone being bought or sold and it might not be true but people are boiling over about it during the day. When you look back over thirty years it brings a sense of proportion to it. When the football fanzines started there was the music press and fanzines, but in football there wasn't really anything – maybe a fan letter in a programme, the pink sports editions of the newspapers once a week with letter columns, often from mad people. What else did you have? Some commentaries on the radio, no fan things though, and certainly nothing on TV. There wasn't anywhere for fans to have their say at the end of the eighties. It's amazing really, it was only thirty years ago.

Final question – what makes a fanzine, what are the defining elements?

It's got to be a magazine made by fans, for fans. If someone sends me something, whether I think it's good or not, I'll think, 'They're a fan, the fanzine is their outlet', so I'll put it in. So that's the difference, it's a channel and it brings us closer. As editor I just put things together.

14

SASKIA HOLLING

interviewed by Hamish Ironside

In the 'About the Author' section of Saskia Holling's brilliant book *Girlsville* (Spinout Publications, 2021), it states that Saskia 'was a pretty normal teenager growing up in the Isle of Lewis and then a pretty normal student in Edinburgh. Riot Grrrl changed all that, and in the early 1990s she began to put on gigs, write fanzines and play in bands.'

The fanzine was called *Heavy Flow*, and it appeared in six A5 issues between 1993 and 1996. The zine's attitude and content are very much in tune with the opening lines of Kathleen Hanna's famous 'Riot Grrrl Manifesto' of 1991:

> BECAUSE us girls crave records and books and fanzines that speak to US that WE feel included in and can understand in our own ways. BECAUSE we wanna make it easier for girls to see/hear each other's work so that we can share strategies and criticize-applaud each other. BECAUSE we must take over the means of production in order to create our own moanings.

Heavy Flow is mentioned by Teal Triggs in the 'Girl Power and Personal Politics 1990–1997' chapter of her *Fanzines* volume (Thames & Hudson, 2010), where Teal writes: 'Menstruation has long been a feminist issue, but the riot grrl movement gave it an angry and often hilarious spin.' This was also the period (no pun intended) when Julie Doucet began her peerless *Dirty Plotte* comic, another publication that delighted in subverting society's treatment of menstruation as a taboo topic.

While menstruation forms a kind of leitmotif across the run of the zine, *Heavy Flow* is an entertainingly diverse mixture of interviews, record reviews, local (Edinburgh) matters, poetry, and short essays or discussions on whatever issues Saskia and her contributors care to tackle. These range from a 'Muzakal Recipe for a Gurl Cabaret' (issue 1) to Saskia's very powerful first-hand account of harassment following the end of a relationship (issue 6).

Also in issue 6 is an interview with Kerry of Gilded Lil, which includes this telling exchange:

> Kerry: My dad used to bring home lots of folk instruments, he can't read music and neither can I but we just used to play. He taught me how to play guitar, Here Comes the Sun was first and then he taught me the Blues.
> Saskia: Your lucky. My dad was a musician but didn't teach me anything when I was younger. He taught my brother . . .

By the time issue 6 was published, Saskia was singing and playing bass in Sally Skull, along with Clare Scrivener on guitar and vocals, and Phil Bull on drums. As the band gathered momentum with gigs and recording, the zine fell by the wayside (alas).

In the following years Saskia took a break from music as she started a web-based business and also started a family with her husband, Russ Wilkins (best known as a member of the Milkshakes), and they moved from Edinburgh to the countryside around Dumfries. In 2016 Saskia reunited with her old bandmate Clare Scrivener (as well as Angus McPake and Catriona Donaldson) to form the Nettelles, whose recordings were released on the *Do You Believe in . . .* album on the Back to Beat label (the same label is due to release a Sally Skull retrospective in the next year).

Over the last five years Saskia also returned to writing with the aforementioned *Girlsville* book, which has been as much a labour of love as the book you hold in your hands. It involved around four years of research and writing to tell the story of the Delmonas and the Headcoatees, two of the most acclaimed bands of the Medway scene that emerged in the 1980s and 1990s. Without disparaging Billy Childish's role in their activities, the book challenges the lazy assumption that these bands were merely a Billy Childish side project,

Saskia Holling in sunny Edinburgh, March 2022.

and gives detailed portraits of the six women involved in the two bands: Hilary Bockham, Louise Baker, Sarah Crouch, Debbie Greensmith, Holly Smith and Kyra De Coninck.

What I especially liked about the book is that it reads more like a fanzine than a conventional biography. As with *Heavy Flow*, the book is imbued with Saskia's voice, but never intrusively so, and the insights into her own experience are so fleeting as to leave you wanting more. The book combines chapters devoted to each of the band members' life stories, told in their own words, with detailed analysis of the mainstream music press of the time, and how they covered these bands' recordings and performances. In doing so, the book not only demonstrates that sexism was alive and well in music journalism well into the 1990s, but also gives a compelling account of how the Headcoatees in particular succeeded in dovetailing the Medway sound with the spirit of riot grrrl.

I met Saskia in Edinburgh in late March of 2022, having travelled up from London on the overnight Megabus for the ridiculously low price of £9.99. We had lunch in the garden of a pub in the Meadows area of the city. At this point Covid restrictions had been relaxed in England, but were still strictly enforced in Scotland. I inevitably kept making the tourist's blunder of entering the building without a mask.

The effects of the Megabus are my excuse for not having been 'the best version of myself' for this interview, as became painfully apparent when I listened back to the recording later. At one point, to my horror, I heard myself saying that my impression was that women had never been marginalised 'in the recorded era'. What can have prompted this outburst of pure bollocks?

I think it was simply a strong feeling that the best music of the current millennium is mostly being produced by women – Julia Holter, Joanna Newsom, Jocelyn West, Mitski, Regina Spektor ... therefore, surely, sisters are doing it for themselves! Having recovered from the Megabus ordeal, I can see the flaws in this argument. For one thing, Julia Holter *et al.* are not *bands*. Where are the new Delmonas, the new Headcoatees? Why are all-female bands still regarded as a novelty? I urge the reader to read *Girlsville*, which may shed some light.

One curious thing about issue 1 was in the back it says 'Heavy Flow issues 2, 3 and 4 out now' – how come it says that in issue 1? They weren't all available when issue 1 appeared?

No, no they weren't. I must have just added that later. I was probably still selling old ones when I was selling the new ones as well.

So if you ran out of one you'd print up a few more of that issue?

Yeah. Because they always seemed to sell.

Would you get a little initial run done from a printer, or something like that?

No, probably ... it would depend at the time – I used to temp, do temping jobs, in offices. And if I could access the photocopier for that temp job I would sneak in my paste-ups and make up copies.

You must have done the classic error of leaving the originals in there and someone else finding them?

Never did that. I was never caught. And I think by the time I was doing number 3 I actually had a part-time job in an office, so I did have access to a photocopier. I think I was able to use that for 3, 4 and 5, and I think for the last one I had to get them printed up because I wasn't working.

And did you still have to sneak it when you were doing your part-time job, or did they know?

No, they didn't know. It was all done clandestinely. Part of the fun!

Some of the issues aren't dated, but I tried to figure out when they came out. It's not clear about the first one, but it's sometime in 1993.

Yeah. That would be probably my guess.

You were probably in your mid-twenties then?

Yeah. I was quite a late developer [laughs]. I was an older riot grrrl.

But you were already involved in reading fanzines and stuff? I got the impression you started it because you were running some events, and it kind of tied in with that?

Yeah, so that [handing me a flyer] would have been the event for the first one.

Okay. And at that point was Sally Skull going?

No, this was my other band, my first band.

Fud?

Yes. And so . . . I organised the gig, and then put together the fanzine to sell at the gig.

And do you remember how it sold there?

I can't remember how any of them sold, I just know that I did reprints. I maybe just printed up 40 or 50.

And were you selling them other places as well, or trading with other people?

Yes, I would put them into comic shops and record shops, and probably send them down to people like Slant in Newcastle. Maybe took them over to Glasgow as well. And there was swapping of fanzines all the time, of course.

I was at a friend's yesterday and she gave me this [handing me another flyer], which I'd forgotten all about. I used to put adverts up for the fanzine as well.

That's interesting, it's got the prices on, because they're not on the front of the zines. 40p for the first one – that's very cheap . . .

Isn't it?

And 60p for the second . . . these are very good prices!

Especially looking back at the amount of work that went into them. Ah well . . .

I couldn't believe, looking at my own, that one with the blue pages [*Saudade* issue 3] is 96 pages – I was selling it for a pound. I must have been losing money on what I paid for the printing.

But we weren't in it for the money, were we?

No, we weren't. And in terms of calling it *Heavy Flow* and having menstruation as a sort of theme to centre around, you know,

discussions about feminism and sexism, I immediately associated that with Julie Doucet, and she's on the cover of your first one . . . and you've obviously used that without asking her permission, because it says 'Hope it's OK Julie'! I think she subsequently gave it her blessing, didn't she?

Yes, she did, I got a letter back from her, saying 'Yes, that's fine'.

Was that where the idea came from for that as a theme?

Possibly, but Heavy Flow is actually quite personal because I did have very heavy flow, and so it came from a kind of monthly anger at having to spend so much on sanitary products, as a woman, which other genders didn't have to do. And so it was a political statement that because of my heavy flow I was having to expend money, which I didn't have very much of at the time, while other people didn't have to. It was partly from that, and probably because I'd seen Julie's comic as well, so a combination of the two probably led to this.

Am I right in thinking you were initially stealing tampons, almost as a matter of principle?

Yes, I was.

And where were you stealing them from?

Mainly just big supermarkets, so that it didn't hurt the shopkeepers themselves.

And at some point you moved over to using natural sponges?

I did, yes.

I quite like the way the run of the zines traces these things as a sort of . . .

A kind of story of my periods? Yes!

And I guess it also forms a kind of focal point for related things, like you had a lot of contributions from other people about their experiences of harassment, and things like that. How were you getting those contributions?

Initially it would be people I knew, I'd be asking them to contribute, and then I would get people sending me stuff, as the zine got better known. So people were actually actively contacting me to have their stuff included in the fanzine.

Getting back to the subject of menstruation and the stealing of sanitary products, I was actually contacted last year by a government department. The University of St Andrews were working with the government to talk about period poverty, and they were putting together a study, which pre-empted the whole free tampons and towels thing now happening in Scotland. Because the Scottish government have now recognised period poverty. So they contacted me to talk about the issues I had raised 30 years ago, which they were now working with.*

How did they become aware of your fanzine?

The found it in Glasgow Women's Library.

Ah, right. So that's a really good resource, isn't it?

The Women's Library is, yeah. You can look up their archives online.

Yeah, that's where I first saw *Heavy Flow*. So you were mentioning riot grrrl, you saw yourself as very much part of the riot grrrl movement.

I think I did, yes. I felt quite inspired by it. Even though I felt I was older than a lot of the people they were trying to talk to, I was still inspired.

I mean, it seems like there was a definite movement in that there were a lot of zines covering related issues ... it's interesting to me that it was seen as having happened at that period of a few years, and I wonder what your perception of it is – where did that go? Has anything improved since then, or has there been a sort of loss of momentum?

I don't know. It's a very different world now, isn't it? I mean, social media has changed the world irrevocably, and the way people communicate with each other and vent their energy, vent their spleen, is very ... it seems quite different. It's a lot more short-lived, it seems. You

* The same researchers also published an article on Saskia's zine; see Helena Neimann Erikstrup and Camilla Mørk Røstvik, 'Menstruation in the 1990s: Feminist Resistance in Saskia's Heavy Flow Zine', *Nursing Clio*, 7 August 2018, https://nursingclio.org/2018/08/07/menstruation-in-the-1990s-feminist-resistance-in-saskias-heavy-flow-zine.

know, you could splurge your anger into a fanzine, and it was a longer process, and took longer to filter through. And now you can reach people immediately, and everyone moves on to the next thing.

Yeah. You get an instant response – can be quite a big response – but then it's so ephemeral, isn't it? That's the thing about the internet, there was this impression of permanence, that once it's on there it's on there forever. But it isn't, because things are harder to find, and in the end . . . I mean, you can still give me a copy of the paper version of Heavy Flow, whereas it's quite a hassle maintaining a website. I mean, it's an expense as well.

Yeah. Although that's what my business is, because I have started a website business – but that's another thing altogether. That's how I've made my living for the last 20 years.

Coming back to 'where did riot grrrl go?' – well, it was killed by the media. The music press at the time, they literally said 'riot grrrl is dead', and replaced it in their papers with Britpop and lad culture.

When you say that, I can remember that was the order of things – there was riot grrrl and then there was Britpop – but how did that manifest itself in them actually killing it?

I wrote about this [in Girlsville] – One of them literally says 'Riot grrrl is dead' – that's the headline [in NME, 17 September 1994]. And then everything . . . all those months of loads of women in the music press – the features, the reviews – all of that information just went.

One thing that comes over in the fanzine is that Joan Jett's band the Runaways were a big influence.

Yes, exactly. Well, I keep mentioning riot grrrl, but it did have such an influence on me, because it also made me kind of focus on women in music and made me realise that there was quite a long history of women in music that wasn't necessarily talked about a lot. So I started investigating – charity shops, car boot sales, anything with women on the cover, any records, I would be hoarding them up. So I had a huge Runaways collection. Suzi Quatro, Bobbie Gentry . . .

I love Bobbie Gentry.

Yeah . . . Wanda Jackson . . . All the kind of blues queens as well . . .

Heavy Flow issue 1, from late 1993. The cover artist ('cover girl') is Julie Doucet.

Heavy Flow issue 2, early 1994. Cover girl is Saskia.

So I was just opening up this big Pandora's box of women in music. I wasn't aware that there had been so many. It was nice to discover. Everything was feeding in to what I was doing. I was feeling more empowered by everything I was discovering, and everything I was doing as well.

I just want to pick out a few things from particular issues.

Oh no! Okay!

So, one of the things you've got in all the issues is 'Hunk of the Time of the Month', and in the first two issues it's George Best!

Yes! [laughs]

And, uh ... what was that all about?

I think I was just making fun of the whole Page 3 thing. It was my version of Page 3.

I wasn't sure if you genuinely liked George Best or if he was the most ludicrous figure you could imagine.

I think it was a combination of the two. I do quite like him, but he is quite ludicrous as well. So that was the thinking behind that. And then I think I put a call out to people to see if they wanted to include anyone – I ended up with a pencil drawing of a footballer

[Peter Bonetti] . . .

Yeah, that's right . . . And then issue 2 I think is early 1994, and you'd just come back from Western Australia. What was that trip?

I was visiting my mother, who lived in Australia at the time. It was a couple of months – two or three months? I can't remember. That was an experience.

I found that quite interesting, I wasn't expecting that at all. Was that the only time you'd been to Australia?

I had been prior to that, when I was younger. I'd worked in a casino in Western Australia. But this was me going back much more politically aware. I could see things that I hadn't actually seen last time, to do with gender politics.

Yeah. I kind of got the impression it was like, 'This is even worse than in Scotland!'

It was quite . . . on the surface. Yeah, sexism on the surface.

More overt.

More overt, yes. I was trying not to be too harsh on it, so I was including some cultural things in there, that I'd found and liked, because I didn't want it to be too negative.

Heavy Flow issue 3, spring 1994. The original cover art was missing so Saskia made this one as a bespoke cover!

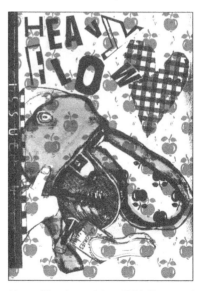

Heavy Flow issue 4, late 1994. Cover girl is Sally Tutill.

Heavy Flow issue 5, September 1995. Cover girls are Melanie Wright and Saskia.

Heavy Flow issue 6, May 1996. Cover girl is Melanie Wright.

How did it come about that your mum moved to Australia?

I grew up in Stornoway on the Isle of Lewis. But I wasn't born there, my parents were from Newcastle, and they moved up there when I was about six. Because they'd been up there for a nice summer holiday, and fell in love with it. The reality of living on a small Scottish island soon kicked in! And my mum left when I was about ... in my early teens. And moved to Edinburgh. And then she started working in casinos. She got a job in an Australian casino and decided to move out there. And then she moved to a casino in New Zealand, so I went back to New Zealand a few times as well. Which was much nicer.

Picking up where we were ... pedantic question: in the article on the Runaways [in *Heavy Flow* issue 3] you mention spellcheck, which I was quite surprised about. Were you doing it in Word?

I don't remember now ...

'Kim Fowley' comes out as 'Kim Phallus' ...

Yes, that's right! [laughs]

I wasn't sure how that happened.

When I was typing up the fanzines I used to pretend I was a student and go into the university, and they had a big computer room, and I used to just go on the Apple Macs there. And that's how I did it. It was all typed up there on the Macs.

Yeah. How would it render 'Fowley' as 'Phallus'?

I don't know. Maybe it didn't, maybe I made that up!

Well, yeah – it didn't seem plausible, to be honest!
Moving on to issue 4, there's a very interesting piece about a centre in Broughton Street where the police invaded it, and I really liked that bit of social documentation of what was going on there. What was your involvement with that centre?

It was the unemployed workers' centre. My boyfriend Tom and I used to go and put on some benefit gigs for them to raise money to keep the centre going. It was a good community place to hang out as well. The idea behind it was to give advice to unemployed people, a bit like Citizens Advice but more community-orientated. And also to provide cheap food for people.

Were they squatting?

They were squatting.

And that's why the police were brought in by the owner of the property, were they?

Yeah, because they were leasing it initially, but then the owner decided that he didn't want to lease it to them anymore, so then they became squatting. And it never reopened anywhere else after it had been closed down.

So then in issue 5 there's the Kim Fowley interview. It's very interesting in the first place that he actually came over to play Edinburgh for a solo gig.

It was Glasgow.

Oh, was it Glasgow?

Yeah, at the Thirteenth Note. I think he had done some other gigs up and down the country. He was on tour.

Yeah. And it seemed like you were drinking to get some Dutch

courage to tackle him?

Absolutely. Yeah.

He's a bit of a sleazy figure, isn't he? Did you already have an impression of that?

Yeah, I didn't really . . . well, you could tell he was a control freak as soon as – because that's his whole stage act. So it was pretty terrifying, going to talk to him in the first place.

But you felt you only learnt that about him from the gig? Because you already knew the Runaways, didn't you?

Yeah, his reputation from the Runaways preceded him. That was what I knew about him most. Plus I'd heard a couple of singles by B. Bumble and the Stingers, things like that, that he'd worked on in the sixties as well. It was pre-internet days, so you just know what you've heard. I didn't know what he was like as a person really until I met him.

It's one of the most powerful and intriguing things I've read in a fanzine, I think.

Well, certainly, I think his personality comes over. And the way he works comes over.

It seems like there's a sort of mixture of megalomania and manipulation, but also a real neediness.

Yes, there was some vulnerability there as well.

It's interesting that in the next issue there's a letter from him where you again get that strange sort of mixture of impressions where he's almost being like a bit of a folksy grandpa figure, but by then you've obviously got no time for him at all.

Well, the fact that he even bothered to reply – that's interesting.

And then in issue 6, the main thing I enjoyed was the interview with Lydia Lunch and Exene Cervenka. What did you make of Lydia Lunch?

She was terrifying as well! And I was having a really weird night that night as well. I just couldn't summon up the courage to talk much, so my friend Louise, who was with me at the time, did most of the interviewing. I don't know . . . it's just one of those nights. But they're only in front of you at that point in time, so you've got to make the most of it.

Were you a fan of Lydia Lunch or was it more like there was just an opportunity to do an interview with her so you might as well?

No, I was a fan of Lydia Lunch. So maybe I was a bit starstruck. More starstruck by her than by Kim Fowley.

She goes off on quite an interesting thing, almost like a fascistic angle, talking about overpopulation – that 'we've just got to keep the good ones' kind of attitude. I felt a bit uncomfortable reading that.

Yes. It was uncomfortable at the time as well.

Were you surprised by that?

There were a lot of surprises that evening . . . yeah. But I just thought I'd keep it all in because it shows that people come from all kinds of different places, don't they? You know, you have an impression of someone but there's so much more going on really.

So you had a run of six issues coming out fairly regularly – was the plan to carry on, or did you feel like, issue 6, 'this is going to be the last one'? I have seen a few fanzines where they do actually say in the fanzine, 'This is going to be the last issue'. But most of them don't, and I think they mostly just peter out. Because people have . . .

. . . have lives! Yeah, no, I think that was just . . . I'd had enough by then. And it was becoming . . . too stressful to put out, I think. I wasn't very well either, I had some health issues. So it just came to a natural close, I think.

What did you find stressful about it?

The kind of pressure to actually put it all together, and for it to be readable, and for people to . . . enjoy reading it. I was quite conscientious, really. Yes, it was just a fanzine, but it was also my little baby fanzine, you know? And I wanted people to enjoy it. So I put the pressure on myself. Nobody else was. Although, having said that, when there were more people contributing, there was then the pressure to make sure that it did come out, because they had given me their contributions to be published into it, so you had to think about that as well.

So the last issue was May 1996. Were you still doing gigs? Were they tying in with gigs at that point?

I wasn't putting on as many gigs, because the band Sally Skull was then actually *getting* gigs, so I didn't have to put them on anymore.

Do you think the band became more your focus rather than the zine?

Possibly. Possibly, because we were quite busy, recording and touring.

And you stopped writing, pretty much, until you did the book?

Yes.

When did you decide you wanted to do the book?

That was probably about six years ago.

Can you remember what inspired it?

I think there's a combination of things, because when I stopped doing the fanzine, I also stopped writing my diary. I'd had a change of relationship, and realised that writing in my diary all the time is kind of destructive in a relationship, because you write everything down instead of talking to the person you're in a relationship with. So I kind of had a change of focus about the way I wrote and what I wrote about.

You stopped writing your diary?

I stopped writing my diary in about '96, '97. And then . . . I also decided I wanted to leave the city, so I moved to the countryside, around '98, '99. And then I had a family. So it was only when the kids grew up that I could think about writing again. So, yeah, about five or six years ago I was ready to write again. So it was trying to think of something to write about, and this seemed like a good thing to write about.

Yeah, absolutely, I think it is. Have you had much response to it?

Yeah, it's been very very positive. Mainly within the musical circle that I'm active in now. It's not mainstream or anything, but it's been well received in that musical circle.

And Sally Skull made a comeback, didn't they, a few years ago?

Yes, we did a reunion gig in 2015 or '16 – we played at a festival in Edinburgh. And then after that gig Clare [Scrivener] and I formed another band, called the Nettelles, and we played in the Nettelles right up until she died in 2020. That was cancer.

Was it? Was that very sudden?

No. I mean, basically, all the time that we were in the Nettelles she was slowly dying of cancer. But it was . . . a band of love of music. Just getting as much out of our relationship – Clare and I's relationship with music – as possible.

I was reading the discography at the back of Girlsville and Holly Golightly's got an album called You Can't Buy a Gun when You're Crying. So that just reminded me that there's a bit of a gun theme going on in Heavy Flow.

in the early Heavy Flows . . .

The early Heavy Flows, yeah. It's almost like . . . you feel women should be allowed to carry guns, in case of harassment.

Yes, I did have that kind of feeling. And I was told off about it in the letters pages!

That was one of the nice things, yeah. Was her name Ruth? She sent a letter in taking you to task for it. I like that, where you get someone slightly challenging something you've written.

Yes, I completely appreciated it and I took what she said on board. I can see that point of view. I don't condone violence, but then I don't condone violence against women. I mean, there's a lot of violence against women.

I didn't know if you attitude was sort of, like, 'Well, she's taking me a bit more seriously than I intended it . . .'

Yeah, I probably didn't mean it seriously . . . but then I probably did as well! Because, as I say, there was a lot of violence against women, and how are we to defend ourselves? Especially if the police aren't defending you, or society isn't defending you. There was the point of anger there, which almost does lead you into violence. I don't actually think that is the answer, but sometimes society makes you kind of say these things as an answer.

I mean, we're such a non-gun culture in this country anyway, so I couldn't really see it happening, but I can see how in the States you might get a case where a woman's being harassed – like, being groped, say, or verbally abused – and she just pulls out a gun and shoots someone dead – whether that would be seen as mitigating circumstances.

Obviously not, really.

But there would come a point where it would be . . .

If your life is in danger, what do you do? If Sarah Everard had had a gun, would things have been different? Again, I'm not condoning it, but you have to ask these questions. The only reason you ask these questions is because of the way society is.

That certainly seems to be an area where there hasn't been any progress since *Heavy Flow* was coming out. The Sarah Everard thing illustrates that.

And there's things I was reading about then, about feeling harassed or threatened which young women are still feeling to this day. But it's about education, really, isn't it? Not about pulling out a gun! But it's a huge job.

Would you ever think of doing another *Heavy Flow*, and revisiting these issues?

It would be interesting, wouldn't it? Now you mention it . . . And people have said it would be interesting to also write about the menopause. Make it more of a publicly acceptable thing . . .

So why not?

Well, there you go – never say never . . .

I'll buy one!

I'll charge more than 40p this time!

15

LAURA MILLWARD AND JANET BROWN

interviewed by Gavin Hogg

Laura Millward and Janet Brown have both been making zines on and off for almost 30 years. Laura started young, distributing her *Just Kids* comic at school in Derby in 1993, while Janet started *Venus* the following year in Bradford. *Venus* ran for seven issues over several years, and in 1995 Janet also started *Release the Pressure*, a poetry/personal zine (perzine).

Janet has continued to create perzines, including a series on reproductive health: *Brick* (2015), *Barren* (2016), *Do You Remember the First Time?* (2018). There are also *Someone, Somewhere: A Perzine* (2017), *Proud Child of Immigrants* (2018) and *Small Town Girl* (2019). Her love of nineties music and pop culture led her to create *Pretty on the Inside*, a Courtney Love fanzine (2019).

Laura's background as a graphic designer means that her zines have higher production values than most. Her series of *Lost & Found* travel comics have been inspired by her trips to Chicago, Holland, Dubrovnik and, more recently, Japan. She has also published *My So-Called Life Zine: The Boiler Room* about the cult teen television show.

After meeting online through the world of blogs, Laura and Janet decided to collaborate and in 2017 they edited the compzine (a compilation of different writers' submissions) *Mixtape*, which focused on their shared love of nineties pop culture. I came across a copy via an online distributor and loved the enthusiasm of the various writers; they covered subjects like Salt-N-Pepa as proto-feminist icons, nineties film soundtracks and learning English from mixtapes. I was interested in their experience of joint editing, perzines and compzines, which were subjects I knew little about. The fanzine world I'd been part of was one of earnest young people writing passionately about bands that anyone outside the world of the weekly music press and John Peel would have been mystified by. They sold their zines at gigs and through the small ads in the music press. It was a time when knowledge about obscure bands and their music was a form of currency, but once all the information you need about the internet generation's version of the Jasmine Minks is readily available, turning inwards to your own experiences or outwards to collaborate with others is the next logical step.

I met Janet and Laura in Nottingham in the autumn of 2018, and began by asking them about when they were introduced to zines.

JANET: For me it was around 1994, seeing adverts in the back of the NME and Melody Maker and not knowing what they were, but they sounded interesting. I'd read about riot grrrl as well so I was interested in getting those zines. I started sending off for them when I was 15 years old. I spent the first year or so thinking I could never do it and suddenly there's a spark and you think 'No, actually I can!' I started making my first zines when I was 16. They were music zines about Britpop and grunge and then I completely abandoned them for years. I started blogging and met Laura through that. We'd both been into zines and were getting back into them.

LAURA: We went to Sheffield Zine Fair together and that's what made us think that we needed to do something. It was such a nice atmosphere.

What kind of time was this?

JANET: About three years ago, fairly recent. [to Laura] You'd done a few comics.

LAURA: I'm quite arty. When I was at junior school I'd made some comics with friends. It was called Just Kids and we used to distribute

Laura Millward (left) and Janet Brown in Nottingham, 2018.

it throughout the school – it had little cartoons and articles in it. I've always enjoyed little DIY projects.

That's quite a young age to start producing zines.

LAURA: When I went to university in Hull I made a zine called *It's Never Dull In Hull*. It was all about the city and how great it was because its reputation at the time wasn't the best. What inspired me to make them again was visiting that fair in Sheffield. I saw a zine about a TV show and that gave me the idea to make one about *My So-Called Life*, a show I liked as a teenager. I talked to other people who said it was a good idea and that inspired me to make a compzine with other people. Janet contributed to that. I posted it on social media to see if anyone else wanted to contribute and loads of people got in touch. There was even one person in LA that sent photos of the house from the show. It was nice making those connections with other people, that was what I really enjoyed about that project. That was the first zine I made in recent years and I started selling them at the fairs. Janet and I shared a table at the Sheffield Zine Fair the year afterwards.

What's that experience like?

JANET: It's always a funny experience, tabling at fairs. I can't say that it's entirely good or fun.

LAURA: Particularly the first time you do it, that's why we wanted to share a table. It's a safe way of trying it! That was a good idea.

JANET: We did the first three fairs together and you feel less exposed. A lot of the zines that I do on my own, the perzines, tend to be on quite sensitive subjects. You put a lot of yourself into it, you're sitting behind this table and people come up and pick up a bit of your soul and put it back down. You feel vulnerable.

It must feel like a slight rejection almost. How much do you edit what you put in them?

JANET: I don't really edit myself. If it's a thought that I think is relevant to the topic, I'll write about it. I've always been like that, even while I was blogging. For me zines feel safer because to some extent you have some control over who sees it. You're selling it at a fair or online whereas a blog could be seen by anyone in the world at any time. If it's a physical item it feels a bit more controlled. It probably isn't at all – a friend of mine distributes my zines so if she's selling them I have no idea who's buying them. So, to go back to the question, I don't edit myself, which is the opposite to how I am in real life. I'm not a very open person with my emotions but when it comes to zines it's all out there.

It sounds like a performer who can go on stage and sing to loads of people but is otherwise very shy.

JANET: Yes, definitely.

LAURA: I think the world of zine fairs is quite supportive. You feel everyone there is a bit of an outsider so people generally are very friendly and encouraging. You get to know people and it feels like a safe world.

JANET: There's a real contradiction in that the people who make zines are the worst possible people to sell at zine fairs. It involves meeting lots of new people, talking to strangers, promoting and selling your own work. Most of us are shy, introverted and socially awkward but because everyone feels a bit like that it feels like a safe and supportive space.

So you'd both done your own zines – how was your experience of doing Mixtape together?

LAURA: It was fun. It can be hard to decide who's doing what bit when you're doing it together but Janet selected things and I helped put them together.

JANET: We'd had the idea and then went away and asked people for pieces. About halfway through the project we had a morning at my house where we laid out everything we had and started to figure out what it might look like. We went away knowing what we were each going to do, but it is difficult, particularly because we don't live in the same city. The process of editing must have taken us about 8 months, it isn't something you can do really quickly.

LAURA: It can take some time to get contributions.

Is it something you think you'll do together again?

LAURA: We might do, I think it's a question of having the time. We have our own projects we work on too.

JANET: We quite often have an idea at a zine fair and we say to each

Mixtape, a compzine edited by Laura and Janet together, was published in 2017 as a one-off issue exploring music, books and fashion from the 1990s.

other, 'No one's done a zine on this, we should do it!' We want to work on it but as Laura said it's finding the time we can both spare. I'm doing a Master's at the moment and that works pretty well in terms of my productivity as there's nothing like making a zine to help you put off writing an essay! I have made quite a few zines on my own over the last year because of that. Doing a larger project together though is harder when you're pressed for time.

LAURA: I also make travel comics with my partner; when we go travelling we take our sketchbooks and publish things from those. We're off to Japan next week so we'll try and make one after that.

So it's like an illustrated travelogue?

LAURA: Yeah, that's right.

I've never seen one of those before, I like the idea.

LAURA: We did some in the previous years, from trips to Chicago and Holland. You get two different perspectives – I did my part and Tom did his. You see the different thought processes about the same trips.

Etsy is really helpful with zines. You can put them on there and sell them worldwide.

Lost in Japan (2019), a 32-page, A5 'travel diary zine' documenting ten days in Tokyo and Kyoto in November 2018 by Laura with her partner, Tom Goodwin. The zine is available for £4.75 through Laura's 'makedoshop' store on Etsy, which had registered a highly impressive total of 274 sales when we visited in July 2022. This zine is part of a series, with other titles having been published following visits to Holland, Chicago and Dubrovnik.

JANET: We've both sold a lot through there, I've been really surprised. I don't remind people about my Etsy page very often but there's a steady stream of orders.

So is that your main way of selling now?

JANET: I would say that I still sell the majority through zine fairs but Etsy is definitely catching up.

LAURA: I've sold more through Etsy. I've sold to lots of other countries like Japan, America, Australia and Canada.

JANET: Yeah, I've sold a lot to Australia recently! What's going on? Four orders in a week, all Australia.

You used to do a fanzine back in the mid-nineties. How did you sell them then? Did you go to gigs?

JANET: No, I didn't do any face-to-face selling then. It was just through the ads in the NME or *Melody Maker* when you'd pay a few pounds for a tiny advert.

You had to pay by the word.

JANET: I used to use teletext too, there were adverts on there. You ended up with a bit of a network. I met some really interesting people through that, when everything was done by post. People would send their pound coins taped to a bit of card.

And you'd swap little flyers around, send them around.

JANET: That's right, my friend in Southampton would put my flyers in with her orders and vice versa.

Fanzines would review other zines too, wouldn't they? It's like you said earlier, there was a supportive network.

JANET: It's really interesting because that aspect hasn't changed, you still have that real sense of community, it's just that the way of selling that has changed.

The subject matter of zines has largely changed. It used to be 95 per cent music, maybe some about gender politics, animal rights – but now there seem to be very few specifically about it. I went to my first zine fair a few weeks ago and from looking around the stalls it

seemed to be about 90 per cent personal zines.

JANET: I wonder what that says about zine culture.

LAURA: That there aren't enough spaces to share personal stories anymore?

Maybe that with social media people feel more open about sharing things. It's less of a taboo to say 'This is me, this is my identity and this is what's important to me.' Also when I was doing zines it was largely a male culture but at the fair I was at about two-thirds of the sellers were women.

JANET: Yeah, that's my experience. There are a lot of men creating but often you find them doing more of the art stuff.

LAURA: Maybe back in the nineties there were more men doing it because there were more bands out there that appealed to them – I don't know.

I went to a record fair earlier this morning and all twenty people queuing to get in were men between 40 and 60. Maybe music had a particular hold over that generation of men that it doesn't have on subsequent generations.

JANET: And there were certain bands that attracted zines like Manic Street Preachers. They had a kind of DIY aesthetic.

I think the riot grrrl movement changed things – a lot of zines were created in the wake of it. Do you think it helped to make zine culture more inclusive?

JANET: I certainly think so. Many zines being made now and the people making them owe a lot to the riot grrrl scene. It still has that influence on the culture, even on people who were born 15 years later.

What were your favourite zines when you first started making your own?

JANET: I can't remember any – that's terrible isn't it! When you got in touch I thought I'd go and find my collection of zines but they're all gone . . . too many house moves! I found three issues of a zine that I'd made but nothing else and I must have had hundreds.

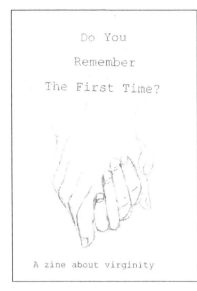

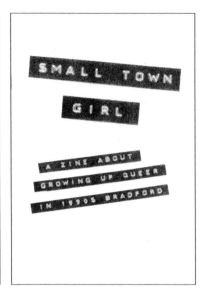

Four zines produced by Janet: *Do You Remember the First Time?* (2018), *Small Town Girl* (2019), *Brick* (2015) and *Barren* (2016). Since our interview Janet has moved on from Etsy and is now selling her zines through Pen Fight Distro (https://penfightdistro.com), a queer and feminist zine and book distributor, which has an impressively wide range of zines on subjects such as birdwatching, street harassment, Asperger's and women in STEM. The site also has event listings, notice boards for trades and correspondence, and many other very handy resources, all of which goes to show that zines are alive and well in 2022.

Were they music ones you were buying?

JANET: Mostly – some that were more feminist and riot grrrl focused. There was a strong overlap with music and Manic Street Preachers zines were always popular.

Laura, you come from a more artistic background. Were you buying music zines or comics?

LAURA: I don't remember seeing that many zines when I was younger. I have a friend who's a similar age and she did a music zine. She wanted to be a music journalist and she saw it as a good way to meet bands and get to write about them. For me, I always liked comics and graphic novels and the chance to publish something and do it all myself was really appealing. Doing a zine with Janet and other people has really made me feel more connected – some of them are now online friends. Libby who did the front cover for *Mixtape* has an embroidery Instagram that's popular now.

How many copies of your zines are printed?

JANET: Over the last few years Thomas, my partner, started doing them for me at work – not a formal arrangement with his employers at all! He'd knock off ten copies and I'd take those to a zine fair. It's got to the point where I'm selling more than that on Etsy. My friend Vicky in Manchester runs a book and zine shop and she does all the copies for me now. It's more formal, I pay and she sends me fifty copies. It's been a rapid change between knowing that if I had ten copies it would last me a year and now I'm printing fifty in a print run. That's a bit weird because I'm not very good at keeping track. My partner gets frustrated with me, I'm so chaotic. He'll ask, 'How many do you have left of this one?'

'I have no idea!'

'Why don't you know?'

LAURA: With the travel comics we only printed fifty copies and eventually they sold out. If felt quite nice to do a limited run – when you've sold them all you feel like you're done with that project.

It's time to move on.

LAURA: The thing that puts me off is the printing process, it's quite a pain to do. If there was just a photocopier somewhere I could use it would be much easier! I go to a print shop sometimes but it can be costly.

JANET: They can be. The ones near me don't have copiers you can just use yourself and I don't like giving random men, it's always a man behind the counter, my zine about abortion to copy. It just doesn't feel comfortable. That's why Thomas did them for so long and now Vicky does them. I can give her any kind of content and she won't look twice. Copy shop guy might think it's a bit weird! The printing part is the worst part of the process and I always put it off.

It's good when you get the finished thing back though isn't it?

JANET: Definitely. Laura's zines always look beautiful, her production values are much higher than mine!

LAURA: I think because I worked as a graphic designer before, I'm a bit of a perfectionist. That can be a bit of a hindrance with zines though, I think they should look imperfect and they don't need to be perfectly set out.

JANET: I'm more from the nineties school of 'glue some bits of paper onto a piece of A4 and photocopy it and it looks shoddy but it's fine'.

LAURA: There's a real variety out there. Some people illustrate their zines beautifully, some people just use text.

JANET: For me that's the beauty of it. If you tell someone you make zines and they don't know what one is they ask, 'What are the rules?' I reply 'Well, there are no rules.' That's quite scary to some people but to me that's the beauty of the medium.

You can go to a zine fair and look at five tables in a row and no one will be selling something that looks similar to the next person. There'll be a difference in the medium that they use, or whether it's hand-drawings or digital or whether it's all text, whether it's coloured or glossy and beautifully presented or some A4 sheets folded in half. I like that about them.

It's very democratic, isn't it? Money or resources, other than at a very basic level, don't really matter. That leads perfectly to one of my questions: when is a zine a zine?

JANET: Good question! There have been some really interesting debates over the last few years. There are producers and artists groups, often working out of London, often coming from art school backgrounds, who will come up with a crowdfunded 'zine'. What they're making is a magazine but it sounds cooler to say 'zine'.

LAURA: It's got to be something you've made yourself – but I guess that could be a magazine too. Because the word comes from fanzine, it needs to be on a topic you're really passionate about.

JANET: For me the DIY aspect is really important. I don't do my own copying but the content is mine, it's made in a low-tech way. It's still basically just photo-copied, made in a simple process. Basically anyone can do it without any training.

LAURA: You sometimes see zine workshops and some of them can be quite pricey. They'll show you how to make a zine for £25 – you don't really need a workshop to learn that unless you want to get inspired by what other people are doing.

That sounds like people seeing a gap in the market! You were talking about magazines before – I guess if there's a company or business involved that stops it being a fanzine.

LAURA: Yeah, if it has advertising . . .

Or a barcode . . .

JANET: And it sounds silly but I think size makes a difference. If it's A4 it's probably not a fanzine; you do see some larger ones but they're often edging towards being a magazine. The larger ones tend to be glossier with full colour. For me a fanzine is A5.

You never see a hardback zine. We can definitely draw the line there!

JANET: I think you could ask fifty zine-makers and you'd get fifty different answers.

We were talking earlier about the co-operative zine. Is that something that is fairly common or is it still unusual to have more than one editor?

LAURA: Sometimes you'll see call-outs on Twitter saying 'I'm making a zine on this subject, does anyone want to contribute?' but it's not that common. It's called a compzine, from 'compilation'. They still tend to have a single editor.

JANET: I'm working on one at the moment with a friend. I say working – everyone else has submitted these great pieces and we've not done much! We still need to put it together and write our own bits. I still think the majority of zines have one creator, one writer.

LAURA: The compzines are good for me because I'm more into the art side. If people submit their writing to me, I can put it together and make it look nice.

JANET: Some subjects really lend themselves to compzines. I did one about a year ago about virginity loss stories. The point was to show there was a diversity of experiences and you clearly can't do that by yourself. It was my favourite thing I've ever made, I was really proud of it.

That was great, some of it was so funny.

JANET: Exactly! Some were funny, some were so sad, some hopeful – a range of experiences. If I'd have just sat down and written a zine about losing my own virginity that would have been a bit weird!

LAURA: I think it's great that people are willing to be so open.

JANET: A woman called Verity did a brilliant comic for it. I'm the flip-side of Laura, I'm a writer not an artist. I draw little comics but they're very bad. It's amazing to do a compzine where I know I'm going to get some beautiful pieces of art from Laura or Verity that I can include.

LAURA: Certain people might have different ways of approaching something. That collaborative process is nice when you've finished the zine because you send it to all the people who've contributed and they can also help you to spread the word about it.

Do you see yourself carrying on producing more zines in the future?

JANET: I think so, I've always got a copy of works in progress on my notes app. There's a list of zine ideas and it just gets constantly added to. Only one in ten of those might get made but I can't see a time when I'm not adding to that list. Like I said it's a great procrastination technique, whether I'm putting off cleaning the house or writing a thesis. It's a really nice community and a good way of presenting ideas so I can't imagine thinking that I won't do it anymore.

What do you think you might do future ones on?

JANET: Good question, what are my ideas at the moment? I can't even remember, I'll have to look at my app!

LAURA: I'll keep doing the travel ones. Also, I've had an idea to do one on 'Who or what was your first weird crush?' so I've been asking people about that. For example, Dogtanian from *The Three Muskehounds*. Some people mentioned strange crushes like that when they were growing up. I started but never completed it so I need to get going on that. It's good to have an end date for a zine – a deadline is really helpful.

JANET: It really is. I tend to almost plan my zine making around the zine fairs. If I know I'm going to one in three months I'll think 'right, what am I going to do?' I did Lincoln a few months ago and having done nothing over the summer, suddenly in the space of a few weeks I got one done. I had a deadline and I needed to do it. I picked up two zines in Lincoln about books. I'm a complete book obsessive; I was an English teacher for a long time, I now work for a book company and it never occurred to me to write about them so that's my latest idea.

And I'm writing a book about zines – we're like yin and yang.
I wanted to go back to a comment about teletext that you made earlier. Was there a page about fanzines?

JANET: It was more like an ads page. I remember meeting someone that I'm still vaguely in touch with because I'd sold her a rare Manics record via Ceefax. It was like the sort of adverts you had in the back of magazines – penpals, things you were selling and people would often mention their fanzine too.

So, how did that work? Did you have to write off to Ceefax?

JANET: I cannot remember!

LAURA: There was a PO box in Bolton you had to write to.

JANET: It was one of those things I'd forgotten until recently when Sarah, who I'd sold the record to, got back in touch and said 'Do you remember me? We knew each other in the nineties.' About a week later than that my friend Kirsty who makes zines tweeted 'Does anyone remember when you could find penpals on Ceefax?' I'd totally forgotten for twenty years that that had existed!

LAURA: That used to be a big part of zine culture, having penpals. I don't think kids now would do that. They have social media for that.

JANET: We used to send mix tapes through the post.

Yeah, I used to buy zines and strike up a bit of a friendship with editors. At some point you'd ask what their favourite music was and swap tapes with them. I got introduced to all kinds of new stuff that way.

You said earlier that you met through blogging. The obvious question that I forgot to ask is why write a fanzine instead of a blog? It sounds like printing is a bit of a pain in the arse.

JANET: I think blogging lost a lot of its community.

LAURA: I started mine around 2005 and it started becoming popular a few years later, lots of people started them. After maybe five or six years when social media took off less people were reading blogs and you didn't get as much interaction. That was nice thing about it; you'd get people commenting and visiting each other's blogs, same thing as the fanzine world really.

JANET: Blogs seem to have become much more commercial. They still exist but the people who get interaction tend to be the big bloggers who make money from it. It kind of lost its appeal for me really. I think what I felt like writing about changed as well. When I was blogging there was always the sense that if you went out somewhere nice for the day you'd have to take some nice photographs, write about where you'd been or think of some insightful comments on recent events. That wasn't what I wanted to do anymore. I wanted to write something more long form where you can explore something at length which works better in a zine than a blog. I also liked the idea of collaboration with other people. It's rare to have other people writing in your blog. Although they get compared a lot, for logical reasons, they are quite different. I feel that what you can do in a zine is very different from what you can do in a blog. Blogs are much more photographs and visual.

A zine can have all sorts of art mediums, which is appealing.

LAURA: I think with the blogging world, because there are so many, there's more competition for attention. People spend less time reading them now. With a zine you can sit and spend some time reading it. You're less likely to be distracted by other things, it's an offline medium.

JANET: It's interesting; you see the same thing with the return of vinyl. By the late nineties people were saying 'Vinyl is dead'.

It's never coming back!

JANET: Exactly – and now you can walk into Tesco's and buy it! It's become a trendier thing. I think there's an appeal, when you live in a world where you can get anything at the touch of a button, to a certain kind of person for something that is more lo-fi, that is made by hand.

It's something that demands more commitment, both by the person who's produced it and the buyer. It was interesting that you talked about the sense of community that you felt was lost from the blogging world but it's still part of the fanzine world.

LAURA: I'd definitely say that, yes.

JANET: It's interesting because the community when I started doing zines in the nineties was, by necessity, about letter-writing and you'd meet up with people sometimes. The community now is mostly online even though the zines are offline. You're keeping in touch with people using Twitter and Instagram and meeting up with them at zine fairs.

So the online world has encroached a bit but it's still ultimately about connection and communication.

BOTH: Yeah.

And that feels like a positive place to end.

16

JASON CREED

interviewed by Hamish Ironside

Like *Smiths Indeed* (Chapter 8), *Pynk Moon* is devoted to a single artist, in this case Nick Drake. It was edited by Jason Creed in a total of 21 issues in A5 format (210 × 148.5 mm), the first 19 of which appeared regularly between 1994 and 2000. In 2011, Jason edited a book, *Nick Drake: The Pink Moon Files* (Omnibus Press), harvesting the best material from those first 19 issues. This was followed by the final two issues of *Pynk Moon* in 2012, since when Jason has maintained a Facebook page as an outlet for his more recent writings about Nick Drake.

Nick Drake's life story is fairly well known now, but to summarise it as briskly as possible: he was born on 19 June 1948 in Rangoon, to parents Rodney and Molly. He had one older sister, the actress Gabrielle Drake, who now controls Nick's estate. The family moved to Tanworth-in-Arden (Warwickshire) when Nick was two years old, and he was privately educated at Marlborough College and Cambridge University. He bought his first guitar in 1965, and just three years later, while still a student, he was recording his first album *Five Leaves Left*, which was released in 1969 by Island Records. This was followed by *Bryter Layter* in 1971 and *Pink Moon* in 1972. All three are masterpieces, as is now widely acknowledged; yet they are thought to have sold little more than a thousand copies each in the first few years after their release.

Their perceived failure was probably a contributing factor in Nick's reserved temperament progressing to severe depression in his last

Jason Creed at his home in Somerton, November 2021. He is holding the full run of *Pynk Moon*, as well as the Omnibus book.

I took a shine to the painting on the wall, which is by Jason's mum. It features what was probably intended as a setting sun, but which naturally struck me as a pink moon.

two to three years, and he died on 25 November 1974, aged just 26, of an overdose of antidepressants. His death did not receive much publicity, and when Jason began *Pynk Moon* twenty years later, Nick was still a relatively obscure figure. Yet the quality of those three albums was becoming increasingly recognised, and interest in his short, rather mysterious life also grew. The first biography (by Patrick Humphries) appeared in 1998, when *Pynk Moon* was already in full swing. Since then further biographies and other books have appeared, most notably including the magnificent *Remembered for a While* (John Murray, 2014), a highly personal compendium instigated by Gabrielle. An 'authorised' biography by Richard Morton Jack is due to be published around the same time as the book you hold in your hand.

Nick Drake is a figure who inspires unusually intense devotion among his fans, much as Morrissey did while with the Smiths, but whereas Morrissey has spent thirty years seemingly bent on having the scales fall from his admirers' eyes, Nick's early death has undoubtedly burnished the legend. The very fact that there is no authenticated film of Nick as an adult has only encouraged people to seek it, so that you can now find on YouTube grainy footage of a few people walking through a festival in the early seventies, with numerous comments discussing whether one of them is Nick.

I should acknowledge that I am one of those in thrall to both the music and the legend, which is probably the main reason why I was keen to talk to Jason about his experience of editing *Pynk Moon*. But I was also curious as to how he managed to put out issues regularly in those pre-internet years, with so little raw material to work from. Like *Smiths Indeed*, *Pynk Moon* seemed one of the most well-run zines of its time, but whereas Mark Taylor was able to harness the excitement of events at the time they were happening, Jason Creed's work was more like detective work, and may have played a significant part in the way Nick Drake became more than a cult figure in the course of the 1990s.

At this juncture, awkwardly, I should address one pedantic point of order, which is that for most of its run, Jason's zine was called *Pink Moon*, exactly the same as Nick's final album. It was only with issue 17 that he began spelling it *Pynk Moon*, with a 'y', as a tribute to the spelling of *Bryter Layter*. The book by Omnibus went with the *Pink Moon* spelling, but we are going with *Pynk Moon* in this chapter, simply because we like it much more!

I visited Jason at his home in Somerset in late November 2021, on the very day that the Omicron variant of SARS-CoV-2 was first reported by the World Health Organization. I tested negative for Covid, but had been poorly for what seemed like ages, and my physical delicacy was becoming increasingly exacerbated by neurosis. I felt like I was taking on some of Nick Drake's traits, almost as if I was engaging in method interviewing. I am very grateful to Jason and his wife Naoko for being such superb hosts when I was in such lousy shape.

You started Pynk Moon when you were 21, in 1993, and I was wondering, were you looking for a fanzine to do and decided Nick Drake was a good subject, but there might have been others that you could have done, or had you not thought of doing a fanzine until you got into Nick Drake?

I was very aware of fanzine culture because I'd been buying them, about Paul Weller and various other bands that were around at that time, and maybe some poetry fanzines as well. I don't think I had any plan to create one myself, though I was enjoying fanzines. And then I discovered Nick Drake, and suddenly, somehow, the two came together. I had a bit of a realisation, the first time I heard Nick Drake, I thought 'I'm going to write about this guy.' I was interested in being a writer at the time. I was reading lots of books – I hadn't really been interested in reading as a kid, but I got into it in my late teens. I was just going mad, devouring books, fanzines, and started writing short stories and poetry. I knew I wanted to write something, I didn't know what at the time, I was just practising – you know when you start finding your way and writing little things? Developing your own style and stuff. And then suddenly I heard Nick Drake, I thought 'I'm going to write about this guy', I had no idea why, it just popped into my head.

I wonder whether part of the attraction was that there was so little information available at the time? And it would be a sort of voyage of discovery, in a way.

It was odd because when I first listened to his music, when I was in my parents' house, laying on the bed, listening to 'Time Has Told Me', and looking at the cover, I didn't know he had passed away. I assumed he was still alive, and I had all these romantic notions in my head. I thought, 'Well, he must have gone away somewhere, because I've never heard of him – I bet he's retired to America! I'll probably have to get a plane to the States! This is going to be really romantic!' You know? 'I can track him down. I bet he lives in some old deserted house tucked away in some place in America, I can go and track him down and interview him immediately', and all of that.

So that was after you got Five Leaves Left, first of all? Because Paul Weller had mentioned it in an interview, or something. And were you able to easily find out that he'd only done three albums, and that sort of thing?

I think – it is a bit hazy now – I got Five Leaves Left . . . and it was not the sort of thing that I would normally listen to. At the same time, I was totally drawn to it. Also just the image of Nick Drake. After that, I think I tracked down a copy of Record Collector magazine. Record Collector used to advertise their back issues for sale, and I think they had a little mention that there was some Nick Drake in there. So I got that. Around that time, I got the Fruit Tree box set, which had a booklet in with a piece by Arthur Lubow. And then some time around then the Way to Blue CD compilation come out. So those were my first bits of information, I think, which opened my eyes a lot, particularly to the fact that he was no longer around.

But this was before any of the biographies had come out, wasn't it?

Yeah, absolutely, there was no books. So that set me off, I think. Once I realised he was gone, and there was no general info out there, I just started putting adverts in NME, I think, just requesting information: 'I'm starting a fanzine about Nick Drake, have you got anything you want to share?'

Got a big response to that?

Yeah, I wouldn't say a huge response, but I was getting a few letters and things each week from people. And then I'd photocopy this old article . . .

Yeah, I was wondering how you were finding that. Was it in libraries and things?

People were sending them to me. The first three fanzines, everything in there came together from my first sort of . . . advertising campaign. The request for info, and the Lubow box set article and stuff. And I borrowed . . . you can see there's a few articles in here, and then I'd just read them and then wrote my own little biography. And then put it into three parts, and that's what filled up these first three fanzines. Everything else had just been sent to me by people. It came together in those three. And, as I mentioned before, I just thought, 'I'll advertise those, and then it's done.' And that's when the interest started coming in – once I'd got these three out, I was getting twenty letters a day.

So, just looking at the timeline – because I know you say you went to Tanworth-in-Arden in '93 – it seems like you already had the idea to do a fanzine then and you were collating all this material, and got three issues' worth. But would that have been over a period of about a year?

I'll be honest with you, it's a little bit hazy. I don't know *exactly* what year I started it, I think it's around whenever I've said in the past it was!

It's alright – if you don't know, you don't know . . .

Yeah, I left home around that time as well, and I started it up . . . when I had the idea for it, I was still at my parents' house. But the actual fanzine, the address of it was my first home when I'd left my parents' house. But again, I don't even have an exact date on that.

And what was your situation at the time? I mean, had you been to university, or anything like that? Or you went straight into work?

No, I was a dropout. I had a terrible time at school. I'd been a normal, happy kid into my early teens, and then . . . I don't know, I got . . . a bit of depression or something. I felt a bit alienated. I didn't fit in at school and I started dropping out and just . . . doing my own thing. I knew I wanted to be creative, but I didn't really know what to do with myself. I went through this whole thing of trying to find a job when I left school, not knowing what I wanted to do, and got into the rut of trying to do things to please other people. Because they would say 'You should go and get a job', or 'You have to do this', and I didn't know what to do, so I was fumbling around in a load of dead-end jobs, really, for a while. And it wasn't until late teens that I started reading, and music inspired me, I think – musicians I admired, they might have said 'I read this book', or whatever, in an interview, and that inspired me to read. And once I found books, I had something that I could aim for. You know, I liked the idea of writing a book, but at the time I didn't have any sort of confidence or feeling I could do that myself. But I think the fanzine, I thought 'I could do that', because by then I was looking at them. I didn't think about it much, it just sort of happened.

And with Nick Drake, was it a case that when you first heard him you thought, 'Wow! This is . . . this is better than Weller!'?

It was something new, yeah. It moved me in a way that I can't say, and I still remember laying on the bed – 'Time Has Told Me' come on, and it was a little bit 'dum, de dum, dum', and I thought, 'This is not something I'd normally listen to.' It's nice, you know? It's good. But then 'River Man' came on, and it's like . . . that was beyond . . . There's that habit, isn't there, of listening to something and getting into the judgement frame of mind, and you think 'What am I listening to? Do I like it?' But with 'River Man' that just went. You know when you hear, or see, an amazing piece of art or something, it's a bit like meditation, you become present, and you don't resist any more, you just take it in. That was what hit me, I think, that day. Hearing 'River Man', it just opened the door for me then.

I totally understand that. So, just to cover the basic sort of production facts, do you remember much about print runs, whether you reprinted, that sort of thing? And how you produced them and all that?

I started off by doing a cut-and-paste, scrapbook version. And then I would take that to a basic photocopying shop, and they would laser print it for me. So then I could just phone up the printers and say, 'Can you do me 20 copies of number 1, can you do me 30 copies of number 2', and I'd literally go down there once a week. Because to start off I had no idea how many . . . so it was a bit more expensive to get it printed on demand.

Yes, exactly. So, did you not have an idea, like, 'If I get 500 done, the unit cost will be lower'?

I didn't really have any money to put into it in the first place, so it was just on a very low budget, and then as long as what was coming in – which was two pound an issue, or whatever – paid for what was going out – which it did, pretty much – you know, maybe left me a bit of spare change for a couple of beers on a Friday or a packet of fags or whatever – it was okay, I didn't really . . . to me, in those days, the idea of running anything like a business or being serious about it wasn't very cool.

Yeah, I think that's like most fanzines, in fact every fanzine I've spoken to.

It just sort of stumbled from issue to issue. I did get organised around issue . . . 17, I think – you can see a slight change. Issue 16 was just a photocopy; 17 is a bit more cardboardy, and these were professionally printed. And I had probably two or three hundred done up in a go.

Right, yeah. Because you say in the book that over the first nineteen issues you sold around 10,000, so that averages about 500 per issue . . . and I'm guessing it built up a lot of momentum – were you doing subscriptions, and things like that, if someone wanted to pay for, like, four issues?

I wouldn't do a subscription but I would – people would just send me money to reserve the next issue. They'd send me a couple of pound, or if they just wanted a notification, just send me a stamped addressed envelope, and I would let them know. But once it got going I would sell a lot of back issues as well. Once people had bought – if they'd come in at issue 12, they would want to buy issues 1 to 11 as well afterwards, once they had read number 12. So they were always available. So seven or eight years after I'd been doing it, you could still buy all the back issues, still for the same price, or slightly discounted if you bought all of them. So it all kept going over that period of time. That's why I think the sale figures were quite high – because number 1 was available . . . for eight or nine years, or whatever.

So the initial run was 19 issues, coming out fairly regularly, and then you say in the introduction to the book that when you did

The complete run of *Pynk Moon*.

number 19 it wasn't intended to be the last at the time – it just kind of worked out that way because you had other interests. But then in another part of the book, the book launch for the Patrick Humphries biography, I think he says to you – I think you say, 'The next issue's going to be the last', and he says, 'You always say that!'

Yeah. I did say it a lot. Yeah. I felt a bit tied down, a bit, at times, because . . . it was only coming out quarterly, but it was quite a lot of work. I think the main amount of work was probably the correspondence. A lot of people would write to me, and I would spend a lot of time writing back. And just the process sometimes of every week going to get the fanzines, put them all in the envelopes and stuff, got a bit of a drag. I wasn't entirely stable at the time, to be honest. I was up and down with my moods, I was drinking too much, I think, in those days. Experimenting with drugs, and not having the most healthy lifestyle.

But it's quite interesting that there's no hint of that in the fanzine. I think a lot of other people – I mean, I was certainly doing the same thing at the same age, but the impression you get with Pynk Moon is it's quite . . . in some ways quite a sort of, um . . . professional job. You know, there's a certain consistency to it.

And if you'd met me at the time, most of the time, you would have thought, 'Oh, here's a healthy, well-grounded, normal young man!' [laughs] But inside I was in a bit of turmoil at the time. So I struggled, really, just to commit to it, but I carried on. At the end I did get distracted. The way I felt about doing it changed, and it did come to a stop. There was a grand plan to turn it into a website and have it all there. And that fell apart.

But was part of it that after the Patrick Humphries biography came out a lot of information was readily available in that, and you were starting to feel like there wasn't that much you could add after that?

Yeah, I don't remember specific feelings like that. Looking back, I'm pretty sure it changed in that it was very ... simple, and organic, and unique to begin with. And then, by the end of it ... you know, everyone was talking about Nick Drake, and there was lots more books available, and there didn't really seem ... that much point in ... you know. Trying to find new things anymore. Maybe I felt like I'd ... Because I'd started it for myself, I guess. It's easy to say now I wanted to, you know, do something for other people, but I'm not sure that's the case. I wanted to find out more about Nick Drake. I was ... I don't know if obsessed is the right word, but I was very very interested, and *moved*, by his whole story and everything. So I did it for myself, in a way. Obviously it came into a fanzine which was for other people, but ... you know, you can't just carry on, I don't think, if you don't really feel like the motivation's there anymore, maybe.

Yeah. So, issue 19 was in the year 2000, and then in 2010 a book came out that collected them all together. But I'm just curious about that decade from 2000 to 2010, whether it was a sort of Nick Drake-free decade – what were you up to then?

I still would have listened to his music. But otherwise ... you know, I got a sort of career going for the first time in my life.

As a gardener?

No, this was in care work, I worked in a care home at the time. As I say, it was a bit up and down in my early years, but I got into yoga and meditation, and that helped balance me. Once I started practising those things, it kind of freed me up a bit and other things came into my life. Care work was one of them. I just walked past a care home one day and went in. Because I needed a job, and I asked, and . . . it escalated quite quickly: I went from being a care assistant to a lead carer and a trainee manager in the space of a few years, and it kind of took over my life a bit, really. I'd even been teaching yoga before that, and that got dropped in favour of the career in the care home.

So you were feeling like there was a real purpose in the care job?

Yeah, looking back, it was very natural. Even though I'd done the fanzine, I never really felt like I'd achieved much in my life. I don't know why, but it was just a feeling I had, that I wasn't particularly good at anything. Probably like Nick Drake, in a way – he produced those albums, didn't he, and he thought he hadn't really done anything with his life. It's ridiculous, really. I look back at the fanzines now and think, 'Well, you've done quite well there. They're pretty good.' But at the time I didn't feel that. But when I went and worked in care, I had this natural rapport with older people, and I was able to help them, or work with them, so easily, I didn't have to think about it, and that was quite a new thing for me. And of course, because I was good at it, everyone said, 'Oh, Jason, you're so good at this – here's this extra responsibility!' You know? 'I don't want to do it – you do it!' And I just . . . I really drained myself trying to please everyone. And I sort of went through this very quick learning curve in the care industry, and pretty much burnt myself out by the time my son was born in 2010. I'd gone through a whole other phase of learning a lot about myself, burning myself out and coming back to square one again. And since then . . . because before I'd dropped the yoga and meditation to concentrate on the career, since then I've kind of . . . been going back the other way again. Doing more stuff that I feel suits me in what I want to do.

You seem to have come to a sort of realisation when your son was born. Do you think there's a connection there?

[pause] Yeah . . . I'm not sure I've ever put two and two together there . . . I suppose it changes the way you look at yourself, and your life, and what you're doing . . . I was definitely in quite an unhappy place prior to him coming, so . . . Depression had been kept in for years, but I was getting to an age where it became . . . you know, starts to manifest as illness. Starting to get tired, starting to . . . you know, stress and anxiety . . . and then physical problems started to come. So it just made

me look at myself, I think – you know, you've got the extra addition in your life of a new person that you've got to support, you've got to be, I guess, in a good place to do that.

I'm probably projecting my feelings on to you there, because that was something I'd felt – I had a total change of my frame of mind when my daughter was born.

But I don't think – in terms of Nick Drake – that period in between the fanzine and the book . . . I still listened to Nick Drake, but I don't think I had any real sort of connection with any writing or anything like that.

So did the book come about because someone approached you?

No, I just had a feeling. I always thought, from day one, once the fanzine started, I wanted to do a book one day. And quite quickly other biographies came out. I always thought, 'Well, what can I do?' You know? I can't really write another biography, it's not going to be any better than anything else. You know, it might be a bit different, or whatever . . . No, it seems odd, really, but I always thought, 'Wouldn't it be nice to have a *Pynk Moon* book?', but never really, I guess, believed I could do it; and then just suddenly one day [clicks fingers] 'Actually, I'm going to try this . . .'

Approached a publisher?

Yeah, I just wrote to half a dozen publishers. Straight away –

And one of them was Omnibus?

Yeah. They wrote back and said, 'This sounds nice.' I think I literally wrote to about ten people, and I think three or four were interested, and a few of them sort of said, 'Wellll, yeah, it's a nice idea, but you really need to convince us – why do we need another Nick Drake book?' But Omnibus didn't say any of that, they just said 'Come and meet us.' I just went and sat down and talked about it. They said, 'We absolutely love it – go away and do it.' It was pretty much done anyway.

Having read the Patrick Humphries biography, you don't get the feeling you don't need this book as well. Because the *Pynk Moon* book, it's so many . . . so many diverse things, you know? It's like you're getting loads of different perspectives.

Yeah. I was quite aware of, you know, I'd interview someone like David Sandison, and I would just put the whole interview in the fanzine – I wouldn't frame it around my own questions, or edit it, or say 'This is what David said . . .', I would just copy it out word for word. Biographies . . . are obviously wonderful, and the biographies that have been written have got so much amazing stuff in, but what I personally don't like about a biography – well, not *don't like*, but – it's because you just get the timeline there, you have to go through . . . who their grandparents were; when they were born; what they were doing when they were five years old; and it's not always that interesting to me, to be honest. With Nick Drake, I want to know about the music years, really, and I want to hear from the people who knew him around that time, and have that image of him, you know?

Sure, yeah. I have to say, I'm really interested in what he was doing when he was five, and things like that.

I know people want to present a more rounded picture, and convince the world that he had a normal life, or whatever, but . . . I want to get close to the person who created the music, really. That's what's my focus, really.

And when you were putting the book together, I wonder if that was the first time you had to confront the fact that quite a lot of the material you were reprinting in the fanzines was copyright material? And did you then have to start seeking permission [to reprint them] – and that's quite interesting because, in strict copyright terms, obviously you should have sought it to put it in a fanzine, but obviously no fanzine editor ever does that. It's almost like there's an understanding that within the world of fanzines . . . you just don't do that sort of thing. But for proper book publishing you have to.

Yeah, yeah. When I started the fanzine I must admit that I didn't even consider it – maybe I *thought* about it at the time, maybe I thought, 'Well, this is probably not *legal*', but it wasn't like . . . I probably thought I was going to sell about ten copies, I didn't think anyone would even notice. I think once the ball had started rolling . . .

You just carried on.

Just carried on. But then I met people – it doesn't count for anything now, unfortunately, but I used to speak to Keith Morris on the phone. I used to send him the fanzines when they came out, and he loved them. He'd phone me up and say, 'Jason, thank you, it's absolutely great. Use whatever you want,' he says, 'all my pictures, free for you to use.'

Oh, really?

But that doesn't count for anything now. I'd have to get permission if I wanted to use his [photographs] . . . but he said to me verbally, 'You can always use my stuff.' There was a lot of that later on. People like David Sandison, he wrote the advert on the back, it's like, 'So happy that you're using this.'

I think most people are just like that. But when you were approaching publishers about the book, were you feeling like 'the permissions are going to be an issue', or was it all a bit of a revelation?

Yeah, it wasn't a problem. It was a fair bit of work. I managed to track down most of the people that had done the articles. Some of them were off in Australia or whatever. They were just people who – not professional writers, just people that had done little articles, memoir things for the fanzine. Yeah, and otherwise having to go to the big publishers, the big companies that owned Melody Maker or whatever – there are still companies that exist that own the rights to those magazines, even though the magazines are gone now. In a couple of cases, a couple of them charged me, like, twenty-five pound for the privilege –

That's what I was wondering, if people charged, yeah . . .

Most of them didn't, so it was . . . I would say it was probably a period of three or four weeks. Phoning, writing . . .

And you were doing all that, rather than the publisher?

Yeah, I did everything. Yeah, absolutely everything on the book. I rewrote it, in a way, because my image of a book of Pynk Moon was just a bigger version of the fanzine, maybe A4 size, with a pink and black cover. And, inside, lots of images reproduced from the fanzine, so you really had an idea of what the fanzine looked like. But when I started making it – when I spoke to Omnibus . . . Chris Charlesworth, I think, was the editor – I can't remember . . . But he said it was probably more likely going to be a normal book, sort of thing . . .

I'm glad he did – I mean, I'm just prejudiced against oversize books! Unless it really, really *has* to be oversize. But I think it's a nice way to do it. And I must say, I think it's a really valuable thing for a fanzine to do, after its run has ended – and there's a few others that have done it – but I think it's what they should do to keep it alive, because a book can stay in print. And it's just a single item, rather than having to reprint, like, nineteen issues.

I think it improved it in terms of the overall read, because, for example, you know, there's information in the book about Nick's live appearances, and that was spread out over all the fanzines. You know, there was little snippets of 'Oh, I saw Nick Drake' here, and then he did the Peel session, and it was all — so what I did when I made the book was put all of the information together in one section. So when you come into the book, you've got stories about mental health, you've got stories about the radio sessions, and so on. It tidied it up.

Absolutely. I think that works very well. I mean, when Sniffin' Glue did a book, they did an actual facsimile, identical to the original fanzines. I think that's another . . . nice thing. I mean, I don't think one's better than the other. But I do like the way you've done it for this.

It would have been much harder if I was going to reproduce the book as a big fanzine, because there was just so many articles and stuff which I *had* just photocopied, which are not in there [i.e. the book], because . . . they don't need to be. You know, like NME articles and stuff were still readily available.

Well, this is one of the things I was wondering, whether you cut out a lot of stuff. Because I've seen only four of the original issues, and I was wondering, was there a lot of stuff that you left out?

Yeah, mainly stuff – probably more in the earlier ones . . . yeah, I don't think really there's anything out of these earlier issues that ended up in the book.

I wasn't sure whether you used to have something like a letters page, or that sort of thing?

I was just taking these articles, which . . . they kind of exist in their own right. They were in magazines like the NME, so they're pretty well known . . . I just thought, you don't need to reproduce them, you can get them on the internet . . . They've been quoted from a million times, so . . . I focused more on material that was original to the fanzine. That I'd created, or people had written for the fanzine, or that I'd interviewed people and found out information myself, rather than just . . . the stuff that other people had. So that's the main difference, I think, between the fanzine and the book.

Well, the next thing that happened, then, is you did two more issues of the fanzine. And they were May 2012 and December 2012. So what prompted you to want to do those?

Two things, I guess. One, because I got involved in editing the book, that had inspired me to get involved with Nick Drake stuff again, and I had some more material that came up. And secondly, I thought that it would be a good advert for the book. Because I know there's a lot of people out there that I can get the fanzine to, and they're going to say, 'Oh look, he's got a book now!' If I advertised it in the fanzine I thought it might help to sell the book.

I thought you might even have made a bit more of it, you kind of tucked it away at the back a little bit, I thought.

Yeah, I was a bit embarrassed about actually doing that, but I still wanted to do it, in a way. Yeah. It didn't really set the world alight, so . . . But I've always got this thing in the back of my head, that it's going to be like Nick Drake, you know? Selling lots later on. By the time I retire it should be selling about a million a year!

17

SELEENA LAVERNE DAYE

interviewed by Gavin Hogg

In October 2018 I went to the Over Here zine fair in Manchester and picked up some copies of *Brown Girls*, a collaborative zine about race, family, food and hair, and *Without You I'm Nothing*, about obsessive fandom of the band Placebo. The enthusiastic and personal nature of both zines appealed greatly, and I felt a sense of connection through the immediacy of the writing. Both zines were produced by Seleena Laverne Daye. She writes directly about subjects that are important to her, and her unfiltered passion for the medium and the outlet zines give is infectious.

Seleena's a retail worker and textile artist, born in Bradford and raised in Manchester. She started writing zines while in her last year of school in the late 1990s, initially inspired by a love of music. Since then she's written many different zines (both independently and collaboratively) on a range of subjects, from a sweetshop she used to run (*Candy Pop* zine) to personal politics (*Poor Lass*), crafting (*Sugar Paper*), celebrity crushes (*Diary of a Teenage Girl Crush*) and even crisps (*What's Your Flavour?*). Her favoured format is the trusty A5, but she's produced a few A6 and some even smaller ones along the way. You can buy Seleena's zines at www.seleenalavernedaye.co.uk, which also features a gallery of her amazing textile art.

She took a break from editing zines in her late teens, feeling that they were something she'd outgrown and perhaps best left to the younger generation, before rediscovering her passion via zine fairs. She's since gone on to run zine-making workshops with different community groups, inspiring others to produce their own issues and share their poetry, politics or passions with others.

The printed version of *Poor Lass* ended after eight issues, but it continues as a podcast, featuring 'real life experiences from the mouths of legit working class people'. To date Seleena and her collaborator Em Ledger have produced almost thirty episodes, covering a variety of topics like favourite working-class TV shows, experiences of the Covid-19 pandemic, and regional dialects and accents.

We met in Middleton, on the outskirts of Manchester, just as the pandemic was turning from something at the outer fringes of conversations into a dystopian movie reality. When we spoke it was at a point when the elbow bumps still seemed too strange and unnecessarily fussy, and for about a year she was the last person I'd shaken hands with.

How did you launch yourself into the world of fanzines?

It's an amalgamation of things really. I was a young teenager and I've got an older sister who was really into the Britpop scene; she went to gigs and bought the weekly music press. In the back of the papers there were adverts for fanzines.

So this would be the mid-nineties?

That's right. She had a couple of friends who wrote fanzines on specific bands which I'd seen and I was really into music magazines. I also used to get a teen magazine called *Just Seventeen* and there was an article on a band called Vyvyan who were from Essex. At the bottom of that piece it said you could make a fanzine and there were some examples. I had a few penpals from teletext and one of them was also getting into zines at the same time on the basis of that article. We decided to make a zine together.

How did that work then, if your penpal didn't live anywhere round Manchester?

Holly lived in Dewsbury, West Yorkshire. She still makes zines now, writing as Holly Casio. I had penpals all over, people at school weren't

Seleena Laverne Daye in Middleton, March 2020, with a small selection of the many titles she has produced.

into the same stuff as me.

What was in those first fanzines? Were they music-based?

Yeah, even now we like fanzines that are fans of things. They were mostly about gigs we were going to, CD reviews, bands we liked – things like that. A lot of the bands were liked wrote zines themselves, like Manda from Bis.

What was the name of that first zine?

I can't remember exactly, it was called something like *The Day Bob* . . . It was an in-joke that no one else could get. We were about 15 then, still at high school.

Was it designed to sell or to give to friends?

We sold them. I'd bought a lot of zines from penpals so I would send them my flyers and they would send them on. I used to see zines advertised on teletext and in the back of magazines but we didn't do that. I think we took them to gigs a few times as well.

What about printing? Did you take them to a printer's or were you just photocopying them as you went on?

For that zine that we did together, Holly got them printed up properly. For a lot of my zines I used to go to Oxfam and print single-sided sheets and staple them together because I couldn't grasp the concept of how to do double-sided printing!

You started making zines relatively early and you still make them now. Do you know how many you've produced over the years?

I did make a list once but I can't remember exactly. I had a short break in my mid-twenties when I thought I was too old for making them! I did zines with Holly and I used to have an accessories stall so I made a zine for that. Then I had a sweetshop so I made a zine for that.

A sweetshop zine? Tell me more about that. What went into it?

It had gig reviews and sweet reviews! I was really into the third wave of emo at the time, even though I was slightly too old and the young people called it 'the emo sweetshop'! I used to get a lot of fifteen- and sixteen-year-olds coming in. I sold a lot of zines in there and the kids used to say they wanted to make them too.

That's amazing. You were helping to inspire the next generation!

I make zines for training tools at work, for charities . . . in short I don't really know [how many I produced]. Probably between thirty and forty. There are some that have never made it out of a drawer.

There are some that you make regularly now. How many issues of Brown Girls have you done?

Four so far.

How often are they?

About two a year. I had that patch when I didn't really make them but then I started making one about crafts called *Sugar Paper* which we made seventeen issues of. I made them with my friend Kandy and we did a spring and a summer themed ones. I always liked doing a series of zines.

Yes, you get a continuity going and the issue numbers.

It gives me more of a theme to work with so it's more likely they'll get done!

You've got *Poor Lass* too. How many of those were made?

Eight altogether but we've stopped now. It was submissions based so it was harder to get an issue finished. We wanted to be more instant so we started a podcast but life gets in the way.

Can we talk about *Poor Lass* and what the idea behind it was?

Me and my friend Em had a conversation about six years ago. We talked about when we were in our early twenties, being in leftist, feminist spaces. For all the right-on politics, everything about class was either glossed over or almost pitied. I was in a meeting once when someone said 'Let's go into working-class areas and teach them about feminism.' Just because someone hasn't read a certain book, doesn't mean they don't know about the subject.

First of all it was an angry response but then we wanted to create a positive space. At the time there were a lot of articles in magazines and papers and there was always someone speaking on behalf of a

Candy Pop issue 1 (*c.*2001)   *Without You I'm Nothing* (2012)

---

working-class person. We thought we should open it up and let people speak in their own voices.

You mentioned the podcast. Tell me about that.

That's a lot of fun. Again, because I can't print double-sided, Em does the technical side of that! I know lots of people are into podcasts, I've never listened to any except ones my friends have made. I think what puts me off a lot of them are people's voices, when I feel I can't relate to them. I think listeners like ours because you hear regional accents.

So you've collaborated on a lot of zines and done your own too. What do you prefer?

Most of the collaborations I've done have been with friends so that's been good. Lately I've been doing a lot of zine-making workshops with refugee charities and LGBTQ groups, and I've really enjoyed those. Though I'm there to facilitate them, I put a few of my own things in. They're not my own work but I love to see people who've never made a zine before get into it. Also, they're people who aren't taking up space or telling their stories so it's good that they have a platform to do that.

What are some of the fanzines that you used to read?

Diary of a Crush (2013)   *Poor Lass* issue 3 (2014)

Any fanzines which are made with passion really, even if it isn't a subject I'm into. If someone has taken time and dedicated it to write about something they love, that'll be a favourite. One of my all-time favourites is called *Colouring Outside the Lines*. It was done by my friend and she interviewed different female artists.

I know that one. It's a chunky one isn't it?

Yeah, really chunky. The interviews were so in-depth and they were with people you wouldn't have known much about, particularly pre-internet.

What defines a fanzine for you? You mentioned passion and enthusiasm earlier so I guess they're important factors.

A lot of zines now are really glossy, they're quite slick looking. When I'm doing workshops I always say that zines are self-published magazines. People sometimes ask if they can make any money out of them but I always reply that they're only done for the love of it, don't expect to make a profit! I'd also say that price-wise it should be pretty cheap, no more than £3 or £4. They're more accessible then, a cheap offering you can pass around. I don't use Photoshop or anything like that. It's cheaper to cut and paste, and the DIY look is a good one. I've seen

301

Brown Girls issue 3 (2017)   *What's Your Flavour* issue 2 (2020)

some quite posh-looking magazines at fairs and they call them zines ... I'm not sure. Perhaps cut-and-paste zines feel right to me because they're the ones I grew up with – technology has moved on so another generation might have different ideas.

I'm with you, I like that older style.

That aesthetic is really in at the minute. I've done some work in universities with fashion and design students and they really like the style but then they want to make them glossy. I want my zines to look as cheap as possible so I can sell them as cheaply as possible.

I was interested in something you said earlier – that you stopped making zines in your twenties because it felt like you'd outgrown it, that it was something you'd done in your teens. What reignited your passion?

I don't know really. I knew a lot of people who wrote zines as a teenager, then everyone went to university and stopped doing them. I didn't have as many penpals then either, I guess people were busier once they'd left home. I don't know exactly when I got back into producing them but I remember there were more zine fairs in the mid noughties so maybe it was that that got me back into it.

When I started taking an interest in zines again a few years ago, the main difference was the amount of fairs. When I used to do it they were advertised in the back of the weekly music papers, which don't exist anymore, or people sold them at gigs, which you rarely see these days. The fanzine world feels a bit more hidden away these days, it's not as noticeable in the culture.

A lot of people ask me how I sell my zines. It's easier now because you can sell online. Once you've found one zine fair, then you can find another one and another one.

Do you tend to sell more at zine fairs or Etsy?

It depends but generally zine fairs. A zine like *Poor Lass* has sold well worldwide and a lot of that is through word of mouth. You don't get that so much with online zines, but with physical copies people are more enthusiastic. Friends would pass them around and it spreads the word. We'd put it online and people would start buying it instantly.

Zine fairs have got bigger and you see a lot of younger people coming now. Older people who used to be into zines now come along with their families.

It feels like there's a new generation of zine writers and readers. You were talking before about fanzines versus blogs. Did you ever consider doing more online?

I think the time when blogs were big were when I lost my interest in zines a bit. I did have a blog for the craft zine, *Sugar Paper*, and I enjoyed writing that but I just like having that tactile thing. I guess things go in waves, like the way vinyl records are back now. I think people just ultimately prefer objects, they'll always come back into fashion.

I think what you said about word of mouth is important. If you pass an object on, people are more likely to engage with it rather than if someone just sends you a link.

I always say that in zine workshops. If someone sends me a link, I'll have good intentions but I probably won't look at it. I'm more likely to pick up a physical object and sit with it for a longer time, it's going to have more impact than scrolling through the internet.

Last night, when I was preparing for this, I took a little stack of

your zines and was flicking through them for half an hour. It was really enjoyable and I wouldn't have done that with blogs.

I've taken fanzines I've got spare copies of to work and set up a little zine library in the staff room. Sometimes I'll sit on my break and not even be looking at my phone and it occurs to me I could be reading. My manager brought one in from a holiday the other day and I was really excited: 'Ooh, what's this? I've not seen this one, I didn't bring this one in!'

Do you think you'll keep writing for many years to come?

I think I will.

Does it feel like part of your personality now?

Yeah, even though in the past few years I've not done as many. I've done more things like the workshops but the more I do my freelance stuff, the more I miss making them. Every year I make a list of zines I want to make in the next twelve months.

Zine-making is a hobby even though it's now infiltrated my job with the workshops! Zines can be used as activism or as a political tool but mostly it's something fun to do.

Tell me a bit more about the workshops.

Last year I did them with LGBTQ community groups in Barnsley, a couple of teenage groups and one for adults. One of the adults used to write poems but never thought about putting them out in the world. After the workshop he sent me a stack of zines, he said he was putting them everywhere, leaving them in the library and everything!

What a nice way to unlock that door for someone.

A big hurdle for people is them thinking that they're not a writer or not creative, but I always say that you don't need a special skill. You just need a piece of paper and a pen.

I wanted to ask whether you self-censor much. There's a lot of your own life in them, things about your family and background.

Not really. My zines are quite personal. I think they're like having a conversation with me, I write how I talk. I'm not good at going back and editing, I like to do something and then for it to be finished.

That gives it an immediacy, doesn't it?

Yeah, and as I get older I think I care less about what I share with people, I'm more comfortable than I would have been ten or fifteen years ago.

Yeah, definitely, you become happier in your own skin as you get older.

The older I've got, the more personal the zines are.

Without getting too psychological about it all, do you think that writing things down helps you to work things out in your own mind?

I think part of it used to be about finding a connection with others, like seeing people wearing the same band T-shirt. Now it's more about taking up some space and letting other people know that it's okay to have those thoughts – if that makes sense. It's still about connection but with the message that 'You can do this too.'

Do you mean people giving each other permission to be how they are?

Yeah, I think particularly with *Poor Lass*, a lot of working class people came out of the woodwork. We had comments saying things like 'I've felt like that years but I've never said anything.'

You said earlier that you had quite a few international readers?

Yeah, I remember one guy reviewed it in America and even though a lot of the stories are British and he didn't get a lot of the slang, he said it still resonated. It's different, people aren't going to be watching *Corrie* and eating a chippie tea, but they can translate it to their own experiences.

I loved your zine about growing up as a Placebo fan. I totally related to it, not particularly about that band, but that experience of being a fan.

Me and Holly are very much people who are fans of things, we either really love something or don't care. A lot of people are embarrassed to be a fan or they act too cool. I love people who are super-fans!

Do you still listen to Placebo much?

Sometimes, usually in the summer for some reason; I'll just need to listen to a certain song.

Did you overdose on them at the time?

I did a bit! But I guess you can still listen to things in a nostalgic way. I know they still exist as a band but they don't in my head. I can't remember when I last went to see them, I think it was more of a feeling of having to go.

You mentioned in the zine about going to see them and they had a drummer who would have been seven when the first album came out. You said you were looking at him but pretending it was the original drummer.

They were part of a particular time period of my life. I'm reading a book at the moment about fangirls, how women get a lot of stick for being fans, it's thought of as a futile thing.

I've never thought of that. Men are allowed to like what they want.

Football fans are just massive fans – but it's seen differently.

'It's alright because it's sport.'

It's true! I'm really interested in fandom and the things people do for fandom.

What next – any other zines or projects on the go?

I made a crisp zine because I love them. It's a submissions-based one and that unearthed lots of crisps fans so I'm currently on the second issue of that. Also, me and Holly want to do a zine on My Chemical Romance, that's another one about fandom. We were older than most of their other fans and we say we'll do it every year. I'd like to do one similar to Colouring Outside the Lines too, featuring different artists. We'll see.

The cogs are always turning. You're never short of ideas are you?

No, I don't think I'll ever stop. There'll always be something to write about.

18

JEANETTE LEECH

interviewed by Hamish Ironside

Kirby was produced in a run of four short issues by Jeanette Leech, a Norvician, between 1996 and 1999. *Kirby* is ostensibly about music, but actually reads as more of a perzine, as the pieces on music are interspersed with all sorts of brief digressions into the life of its creator – no topic is too trivial to digress upon – and even the pieces on music often find a route to digression. It often feels like Jeanette is hell bent on disrupting her own zine even as she writes it.

The Wikipedia 'stub' at https://en.wikipedia.org/wiki/Perzine states that the perzine genre 'has become increasingly popular within the zine community and is probably the largest used format for zines today', offering no evidence whatsoever for this claim . . . but maybe it's true! If so, what distinguishes one perzine from another? For me, it's almost nothing to do with the subject matter, and almost entirely to do with how good a writer the 'per' behind it is.

Jeanette is a top writer, which is why *Kirby* is not only a top perzine but one of my favourite zines of any sort. Each issue is in the classic A5 format, either 16 or 20 pages long, and although the design is very simple, it's also very considered and distinctive, with the text nearly all typed on a manual typewriter, the headings hand-drawn, and the images all of women, cut and pasted from diverse sources, usually nothing to do with the content on the same page. The writing itself has many of the hallmarks of this kind of zine: opinionated, self-deprecating, alternately shy and bolshy, and very whimsical. The tone throughout is like a letter to a friend, or sometimes more like a phone

Jeanette Leech in Love Lane, Canterbury, January 2020. Photographed with a Rollei B35 camera on 160 ASA chrome film (since you asked).

call, as she may address questions to the reader between paragraphs: 'I'm having fun, are you?'

Kirby takes no time at all to hit its stride. After an editorial largely devoted to explaining the complicated procedure involved in writing to either of two addresses, the second page of issue 1 includes a list of 'Reasons why I am happy', including 'I ate plenty of strong cheese for my tea' and 'An ex-best friend of mine is looking rough'. She goes on to explain:

> But I am not happy right now because 1) the fucking t on my typewriter keeps sticking and 2) I am having a paranoia fit about not being very good.

There are postal interviews with the Yummy Fur, Eggplant and Lung Leg. Jeanette's love of music comes across strongly, and it's no surprise that her post-fanzine life has included publishing two acclaimed books – *Seasons They Change* (2011) on acid folk and related genres, and *Fearless* (2017) on post-rock, both published by Jawbone Press. Jeanette has also written for the likes of *Shindig* and *The Wire*.

Alongside *Kirby*, Jeanette produced several one-off publications on an ad hoc basis, such as the wonderful *Badges for All* (subtitled 'growing up in the eighties'), which simply (but very entertainingly) reviews her collection of badges. In 2000 she produced *Amex*, seemingly intended as a regular zine to follow on from *Kirby*, but the first issue is the only one that appeared (hardly a novel circumstance in the world of zines). In more recent years she has done occasional online projects, alongside a career as a social care journalist. She now lives in Ramsgate with her husband, Graham Sutton of Bark Psychosis, but she was still living in the fair city of Canterbury when I interviewed her there in January 2020.

There are no dates on Kirby so I did a little bit of detective work to figure out when they all came out. I think Kirby 1 was 1996? And then they were sort of one a year, so Kirby 2 was '97, Kirby 3 '98, Kirby 4 '99.

That sounds about right.

And I think you were 20 when you started, would that be right?

Yeah.

But in Kirby 3 you refer to several aborted fanzines since age 16, so you had sort of practice, I guess?

Well, yeah, and I think it was about confidence, about not thinking I could do it. So I would try stuff, and then I would just leave it. So maybe it was practice, or maybe it was just I didn't have the confidence to put it out. Partly because I was in Norwich, and Norwich is quite a small place, and everybody worries that people will laugh at them. And I think when I moved to London, to go to university, it was a much more anonymous place.

Yeah. So Kirby was post-university, and the practice ones were before?

I think Kirby 1 actually came out while I was in my final year maybe. I seem to remember doing that in my final year. And I think Kirby 2 came out in the summer after I'd just finished. I'm a bit hazy on dates but I think that's right.

These aborted ones, have you still got them?

No.

No?

No.

What, have they been burnt, or . . . could they be lurking in a box somewhere?

No, they definitely aren't, they will have gone in my dad's house clearance.

Okay, right. That's a shame. I was going to push for a sort of Kirby 0, you know, with all these things in.

I know what you mean, but they were always meant to be ephemeral. I mean, people kept them and I kept them, but . . . you know . . .

That's what I was wondering, whether you were doing those first ones thinking 'I'm going to publish this', or whether it was a bit

Top left: 'Hello my name is Jeanette and this is my first fanzine so I hope you like it.'

Top right: 'Finally made a second issue which is quite astounding. It's as thin as the first one, hope you don't mind.'

Bottom left: 'I think I'd like to start this zine by revealing my surname, cos I'm getting a bit fed up with this one-name deal that quite a lot of underground people have.'

Bottom right: 'Number 4 – my, I am getting into the serious league of fanzines now. And still no-one has heard of it!

311

more like doing a diary, and just doing it in a paginated form, so that you were thinking about design and layout.

Yeah, I was. I think that's true. Like you'll notice they're all done on this same typewriter, and I had that ever since I was a little girl. So I would always type stuff out. And I just quite liked the look of it – it just felt more official.

Okay. I thought it was a series of typewriters. Because you note, like, in one of them it's the 'T' key that isn't working, and then there's another one where it's the 'A' key that doesn't work.

Actually you're right, there was a black one that came, towards the end, I think? God . . . I haven't thought about this stuff for ages . . .

But you write about it quite a bit. It's one of the things I like actually, it's very self-referential. You'll be talking about the mechanics of it even as you're writing it. You know, in one of them you accidentally do one page too many . . . and your solution to that is to write another page about it, explaining how you'd had to take two pages out.

That's quite good actually!

See, I obviously know more about Kirby than you do at this point!

Well, when you asked me for them, I just thought 'Am I going to read these again?' And I don't want to, really.

Why would you not want to? You're not embarrassed?

No, I'm not embarrassed. But it feels like a long time ago, and part of me wants to preserve the feeling of writing it then, rather than look at it with a bit more of a critical eye, I suppose? So it's not embarrassment, I think I'm pretty proud of them.

Yeah, well you should be, because they are great! You know, I've seen so many fanzines and it's one of my absolute favourites.

Ah, thank you, that's good to hear. That's good to hear.

Now, having talked about the pre-Kirby abortive ones, I'm wondering about the 'side fanzines' as well. Because I've got Badges for All –

Which is probably my favourite, out of all the ones I did.

badges for all

aka

growing up in the eighties

Badges for All (c.2000), a one-off zine (or is it?) in which Jeanette reviews her badge collection, as a way to avoid tidying her room.

Yeah – but in *Kirby* you mention *Kapitalist* –

Ah, those – now, I don't know where those are. I think they probably are in my friend's basement. But those were, really . . . I don't think I would even charge for them, they were just really ephemeral things that had no interviews, they had no . . . it was just me . . . banging on! As most of *Kirby* is.

Well, yeah, they read very similar to *Kirby*. And that's one of the things I'm interested in with our book, is deciding what is a fanzine and what isn't. And you can immediately see with *Kirby*, although there are no dates on them or anything, there are issue numbers and it is clearly a periodical of some sort. Whereas *Badges for All* isn't. But that's really the only difference. And *Badges for All*, if you were to say to someone what it is, I think you would say it's a fanzine, wouldn't you?

Yeah, you would. I think that's the last thing I did, *Badges for All*.

Was it? So this would be about 2000, when the internet was just getting more accessible, and I was wondering whether you decide 'If I want to do any more personal writing I'll just do it online instead'?

That's a really interesting question, and funnily enough I did think about that, knowing you were coming. No, not really, I didn't really blog. But a lot of people – a lot of fanzine people – there was this . . . I can't remember what it was called but it was like an online diary thing that a lot of fanzine people did. Something like 'MyJournal' – I'll find out the exact name.* But a lot of people just stopped doing fanzines and migrated to doing that. And I didn't. I think it had just run its course for me at that point.

Yeah. But you did an online thing where you were asking people to recommend a book, and you would read it and blog about it . . .

Yeah. That was brilliant. That was the first time, and only time, I've done something like that.

And I was looking for that online, and I can't find it. And this is what was making me think that, with the internet, people may have been thinking 'Oh, this is an easier way to reach a lot of people', you know: 'People in China could read this!' But then they seem to be more ephemeral, in a way, than the fanzines, because if you haven't taken trouble to keep it on a more permanent site then it's just disappeared.

I agree with you, totally. I think that whole thing, that dream of the internet, that other people in America, people in China can read them, or whatever – you try and search for something that's, say, by one of the authors that I blogged about, you wouldn't be able to find it because everything that comes up is trying to sell you stuff, or Wikipedia, or whatever – there's not really that space for the small voice to come through. With fanzines there was, because I remember at the time going to Tower Records and they had a fanzine section, and you'd get fanzines from America, you'd get fanzines from Canada, and they all shared space with Q magazine.

I mean that was what was great about Tower. But there weren't that many places doing that. I mean, I never got my fanzine . . . I don't think I got it into any shops.

Nor did I.

With *Kirby* 1, you were thinking 'This is going to be published', but

---

were you starting to think of exactly who your audience was?

No. And I really want to say my favourite cliché from *Smash Hits*, which is, like, I'm just doing it for myself, and if anyone else likes it, that's a bonus! Because it really was – I think there were things that I wanted to express. I'd started to read quite a lot of fanzines, and I felt that nothing was really exactly what I wanted to read, and I wanted to express it. So it was kind of like I thought – particularly with having the interviews – I thought that the kind of people that I knew would like it. They went to the same kind of gigs that I did. But I didn't have anyone in particular in mind, and certainly for *Kirby* 1 I had a very small print run, like 25 or 30.

Ah, really?

The other ones had a much bigger print run, but certainly the first one.

Because I was quite impressed, because you did mention that you sold out of *Kirby* 1, and reprinted it! You even implied that there was more than one reprint. But I wondered if it was a really low print run. I did 1,000 of the first issue of my fanzine!

Oh, that's amazing!

I had about 950 left over!

See, that's the thing, if you can brag about a reprint it sounds better.

Oh yeah, you got it right from the start. Start small and grow. Unlike my massive mistake. But I remember you telling me you made use of Ceefax, I think?

That was for the second one. The Ceefax one was really really important, actually, for a personal reason, because that's how I met the person who is still my best friend to this very day, Kathryn. She sent off for my fanzine, and I sent it back, and we just corresponded, and that's a friendship that's now lasted 22 years, and we're as close as ever, which is just amazing.

Yeah. That's brilliant.

And without writing a fanzine that never would have happened. But I don't know why – well, I do know why, because I read the fanzine

315

reviews, and it seems unbelievable now that there would be fanzine reviews on Ceefax, but there were, and I just thought 'Oh well, let's just give it a go, then, they probably won't review it' – and they did! And then I just got loads of mail.

Really, you got loads of it? Because I was aware of Ceefax, but I think even at the time I was thinking 'This is really clunky, I can't believe anyone reads this.' But I never saw any fanzine reviews on it, and I don't know how I would have found them, actually.

I can't even remember which sort of . . . because they were all in sort of suites of pages, weren't they, Ceefax? I think it was in the pop pages.

They had numbers, didn't they? Like 300 was sport, or whatever . . .

Yeah. And they only did it once a week, and I think it would only be up for one day, and then it would go down again.

But that's amazing then, that you got all that response even from it being . . . but I guess it's because everyone's got a telly . . .

And people didn't have instructions of – like, if you wanted to find out information, you'd look on Ceefax! And that just seems like something you couldn't explain to younger people anymore – why would you look at this static page of text?

And yet it's like the internet before the internet was fully formed! A sort of halfway point, isn't it? It's got all the features but it is just really sort of . . . clunky . . . a kind of steam-driven version of the internet.

When the internet first, sort of . . . came out, and my dad became aware of it, he was like, 'I don't know why anyone is bothering with the internet, there's so much on Ceefax!'

Yeah. Exactly! Bring back Ceefax! I think he's right, I hate the internet, and I like to think that one day there'll just be information overload and the whole thing will just stop working. And we'll have to go back to . . . you know, fanzines will be a primary means of communication!

It's interesting, isn't it, because, I mean, I know fanzines are still going on, but it *was* the means of communication if you wanted to put something out yourself. It was really important.

How much were you selling it for, by the way?

50p. Fifty pence in person, fifty pence with an SAE if they wanted me to post it to them.

And was it just at gigs you were selling it in person?

Yes. Mainly on the first one, I relied on mail order. Unless there was a gig I was going to where there was an interview with that band, I would bring it. To say, 'Oh, you're here to see Helen Love – why don't you buy this fanzine?' But I totally remember thinking, 'I'm not talking to them – they look like they're here with their mates.'

So you were approaching, like, the wallflower types.

Yeah. The people who, I thought, they've got no reason to be here other than they really like this band.

I want to talk about your writing style. It felt like it was fully formed right from Kirby 1. I thought it was quite distinctive in that you've got a sort of dual thing going on, where there's the text itself – you'll have a subject – but there's a constant subtext, which is you digressing into these little bits of information about your typewriter. The subtext is your own life, the diary aspect of it. And I really love the fact that there is this one page that starts off as a gig review, and you say nothing about the bands except that one of them's got your next-door neighbour in . . .

Oh, that one, yeah!

And the whole thing's just about how you wonder how you can get out of there without being noticed!

Yeah. And I can't remember why I wrote that night up, but it just seemed so ridiculous, that I . . . I felt I wanted to share it.

It's a great set piece, it's one of the real highlights, it's so funny. But it's not a gig review at all.

I think I got fed up with . . . one of the things that I do . . . later on I used to do reviews for Shindig magazine, and reviews occasionally elsewhere, and I stopped because I was . . . I was a little fed up with the concept of reviews anyway, and I think actually, if I think back to *Kirby* days, I don't do any sort of record reviews and things like that, and a lot of fanzines were full of them. Or gig reviews, things like that. Because . . . I don't see the point of them.

That's what I thought, because everyone was doing that, and you've got your stance and you set it out, and it's really consistent with all four issues. You know, the design's really consistent. And this stance, like ' I don't do these things, I don't do this, I don't do that', you're really clear about what you want to do with it.

It's so interesting hearing you talk about this, because I hadn't realised that there was this thread going through all four.

I think that's because it was your natural style. It's not like you'd read someone else's fanzine and thought 'I'm going to do one just like that.'

No, I didn't like that many other fanzines. There were a few others. There was one I know that was influential on me, it was an American fanzine called *Semibold*.

Yeah, well you do review that, you do have some fanzine reviews.

Semibold was amazing.

I'd really like to see it, but trying to track down an issue of *Semibold* now would probably be really really difficult.

It was hard enough at the time. I think I've only got two of them. The first issue was just her talking about her life, it was brilliant.

And about the neighbour, when you were writing about it, were you not thinking, 'I hope he doesn't get to read this'? I was wondering if your distribution network was such that he could have got to see it. What if he did see it, and knocked on your door?

Unlikely! I don't think he even knew my name. Certainly he knew my face. He might have seen it, but I don't think I cared.

You were working alongside doing the fanzine. What were you doing at that time?

You mentioned one of the side fanzines, *Kapitalist* – that was when I was working in a really bad job, the first one after university, for a travel insurance firm. I was really really unhappy. Then I worked in Oddbins for a time – I think that's when I knew you, wasn't it?

I was working in Blackwell's, but I wasn't thinking of myself as a career bookseller or anything, it was sort of like my work was secondary to everything else I was doing. I was wondering if that was what it was like for you.

Oh, certainly work gave me no definition in those days. A little bit later when I started working for the voluntary sector, that was different, but certainly in those days it was a bit like, I didn't want to work, I didn't want to be there. It was just for the money. It gave me no sense of identity.

There's one memory that I have, thinking about this – how embarrassed I was about photocopying it. Because in those days there weren't that many of those self-service copiers that did double-sided, so you would have to give them to a staff member. And I hated doing that. Because people would be just, like, 'Oh, what's this?'

Like at work?

No, I didn't have access to a photocopier at work, I had to go into one of these sort of quick copy places – I know a lot of people photocopied them at school or at work, and that was much better because you've got your privacy, and it's free . . . but, yeah, I remember that quite strongly, every single time, just thinking 'I don't want to do this.'

Were you just worrying that they'd say 'What's this?' or were they actually saying to you 'What's this?'

No, it was just all worry! It was all in my head.

Yeah. That reminds me of how in Kirby you are always picking up on your own little idiosyncrasies or mistakes. It's sort of simultaneously castigating yourself but also . . . saying how cool you are in some respects!

I think that's probably fair enough. I don't want to sound arrogant but I did think Kirby was better than a lot of stuff that was there, otherwise I wouldn't have done it.

I think that's part of, like, the whole fanzine attitude as well, is that you have really strong opinions about everything, what you like and dislike. And you know, I was thinking, in contrast, magazines like Mojo and stuff, you know when they do their reviews, out of five stars? Almost everything gets either three or four stars. You think, 'Why use five stars when you hardly ever give either five stars or one star?' I think it just typifies these corporate magazines, that they have this sort of bland level of enthusiasm. That's why I like fanzines more, because I'd prefer some good honest enthusiasm.

You're in nobody's pocket either. It's not like you've got to keep record companies sweet, otherwise you won't get the interviews with big stars or things like that. You are completely your own master. And that's really really important, and that's why you can slag things off at will, and enthuse about stuff. That's what I love about fanzines. They don't have that agenda.

Yeah. But then I was doing mine partly to get free stuff! I was getting lots of free records. I did feel like I'm not going to be swayed by that. But there were a few people I got records from, like Shimmy Disc records and stuff –

Shimmy Disc! That's pretty good!

Yeah, and I kind of would like everything that came out on Shimmy Disc anyway, but there was the odd one that came out where I thought, 'This isn't very good, but I've got to say something nice about it because it's Shimmy Disc.'

I got barely any free stuff.

You could have if you'd asked for it though. You must have been aware of that.

Yeah, and I seem to remember thinking, 'I don't want to be in people's pay.' To me it wasn't a stepping stone to anything, it was an end in itself. It wasn't a stepping stone to being a music journalist or being in a band.

For the interviews in Kirby, am I right in thinking they're all postal ones until Marine Research in Kirby 4?

Yeah.

Is that the first and only one in Kirby that was from an actual face-to-face interview?

Yeah, and that was my first face-to-face interview ever with a musician. And I didn't have any of that [pointing to my tape recorder], and me and Kathryn did it. Kathryn was listening as well, and then we went back to the pub to try and remember it.

Oh, you didn't have a tape recorder?

No! [Laughs]

Were you making notes then, writing it down?

I think I probably must have made some notes. But maybe just the odd word or something. Because certainly I do remember going to the pub immediately afterward, saying 'We have to get this down!' But yeah, no recording.

Oh, that's brilliant!

I don't know *why* they trusted me! And Marine Research, as a band, they weren't particularly big, but they did have members of Heavenly and Talulah Gosh, who were very well thought of in the indie scene. So it was quite a big thing really.

It's interesting that the period when you were doing Kirby was a period when I wasn't really listening to new music, I kind of feel like I dropped out, and I'm finding out about all these bands that I want to listen to now, and they are new bands to me, Helen Love and things like that.

Helen Love are still going actually.

Do you still buy all their stuff?

No. I was thinking about the bands from that era that I still listen to – there are a few, but Helen Love I don't. Bikini Kill I listen to on a very regular basis. My love for them has never gone, really. The Yummy Fur as well. I still listen to Miranda July, who I think I wrote about in one issue, I listen to her a lot still.

There's a great article in Kirby 3 where you're writing about that

I can hide it from my eyes

But how can I hide it from my heart?

amex

Like all Jeanette's other zines, *Amex* is undated, but internal evidence suggests it's from about 2000, when Jeanette was living in Hackney. Articles include 'Shopping On The Internet – who fucking needs it?' Amazon were only 6 years old at the time, but were already getting short shrift: '<u>Do not</u> use Amazon. They suck.'

No change there then!

---

sort of situation where you like a band but you're aware that their new releases aren't as good, and basically they're going crap, but you keep buying their records for quite a long time after you're aware they've gone crap!

Yeah . . .

And you say this is typified by your Madonna interest, which . . . I was really surprised to read you were ever into Madonna. But you kept buying her even up to the point of 'Hanky Panky', I think?

Yeah, I've still got some! I didn't buy the two most recent albums, but I bought *Hard Candy*, I bought *Confessions on a Dance Floor* . . . It's really hard to break the loyalty bonds.

After *Kirby 4* you did *Amex* – it's got 'Amex' on the cover but 'Amix' inside, so I wasn't sure which of the two it was meant to be, or where the name came from . . .

I cannot remember the thought process behind that, or why I didn't do *Kirby 5*. I think I just wanted a fresh look, maybe? But as with most rebrandings, it didn't work that well!

Why not?

I didn't feel it was as interesting, that fanzine, as the *Kirbies*. I don't

322

know – as soon as I put it out I barely looked at it.

Oh really? I like it, I feel it is quite consistent, to the point that I think it could have been *Kirby 5*. But in *Kirby 4* you were already saying 'I think I'm going to call my next one Kinky'. So you were obviously getting kind of bored with the *Kirby* thing.

I genuinely don't know why.

Okay, now my final question: what would it take to bring back *Kirby*? If I were to do a petition, how many signatures would I need to convince you to do it?

Like Big Ben bonging for Brexit, it wouldn't happen.

No?

No. No.

Nothing could induce you?

No, I don't think so.

A million pounds?

[Pause] Is that an offer?

If I had it to give.

No, it is what I said: if I don't have anything to say . . . I won't say it! One of the things that bothers me – and it's related almost to that thing of bands after they've gone crap – what bothers me is when bands are just contracted to do something, and they churn it out. And it's like – they're not happy with it, the fans aren't happy with it, it's just product. And for me one of the things that's there in those *Kirbies* is that I really wanted to do it, so it's not just like I feel I have to put one out. That's probably why they're so sparse – one a year, or whatever. But it was only when I felt I'd got something to say that I would say it.

19

ELIAS NEBULA

*interviewed by Gavin Hogg
and Hamish Ironside*

Elias Nebula's output is perhaps the most idiosyncratic of any zine editor, and it takes some explaining. He began making zines towards the end of the last millennium, in his mid-twenties. If he was somewhat of a late starter by zine standards, he has certainly made up for it over the past twenty years, having edited over 150 individual issues of various titles. Furthermore, he has written the vast majority of every issue himself. And he shows no sign of slowing down.

It's difficult even to convey what the content of most of the zines consists of. Before we tackle that, then, let us try to account for the formal aspects of it. Nebula has concurrently edited two main titles: *The Hegelian* and *Curiosa Rubberlineana*. Issues of *The Hegelian* have appeared in A4, A5, A6 and other formats; a couple have been on CD. The format has been standardised over the last few years as 24 pages in A6 format (148.5 × 105 mm), produced as A4 photocopied sheets folded and stapled. The folded pages are left uncut, like an eighteenth-century book, so the reader has to cut them loose to be able to read the content. Seven issues of *The Hegelian* have been produced by guest editors, one of which was compiled without Nebula's knowledge, as a gift for his wedding; another was produced as a website (no longer accessible). These guest-edited issues seem to have been accepted into the canon, although the dating and numbering of issues would probably defeat the subtlest of bibliographers (we note in passing that issue 23 appeared in July 2004, around 2½ years before issue 22). At the time of writing the series is up to issue 65 (although issues 25 and 50 are yet to appear).

Nebula's parallel publication, *Curiosa Rubberlineana*, gets its name from its editor's previous pseudonym: Dauntless Rubberline. The main thing that distinguishes the *Curiosa* from *The Hegelian* is its form, which is more that of a newsletter than a magazine. They are published in a volume consisting of (usually) twelve monthly issues, and each issue consists of a single folded sheet of coloured A3 paper, always with an 'errata slip' stapled to it – although the contents of the errata slip are usually not errata; and sometimes the errata slip is longer than the rest of the issue. For that matter, many issues of the *Curiosa* are not A4 but some American variant, and they may be folded once or twice; or sometimes not at all; and sometimes they are actually more than one sheet! (Readers with a low boredom threshold will be pleased to learn that there is not too much more bibliographic minutiae to go.)

In addition to the two main titles, there have been others that have appeared for one or two issues, or perhaps a single volume, including *Colloctanea Minora*, the *Peach Crate Sender*, *Decoy Duck Fancier*, the *Journal of Hughesian Folklore* and the *Libeller's Almanac*. The latter was notable as an attempt to 'go legitimate' by producing a relatively conventional fanzine, with relatively conventional distribution. Nebula even edited the *Libeller's Almanac* under his real name.

The fact that there were only two issues of the *Libeller's Almanac* (one in 2001, one in 2006/7) goes to show that the bid for legitimacy was always somewhat half-hearted. If zines generally are against the establishment – against 'selling out' – then Nebula's zines take this tendency to some kind of an extreme, almost revelling in their own obscurity. The majority have been produced in runs of fewer than ten, most of which go to a small set of 'subscribers', who pay nothing for their subscriptions, however. Nebula makes little or no effort to even make them known to a wider public. The arrangement is somewhat like that of SF zines, where the tradition of 'the usual' holds; but whereas the readership of the SF zines uphold their end of the bargain by offering 'letters of comment' (LoCs) or copies of their own zines (or both), Nebula's readers have tended to receive a new issue at a gathering in a

'Who will buy?' Elias Nebula in the garden of the Elephant pub, Pangbourne, in August 2021, with the church of St James the Less in the background.

pub, and after briefly scouring the contents for mentions of their own names, most of them gave the thing no more thought. At some point this resulted in the early group of subscribers being 'winnowed'; issue 16 of *The Hegelian* even featured 'The Great *Curiosa Rubberlineana* Vote-Out' (mentioned by Nebula below), where subscribers had to decide whether to eject Harry Metcalf or 'Scott at UEA' from the list.

The readership has continued to dwindle over the years, a situation Nebula seems happy with, or at least resigned to. During the Covid pandemic, Nebula continued issuing zines at a steady rate, but his 'anti-marketing' approach progressed to a new level of perverseness, as he only announced new issues on a YouTube channel that had no subscribers, offering copies free on request for a limited period, after which time they would only be available at an extremely high price, which would steadily rise. Two volumes of the *Curiosa* appeared in this way in 2020, with no one knowing about them until after the 'free on request' deadline; since then it is understood that one subscriber, having found out about them, has paid £200 to secure both volumes. Issues of *The Hegelian* also appear regularly, in editions of just eight copies, announced on Nebula's YouTube channel (sometimes supplemented with an Instagram post showing a photo of the issue). Even as this book is published, there is a fair chance that you could have a free copy if you would only seek out Nebula's YouTube channel and check for updates now and then.

The natural end of the anti-marketing trend may be for Nebula to produce his zines in editions of a single issue, solely for his own archive. Would that even count as publishing? We leave that for the philosophers to discuss; for our part, we simply regret that so few people are reading such fine writing. It brings to mind the case of the Monteverdi Hai: the most beautiful car ever built, yet they only ever made four of them!

As for the content of his zines, Nebula cites American zines like *Cometbus*, *Motorbooty*, *Bananafish* and *Breakfast Without Meat* as more of an influence than any British zines. His subject matter could be almost anything – the only thing you can be certain of with *The Hegelian* is that it won't mention Hegel. Typical long-running interests include the Padstow Obby Oss, Marvel comics, Thomas Pynchon,

Japanese films, Dog the Bounty Hunter – but the predominant topic is the editor's circle of friends, representing another similarity to the fannish SF zines. It might be thought that this would alienate readers outside of that circle, but this seems not to be the case – which seems to prove that jokes are sometimes funnier when you don't understand them.

And humour is indeed the over-riding aim of all of Nebula's zines. His belief seems to be that the worth of any zine is in how much it makes you laugh, and it's hard to argue with that. Moreover, just as Nebula's marketing is anti-marketing, so the humour is often more like anti-humour. Anything that comes too close to 'commercial humour' is to be avoided, or at least comes loaded with an apology. This can make the 'jokes' elliptic – nebulous, even – and then there is the fact that a fair amount of the content doesn't even strive to be funny. And yet every issue evinces a few 'belly laughs', or even the sort of silent weeping with laughter that we most associate with Laurence Rémila.

Elias Nebula was living in London when he began producing his zines, since when he has lived in Norwich, then in the US for the best part of a decade, first in New York and later in Los Angeles, before moving back to England in 2017. He now lives with his wife in Pangbourne (Berkshire), overlooking the River Thames. We travelled to Pangbourne in August 2021 to interview Nebula together.

GAVIN: Let's start at the beginning – what I'd like to know first is your personal history with zines in terms of when you discovered them and when the world of zines opened up to you.

I was always interested in music magazines. The first zines I remember . . . I used to get *Factsheet Five*.

GAVIN: That was an American zine, yeah?

It was like a directory. He [Mike Gunderloy] reviewed everything. He reviewed mail art, he reviewed zines – it was amazing. You just had to send off for them, and that was really kind of a gateway to loads of things.

GAVIN: What kind of year was this? Are we talking mid-eighties?

That was the late eighties. Then, you know, there was *Maximumrocknroll*, I really liked *Maximumrocknroll*. The ones I really still think of as the best are things like *Forced Exposure* and *Rollerderby*, those two in particular. American ones – you know, you'd go to the Rough Trade shop or Tower Records, *Ben Is Dead*, things like that.

GAVIN: **So is that how you were finding out about them? Through reviews, or just browsing in record shops?**

Yeah. I mean, there wasn't much in Reading – that's how I saw *Maximumrocknroll* – but then when you went into London and you're in the Tower Records basement, there was tonnes of stuff. It's a shame that's gone. Because that was where you'd meet people – a prearranged meeting place, just leafing through the zines.

GAVIN: **Did you go to many gigs at that time? Did you buy any at gigs?**

No. No I didn't. I've *sold* them at gigs – I haven't bought them at gigs, to my recollection.

GAVIN: **Was there any particular reason for that?**

I don't think the gigs I went to had merch stands very much – I came across that as a phenomenon much more in America. By which time I was doing them myself. It wasn't that I refused to buy them.

GAVIN: **Not a principled standpoint then?**

No, you just didn't see them much unless you went to the shops in London.

GAVIN: **You just mentioned your zines so let's talk about those. I'm curious to know about the history of them because I think there are a few different strands and different formats. What was the first fanzine you did and why start doing it in the first place?**

I was planning one when I was still doing my A levels, and I actually interviewed people for that. It would have been a good, proper zine – it wouldn't have been like I ended up doing! It was always a case of having enough money – you have to save up the money to do it, and I was working as a trolley boy on the weekends and spending my money, I could just never save it. I *planned* this thing for years and didn't do anything with it. I had interviewed Lisa Carver, interviewed Sebadoh, did all these really good interviews, and didn't use them. The first *Hegelian* ended up coming out in a flippant moment – I called it *The Hegelian* flippantly – obviously I thought I'd give it the most sort of over-intellectual title I could. I was leaving this job and I was leaving London because we'd been evicted suddenly. I was mucking around on the photocopier at work, and I was meeting people in the pub later, so I did the first issue of The Hegelian like that – you know, a few copies to hand out to people. It really is . . . crude. It's got drawings I did randomly . . . so crude and dumb . . . These early issues are the ones I think are garbage. They're really awful.

GAVIN: What is it about them you don't like?

They make me cringe. Well, one thing is I started to read lots of stuff in American dialect from the nineteenth century, which was going to be my PhD. And . . . I'm really impressionable – or I *have* been impressionable – by the style of the writer I'm reading. I did that when I was reading Ezra Pound's letters, I did it when I used to read R. Meltzer and Byron Coley. It just gets into me. I think it's also that I was drinking a lot at the time and in the thick of it you don't realise, you think it's really inspired.

GAVIN: And then in the cold light of day it seems to be lacking a bit of discipline?

It wasn't even the cold light of day, it was years later I'd look back on it and thought it was rubbish! It was also, it wasn't intended to be read back. I didn't think it was going to be a big deal.

GAVIN: So the target audience was just people you knew down the pub?

Yeah, very much. There was a guy I used to work with, Damian. I can't remember how many copies I did for the first one – three or four at the most. Then I went to university a few months later . . . and then I met other people. One housemate in particular was American and knew about zine culture and that sort of thing. He was excited by it . . . so then it picked up again. But it didn't get any better! Looking back on them, because I was doing this interview, I didn't realise how many I did in quite a short amount of time.

HAMISH: I was looking at the dates and *Hegelian* number 1 was July 1999 and *Curiosa* number 1 was April 2000. Then *Hegelian* and *Curiosa* are running concurrently – I'd say they're formally different but the material overlaps quite a lot.

Yeah. In my head I think the *Curiosa* had the better stuff. I think I say it in one of the issues: the best stuff goes in the *Curiosa* . . .

HAMISH: And how would you make that decision?

I don't know, it almost implies that I think I'm getting better with the *Curiosa*. But when I read it . . . [laughs] Well, there's actually a point where I think it does get better. With both of them. Like, it's volume 3 of the *Curiosa* I quite like. And after issue 17 of *Hegelian* I think it's not as toe-curling. There's the odd joke in there that's not done in dialect, and it's tolerable.

HAMISH: Just to briefly cover the main sort of runs of what you did – because I think of *The Hegelian* and the *Curiosa* forming sort of 95 per cent of it, in sort of equal amounts. We'll probably have to explain *The Hegelian* is always like a magazine format, stapled usually, most of them A6 size, but the first one was like A4, and a few have been A5, and stuff like that . . .

And there's one . . . did I send you that really long one? Issue 39?

GAVIN: Yes.

A guy in Brooklyn [Gabe Fowler, who runs Desert Island comics shop] refused to stock that one because it was too long. We had a row. Then I wrote him a really scathing review on Yelp! He then apologised – first he laid into me, then he apologised and wanted to pay me. We got into this really weird thing, and all because of the size of that issue. The format always changes. Which is annoying for people who want to keep it all in one shoe box.

GAVIN: What's the reason for the changes in the format? Is it just what you want to do at the time?

Yeah, yeah. Definitely.

GAVIN: Is it also partly something about not wanting to be too predictable?

Yeah. There was one I did that was about Will Oldham, a one-off, because everyone in this crowd liked Will Oldham. So I was saying 'Okay, what's your top ten Will Oldham records?', and reflections on Will Oldham. And that's folded up into this triangle shape. [laughs]

GAVIN: They hate triangles, the Will Oldham fans, don't they?

HAMISH: Is that *Peach Crate Sender*? Which was October 2000, so there's lots of different things coming out around the same time, because in August 2000 there was the *Journal of Hughesian Folklore*, which was again just a single issue.

There are a lot of one-offs. There's the *Decoy Duck Fancier* – I can't even look at that.

HAMISH: The *Journal of Hughesian Folklore*, that was one where it's about one of the readers –anecdotes about one of the readers.

Well, he wasn't even a reader, that's the thing, it was just a person we knew. We all used to work at Foyles [in Charing Cross Road, London], most of us in that scene. He is a friend – I hadn't seen him in a while, he'd never read the zines . . . he's quite self-absorbed, I don't think he wants to read about anyone else; so I did a zine about him! None of us had seen him for quite a while. He used to tell the same stories over and over again, so I said, 'Well, we should just collect some of the stories he used to tell.' By this point I was in academia, so it was in the style of these academic journals that I'd seen in the library.

That was what the *Curiosa* was based on, in fact. I was doing research into a nineteenth-century humourist from the state of Maine, called Artemus Ward. He came from this little village called Waterford. So I went up there, and I was in correspondence with people in Maine, and they had a village bulletin. That was the format of the village bulletin – it's a really nice-looking thing, and I said, 'I'm gonna do something that's a total tribute to that', in the same format. That's why it took the form it did, and the *Curiosa* was meant to be more consistent. It changes between volumes but doesn't change from issue to issue. The *Hughesiana* is in the same kind of format as the *Curiosa*.

HAMISH: But formally, where *Hegelian* is a stapled magazine and numbered without volumes, just issues, *Curiosa* was always in volumes, and a lot shorter, and always on coloured paper and folded

The Hegelian issues 1–58. Issues 25 and 50 have not yet appeared. On the other hand there is more than one version for some issue numbers: I counted 59 issues in this photograph. This was the complete run when the photograph was taken in Ferbuary 2022. However, another 7 issues have appeared since then . . .

up, so it had this distinct format. That's what I think, for me, distinguishes the two things. It's more the form than the material within
it, you know?

There is also the thing where I might say, 'I've got this many pieces
written; I don't have enough to do a volume of the *Curiosa*; I can't see
me keeping doing this for this long, but I could get out one issue' –
so sometimes there is no difference. Like the recent volumes of the
Curiosa, I think, were because I was generating a lot of material
regularly. And I thought, 'This could run and run'. So it was . . . doable.
And it was an overflow, so I did a couple of issues of *The Hegelian* as
well. I thought, while lockdown was going on, I wanted to do as much
as possible. So I was going to get *The Hegelian* up to 50, and I was going
to do a few volumes of the *Curiosa*, so . . . I did.

**HAMISH: I'm quite interested in the fact that it all started in July
1999 and then by 2000 The Hegelian and the Curiosa were both well
under way, and you were also doing these one-offs of other things.
It's almost like you became intensely productive very quickly
around that time, just around the turn of the millennium.**

The other thing is, I got funding to do research. So I wasn't having
to work, for the first time in years. I don't know if it was a good idea
doing all these, because I was wasting the time when I should have
been writing and researching. Doing this – it became much, much too
important to me. It took over at times. I just got more interested in
this than actually doing my PhD.

**HAMISH: But taking the longer view, don't you think maybe this is
equally valid, if not more so?**

No. No, that's what I mean, I don't think it's well-written enough,
that's the trouble.

HAMISH: Okay. But when it's at its best, though?

Yeah. Yeah, but the thing that worries me is, whenever I do it, I think
it's good *then* – the test is down the line.

HAMISH: Yeah. But every writer has that to face, don't they?

Now when I look back at issues of a certain vintage – when I'm in New

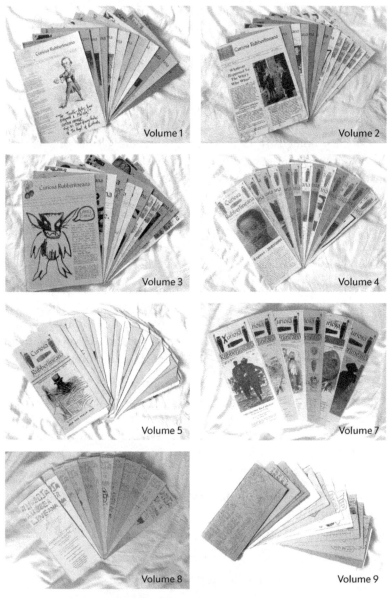

The complete *Curiosa Rubberlineana* thus far. Publication dates are as follows: volume 1, April 2000 to March 2001 (12 issues); volume 2, April 2001 to March 2002 (13 issues); volume 3, April 2002 to March 2003 (12 issues); volume 4, April 2005 to March 2006 (12 issues); volume 5, April 2007 to March 2008 (12 issues); volume 7, April 2017 (6 issues); volume 8, March 2020 to February 2021 (12 issues); volume 9, March 2021 to February 2022 (12 issues). Note that volume 6 is yet to appear . . .

York – I still think that stuff's really good. I think the LA stuff's good, I think the New York stuff's generally good. So I do think there is a point at which it gets better.

HAMISH: Yeah. I think every fanzine producer, they cringe at some of the stuff in their earlier fanzines. [To Gavin] Don't you? Not that you should!

GAVIN: No, no, I should, and I do! Because it's . . . I mean, I wrote it when I was about 19 or 20, and it just seems so toe-curling now.

But I think both of you invested more money in your own zines when you were doing them than I did. I think that's why I could be so flippant and do such a slapdash job early on, because I wasn't losing any money on it.

GAVIN: Well, let's talk about that. How did you fund it, or were you just photocopying it on the work machine?

It depended – I mean, sometimes you'd go down Ryman's. And then when I was teaching at the university I got photocopy privileges. But then they found out that I was doing it, I got into real trouble with my supervisor. I also left a page of the zine in the photocopier . . .

GAVIN: Rookie error, mate!

One of the secretaries found it and unfortunately it was a page where I was being really cynical about academic study as well.

GAVIN: A double blow.

It was a funny article, that was the only good thing about it, still funny to me now. Then my wife, in New York, worked at Penguin, so we'd go in on the weekends and use the Penguin copier.

GAVIN: On the Penguin dollar!

Yeah, I could do high print numbers of some of the New York ones for that reason, I didn't have to pay for it. But I did pay for the two *Libeller's Almanacs* – they were the two . . . my legitimate zines, as it were.

HAMISH: So that's like you being a bit more commercial, producing something that you could sell in shops?

That was the idea! [laughs] It was on the back of interviews – like I

Miscellaneous zines produced by Elias Nebula, including both editions of the *Libeller's Almanac*, the closest the editor has come to courting a readership.

thought that Huggy Bear interview was really good, but it was 20 years after riot grrrl.

HAMISH: Yeah, so what period was that? '94 or something?

When *was* riot grrrl? '92, '93? But I actually published the *Libeller's Almanac* just before I left for America, so it was like 2001. So it was, like, *years* later. There were still people that were really interested in Huggy Bear. Because there weren't many good interviews with them – and it is a good interview. The next one I did was with the No Neck Blues Band, and they always refused interviews. I said, 'Okay, we won't talk about music whatsoever', because I didn't care about their music that much. I knew they liked literature, and I like literature, so I said we'd just talk about books the whole time. So we did that, and I like it, I think that's a really good interview. That second issue I pretty much stand by, I think it's quite a good issue.

I was thinking that one of the things that almost disqualifies me from being a legitimate zine writer is that I don't disseminate them in the classic way. I think it's embarrassment, you know, the thing of going up to people and saying, 'Do you want to buy my zine?' I never *ever* wanted to do that. Like at football matches, people with their zines going round – I couldn't do that *ever*. But I did in shops in Brooklyn, because . . . having been in London, there doesn't seem to be much of a scene in London. It doesn't support zines, Tower Records had shut down. And when I got to Brooklyn, there were shops on every corner selling zines, and people were producing zines, and there were people in bands, and it was amazing.

GAVIN: It felt like a much healthier culture?

Oh yeah, it was brilliant. I started selling them then, I'd go into a shop and they'd have my zines. At that point I would sell them in shops in Manhattan and in Brooklyn.

GAVIN: How much did you sell them for?

I think they were a dollar or two dollars, for the *Curiosa*. I think *The Hegelian* has always been the bastard stepchild, of the two. Like, you know, I don't take good care of the format, I don't . . . I think I made a better note of how many I produced of the *Curiosa*.

GAVIN: I mean, what kind of runs would you typically do, or is there not really an average?

It really does vary. The first ones, you could count up in your head who you would give it to and then do a few extra for random people. Every time I would think about people who might want it and who I thought deserved a copy, and so it would be down to that – it would be a figure of seventeen, or something like that, so I'd have some spares. But I think with the Libeller's Almanac I made two hundred or three hundred of it.

GAVIN: And when did you go to America?

2001.

GAVIN: Do you think your writing changed much then? Did it change the subject matter?

It definitely varied . . . because I'd come from doing stuff in Norwich, in an academic setting. And I think there was a lot of good material there, because academics are so funny – inadvertently, you know, their sort of mannerisms. I think Norwich is better for me as a writer than New York, in some ways, because there was more humour to be had. I don't mean that as a putdown on Norwich, it was a good scene. People studying James Joyce . . . these self-important people were easy prey! Whereas when I was in New York it was kind of predictable – Englishman abroad discovering new things about this country, in the city that everyone goes to, you know – which can be very interesting; but I think it's when you get to know a place, then you become more interesting.

GAVIN: **You can find a seam in it to mine?**

Yeah. It was when I was living there and watching TV, and it had become my normal life, that I started to really enjoy the writing.

GAVIN: **What were you doing out there? How were you spending your time?**

I was . . . a house husband. [laughs] I was a freelancer. I was editing audio books, but that was part-time. I was trying to turn my PhD into a book, which became so huge . . .

The problem was that the more I studied . . . I wasn't able to pare it down, it kept metastasising into something bigger. So I was thinking, 'Okay, this is going to have to be a trilogy of books . . .' I was studying, researching, every day, in the New York Public Library, for years – it was lovely, but I wasn't writing, I wasn't getting enough written, I just kept absorbing material.

GAVIN: **And the boundaries kept stretching out further?**

Yeah, because you discover things and it was a revelation. I think the reading I was doing then was really my education, because it was journalism that was completely forgotten. The main person, Artemus Ward, was writing a daily column, an editorial column that was about what's going on around Cleveland. He had to do it every day, whether something happened or not, so it's fascinating. I was reading all of these, and that became the voice in my head. It was something nobody else had read for over 100 years, and it was completely original to me. I think I picked up stuff from that that was more beneficial to me than anything I'd read before. Definitely. And it was nice because nobody else had read this stuff or knew it, they were all dead.

HAMISH: **So these were writers that were, like, just before Mark Twain – is that a good way to provide context?**

Yeah – particularly Artemus Ward, because Mark Twain was briefly his protégé, and Mark Twain gained a profile by his association with Artemus Ward. But the difference was that Mark Twain became a novelist, and the novel became the dominant medium that people remembered – all these other people, they were bohemian journalists, they became completely forgotten. They only existed in the newspaper archives. I'd have to go to Yale to see one guy's writing. It was great, I knew I was the only person who was into this stuff and it was really good. I still want to write the book.

It was almost like, 'This is the stuff I'm doing while I'm doing this serious work.' I mean, I kind of equated it in my head with this thing you hear about Stan Lee, why he didn't use his real name [Stanley Lieber]. He wanted to save his real name for when he wrote the great American novel, whereas he thought that the Fantastic Four or whatever was this superficial, ephemeral stuff, and it didn't matter, it would be forgotten, so he didn't want his real name associated with it. It was kind of like that, the fact that I never put my [real] name to this stuff. Now you could say it's because I'm trying to avoid being in trouble – and there probably was an element of that – but there's also flippancy, and that's my *problem* with it as well. Because it was so flippant – that's a good thing about it and a bad thing about it, you know, it's a fine line. You can really enjoy being flippant about something – like telling a joke that peters out; it's got the promise of being funny and then it goes away from that. That's something that I became obsessed with: non-jokes.

GAVIN: **There's a freedom to that, isn't there?**

I think that's the thing, in the earliest years when I'm doing these punchlines, I find it wearisome to reread because I think . . . that wrote itself. It's boring to me. I really don't want to ever read it again. Whereas when I don't know how I'm going to end it, that's much more interesting – when it ends on a completely different note, when it's not a joke at all.

HAMISH: **You want it to be all great from start to finish, but I don't think any publications are. I mean, there's a lot of publications that I like a lot but I'll know I'm going to skip some of it, you know – like, some zines I'll avoid the record reviews, I'll only read the interviews or something like that.**

Yeah, that's the difference, I think, between the writer and the reader, isn't it?

HAMISH: Yeah, exactly, that's why I'm saying I think you're too hard on yourself – because if the reader looks at it and they think half of it is brilliant and the other half is just so-so, or they don't really get it, that's still a success.

GAVIN: Yeah, that's still really good.

I know, but as writers, you both know that it's the half they don't like that gets to you.

GAVIN: You think 'I could have made that better'.

It just bugs you they didn't get it.

HAMISH: I mean, some of them, you could say you could say there's like fifty or eighty items, whereas in a typical zine you might have, like, three interviews and ten record reviews, or something like that. In your fifty little sketches, some of them are just one-liners. That's what I think is great – there are always going to be *some* that are great.

GAVIN: Reading them feels very much like a peek inside your mind. Well, I guess it's your mind – is it definitely you, it's not a character you've created?

No. I think there's that sort of thing, of saying some things that you wouldn't necessarily say out loud – but I don't think I do that much anymore. I think most of it's much more observation now, which is as close to the reality as you can get it.

GAVIN: I liked the little haiku about Dennis Waterman being the drummer from the Jam. I like those little bursts, they're like snaps from your brain.

That's how it has seemed to evolve. I prefer doing that.

GAVIN: We were talking about audience just before. Do you have any kind of idea of an audience's expectations or doesn't that come into it at all?

When I knew exactly who I was going to give the issues to, the early ones, it was almost like telling a joke – you knew you could aim this joke for that person, this joke for that person. It's incredibly neurotic in a way: 'I expect this person to like that joke, and this person to find that one funny.' That's not necessarily a healthy way of writing. The more people that became interested in it – there was a point when I was sending them back to England, and I had readers in New York. The people in New York were quite enthusiastic about it as well, so you could get more carried away then. I was selling those as well, and I knew when I did it I'd sell them in Williamsburg, in Saint Mark's. So yeah, there were things that were intended commercially, but there were also things that were sort of defiantly uncommercial. Which I'm glad I stuck by, really, although I think it's probably a problem as well – like the joke about *Neighbours* in the *Libeller's Almanac*. [laughs] What's the point?

HAMISH: I always liked it when I was reading American zines and there were references I didn't get – they're probably better if you don't get them.

They're more tantalising.

HAMISH: And later, when you were in LA, did the zines take on a different character there, do you think? How much does the place affect them?

I didn't write much in LA. We knew we were leaving, and I wanted to do a volume, so I did the whole volume at once. That's an example of this material I'd stacked up and I didn't know what I would do with it. That volume's only six issues, not as long as the others . . . and so I did them all at once – it wasn't done once a month or whatever. I just knocked them out because I wanted to sell something in LA before we left and it suddenly became a race against time.

HAMISH: You were also writing stuff online, weren't you? Because you were doing stuff like a whole blog on Dog the Bounty Hunter. But then there was also other stuff on Trump, and then eventually that found its way into your print stuff.

Yeah, well, the Trump stuff is a very limited edition, but I wanted to do it before Trump left office. So I was doing it very last minute as well, getting it out before he left the White House. Yes, I was doing a lot online. I don't think many people read it. But, again, it didn't matter much, you know? It was a kind of place to record your ideas.

HAMISH: **Just getting it out there is enough?**

You refine it because you are publishing it. It is, technically, publishing. I hold myself to a certain standard. I'll reread it, I'll check for mistakes and then I'll rewrite it as I go. So it forces you into a process of rewriting and rethinking in a way that keeping a diary wouldn't. I've never been able to keep a diary for very long – I think it's because I don't want to do it every day.

HAMISH: **You don't have to, there's no law.**

GAVIN: **Do you feel like these zines are almost a diary?**

No, I don't, but it's been said!

GAVIN: **I mean, it seems like one to me, you know, because you've got stuff about friends and stuff you're watching on telly.**

HAMISH: **Although the recent volumes, it seems like there doesn't need to be a punchline after everything, some of them are just observations.**

I think it's rare that there's no humour in it. If I find myself simply making a statement I usually throw it away because I could make a really boring remark about academics or something, get on my soap box and it turns into a polemic, and I definitely don't want to do that. They're the most boring things – when written by me, particularly – to read.

HAMISH: **See, I think humour is undervalued in literature because sometimes I think people see it as a low form. One of the things I like about all your zines is that the highest thing you can get out of it is a good laugh. I like Updike, for example, because he's funny, but no one ever says that about Updike.**

No one says it about *anyone*. I think part of the reason is that critics are a humourless bunch and they don't realise if things are funny.

HAMISH: **They think there's something slightly *shameful* about being funny, that it doesn't have literary weight, that it's froth.**

When somebody is joking, they can't detect it a lot of the time. People like Harold Bloom...

GAVIN: What's the best feedback you've had from a reader?

I seldom get feedback – it's a recurring theme in my writing, my irritation at the readers because they don't say anything. What used to happen is if we went up to London, I'd get a bunch of people out and hand out the new issue. It would get passed around, people would get drunk, maybe read it on the tube home or whatever...

GAVIN: You'd never hear about it again?

I'd never hear anything else. I'd always turn up with this thing, they'd take it and I'd think, 'This is stupid.' I'd thought it was quite a recent resentment, but actually reading old issues I realised it's been a resentment for years! I just forgot. There was one issue where the whole issue was me getting everyone to vote off one of the subscribers. 'One of these people isn't going to receive it anymore!'

HAMISH: Anyway, in due course everyone got off the list!

Well, that was it, it was like, 'This is a diminishing return.' I still enjoyed doing it. I like the format. I like ... I almost like the idea of it not simply as a piece of writing or as a piece of art but as a kind of combination. It's a unit. And I like doing it. That was another thing: I became inspired by writers who had failed in the classical perception of things, like George Arnold, who wrote lots of short stories and articles in newspapers, but they weren't published in book form. And I came across them again and again, these nineteenth-century writers, who had great reputations but they never got published as books. We privilege books as the form that's paramount – or at least we used to, I don't know if that's still true.

HAMISH: I still do.

There was a sort of fetishism about the novel, which I agree with to an extent. All the time I've been doing this I've been writing a novel, which is like my book on the Bohemians: it's always getting bigger, but it never gets resolved. These little outbursts [i.e. the zines] are things that *do* get finished, they're doable ... and they're not a chore for me to do.

345

GAVIN: So they're just little achievable things you can do.

Yeah, and when you add it all up . . . To get back to my subject, there were these writers who wanted to have these books out, but it didn't work. They did really great stuff, and you realise that the work that gets canonised is not the best – it's a common enough idea in the academy, but it's usually judged on a sociological level.

HAMISH: But the canon is always changing, isn't it? I mean, in the time I've been following literature, which is about 30 years really, in English poetry, there are people who are talked about now who weren't really talked about 30 years ago – from times gone past I mean, from a long time ago.

Well, Melville was forgotten. And then he was rediscovered in the 1920s. He ended his days working as a clerk.

HAMISH: And that's why I think for writers and artists it's a reason not to get disheartened, because you never know what could happen with your legacy. It also happens in reverse – I mean Southey was the biggest poet of his time and now he's not in print anywhere.

Exactly. One of the major figures of the period I'm talking about was Bayard Taylor. No one knows who he is now. I found that freeing. I don't know if it was sour grapes: 'I fucked it up as a novelist, I'm never going to be a popular novelist, but that frees me to write whatever I want!' But in a way, that's *not* just sour grapes. But if you get to the point where no one's reading it . . . and you're still doing it . . . that's the point I've reached.

HAMISH: So, you've announced these new volumes of your work on a YouTube channel that, like – there were no subscribers, as far as I'm aware – but you announced that people could have them for free if they were able to get in contact with you.

I think I also put them on a blog that I hadn't really done anything with for a few years. [laughs] I'd done a lot of writing on that in America –Elias Nebula: What He Says – and I'd done a sort of farewell entry on that blog. Then a few years later I put a few more adverts on there – it was kind of sarcastic as I knew no one was going to look at it. I thought I could also say, 'Well, I did *say* . . .' And that's why I then said,

'You can get them for free for this period and after that you are going to have to pay a hundred pounds for the volume.' Because I was doing such a low run as well – if you did an art piece, if you did a print, no one would look twice if you said it was a hundred quid for a numbered print. And it was a smaller number than most people do lithographs in, so why not?

HAMISH: What is the edition, specifically?

Eight.

HAMISH: For both volumes?

For everything. I'm now fixated on the number eight because there's mystical meaning!

HAMISH: Okay, so there were two volumes of *Curiosa*, with twelve issues per volume. There were also several *Hegelians* which were only announced in a similar way.

Yeah.

HAMISH: Three issues, and that takes us up to 49?

Yeah, 49. And I will point out that if anybody had asked me, 'Well, what are you doing, are you writing anything at the moment?', I would have then let them have a copy – there were certain conditions that they would have to have met, but if there was any interest whatsoever . . .

HAMISH: That's actually how I found out about it, because you did one Instagram post where there was an image of the new *Hegelian* and that was what got me on to it. Now, the two latest volumes of the *Curiosa* are officially for sale at £100 each . . .

They're now £110. I sold one volume to a private collector. One of the conditions of that private collector was that I should never give them away to anybody under any circumstances. I said, 'That's fine, I don't intend to.'

HAMISH: Well, as the edition becomes smaller the price would naturally go up.

That's what I thought, yeah.

GAVIN: Simple marketplace economics.

HAMISH: The edition of eight includes your own issues? Do you archive just one copy?

I think I keep two for myself.

HAMISH: So there's really only six copies?

No, there's five, because there's one that I'm putting aside to give to a major library that I've not determined yet. So that was one thing – I gave everything I'd done to the British Library. I don't know if it was a good idea or not.

GAVIN: No feedback from them?

No, the guy that I had dealings with left. I was looking him up online and there was a film of him being attacked on stage because he was involved in something to do with Palestine and Israel – he was being attacked on stage by a pro-Israel person.

HAMISH: So was he all enthusiastic about it, when you approached him?

Slightly. I don't know ... it all felt a bit grudging, but he said 'Yeah, we'll take it, we do have a zine archive.'

HAMISH: 'We've got a paper shredder we can put it into ...'

Well, I mean, I kind of hope they did now! I don't want people to be able to access some of the stuff, when I think about it. The thing was – some of the material was about porn, and things like that, and I was cringing to read it, so I thought, 'Okay, I'm not going to give this to the British Library'. So ... I rewrote history. I redid them. I just redid them outright.

GAVIN: How long do you think you're going to keep producing zines? Will a novel get in the way?

No, I don't think it would. It does a separate thing. At this point, things that would be intended for the novel just go into the novel, things that are intended for the zine go into the zine – I keep them separate. Apart from anything else, the novel is fiction.

GAVIN: But I meant in terms of time that you spend on it.

Oh, well ... clearly I'm not managing my time properly! I'm not getting my novel done, I'm not getting my book written – but I keep churning out zines! Forecasting my future, I'll keep doing zines.

GAVIN: Do you have notebooks full of this stuff, as ideas occur, or is it stored in your head?

I write them down, but usually on bits of paper. Once I've written them into the computer I can scrunch them up.

HAMISH: If you're on a walk do you do voice memos?

I have done. I've got a bunch of voice memos that I haven't gone back to, they haven't been incorporated.

GAVIN: You could do Hegelian, the audio book . . .

That's what I was going to do for issue 50 – I was going to choose a minute's worth of talking from every issue. It was based on a John Cage thing called Indeterminacies where he used to write these short stories that were quite pithy. He used to read them at some of his concerts, and he did a collection with David Tudor doing music in another room, using some of John Cage's back catalogue of music. It was random, so he didn't know what Tudor was playing. There's a Folkways double album of him reading these, and it's incredible. And I was thinking, 'Well, it would be nice to do something like that.' That was what got me reading the first issues again, but I was thinking 'There is not a minute's worth of text here that I could use. Not one minute's worth!' But that was my idea for issue 50.

HAMISH: So what format would that have been?

I was thinking of doing it as a tape. Because I did issue 15 as a CD, which was me and two other people [Wash Cowie and Larry Arkansas] doing folk songs. We did the same thing with issue 20, and issue 25, which hasn't been released. But they're CDs – CDs are already falling to pieces, aren't they? Like a really old CD starts to skip and stuff.

GAVIN: Well, mine have been okay so far – they don't look great but they play okay.

HAMISH: But they're not as permanent as we were told at the time – that you could spread jam on them and that sort of thing. Nothing's permanent, is it? Paper, I think, is as good as we got.

GAVIN: I think we peaked at paper.

Unless we do inscriptions on stone tablets.

GAVIN: That might be the way forward. We're in a churchyard right now, you could start chiselling the latest issue out. Talking about formats, when is a zine a zine?

Well, I think part of it is the self-published element. For me – I'm quite a purist – black and white, done on a photocopier. Anything glossy isn't . . . I mean, there are exceptions: *Forced Exposure* had a glossy cover.

HAMISH: *Maximumrocknroll* – I don't really think of that as a zine, though I know there's a case to be made for it. But it's such a big, collaborative enterprise.

It's a successful zine, that's all.

HAMISH: But it's a *big* one, and there's lots of writers, aren't there?

Well, there are, but I don't think that disqualifies it. That's an interesting . . . you think it should just be the work of an individual?

HAMISH: There are some that I know, ones about single artists, that tend to have loads of fans submitting their stuff. On the other hand you've got the other kind of fanzine, which is more like your sort, and like *Kirby*, which is like one person sitting at home and just writing all their thoughts.

Well, it's not a *fanzine*, for one thing. I don't think I've ever called it a fanzine. Because I'm not a fan.

HAMISH: No, I know, we imposed that on you!

Well, I think the word 'fan' was separated from the word 'zine' for a reason, wasn't it?

HAMISH: Yeah, we started off doing the book like . . . we were saying you [Gavin] always use the term fanzine. I think it was me who said we should use just 'zine' because what people are doing these days, you know . . .

GAVIN: These young people! See, in my head they're still fanzines. And I still call yours a fanzine.

What am I a fan of?

GAVIN: Your own thoughts!

HAMISH: A fan of yourself.

That might be true. I'm my biggest fan.

GAVIN: But that's not a bad thing! That's alright.

HAMISH: But now they use the term 'perzine', don't they, and everyone who does a perzine, that's basically what they're doing, and it's more like a diary.

I think that's a terrible name.

HAMISH: It's not great. We could do with a better term for it, but it categorises a certain sort of zine, which is perhaps the sort that I like more than any other. Like, the person just doing it on their own, the whole production, start to finish. That's what I feel like is the most pure kind of zine.

But you don't want it to be . . . sort of solipsistic, like you're reading them journalling.

HAMISH: Like, thinking again about Kirby, Jeanette was writing a lot about her own life, but also about music, and there were some interviews in there. That for me is a kind of model of the zine. And I'm also partly thinking, because other people have done books on zines, they always focus on the massively successful zines that ended up printing thousands of copies.

You couldn't be further from that with me.

HAMISH: And the majority of zines never get to anything like that. That's what I like, in a way, that you've gone to a real extreme with that in doing such tiny editions.

I know, but . . . I don't think anyone has ever chanced upon me, and written to me and said, 'I really like this and I'd like to write about it', and I don't think that would have happened. Which means I don't take it too seriously, but that might be a good thing.

GAVIN: Yeah, I think it is. It's also kept a certain purity in what you're doing. It's not been diluted by thinking about whether you could sell more by doing this or that.

I think it's funny that I keep on doing it. I don't even know why I keep doing it – I just do.

GAVIN: That was one of my questions – why do you keep on doing it?

I don't know. That's the thing, sometimes I just feel like doing one. It's like . . . I've built up enough material. I mean, I've got into a thing now where it is quite uniform – it's twenty-four pages, it's A6. At the moment I like that size and I'm sticking with it.

20

ARLO LIPPIATT

interviewed by Hamish Ironside

To the best of our knowledge, the only good thing to have come out of the Covid-19 pandemic is *Pint-Sized Punk*, a zine that emerged in June 2020 from the hinterland between Bath and Bristol. While almost everything else was closing down during lockdown, *Pint-Sized Punk* came out swinging, with three issues published in three short months by the time Boatwhistle headed west in August 2020 to investigate further.

Pint-Sized Punk is exceptional in several ways. Most notably, it has by far the youngest editor of any zine that we've encountered: ten-year-old Arlo Lippiatt. Furthermore, while most zines have to contend with a public response somewhere between apathy and disdain, *Pint-Sized Punk* met with instant and widespread acclaim, far in excess of what Arlo had anticipated. Being so successful is rewarding, of course, but also brings a certain amount of tribulation. It must be a little discombobulating to set out steeling yourself to pester other people, only to find that it's soon other people who are pestering you.

Pint-Sized Punk declares itself 'A 10 year old's guide to life and music'. The main part of each issue consists of interviews by Arlo with bands such as Idles, Fontaines DC and Dream Wife, alongside which are regular instalments of Arlo's own computer-generated comic strip, 'Death Pigs', drawings by Arlo, record reviews, and in issue 3 even a bread recipe by John Newton of JOHN. Each issue ends with a chart showing whether the featured artists love or hate Marmite.

Arlo Lippiatt at his home in Keynsham, August 2020.

Issue 1 of *Pint-Sized Punk* has the appearance of a traditional fanzine: black and white printing throughout on white paper for the inner pages and coloured paper for the cover. But subsequent issues are full colour throughout, printed on glossy paper, designed digitally, making it quite a contrast to old-school zines constructed using Letraset, typewriter and glue. And (in case it wasn't already obvious enough) gone are the days of sellotaping 50p to a piece of cardboard and trusting to the post: *Pint-Sized Punk* does not even have a physical address printed for Luddite readers to write to. If you want to order a copy you either get it in a shop or order it online (available from https://pintsizedpunkzine.bandcamp.com at time of writing), and readers are encouraged to engage with the zine through all the usual social media channels.

The use of technology extends to the streamlined system for recording and transcribing interviews, as we see below. But I am pleased to report that the attitude throughout is very much that of the best punk zines, with much wit, irreverence and randomness enlivening the interviews, and the reviews characterised by appropriate levels of enthusiasm and hyperbole.

I met up with Arlo and his mum (Hannah) at their home soon after Covid lockdown restrictions had eased, at which point issue 3 had been published and issue 4 was in preparation. Since the interview Arlo kept up the frankly incredible work rate for a full year, with issues appearing every month up to issue 12 in May 2021, after which they have become more sporadic. At the time of writing the latest issue is number 15, produced in May 2022 by a now twelve-year-old Arlo. The interviews have continued to be the main feature of the zine – artists Arlo has talked to in issues 4–12 include Slowthai, Bob Vylan and Wet Leg – and there have been special issues for Alcopop Records (issue 10) and for Bristol (issue 13), although in truth all the issues evince a strong loyalty to the city. The 'Death Pigs' serial reached its dramatic conclusion in issue 9. And the Marmite lovers now greatly outnumber the haters (despite the release of truffle-flavoured Marmite in May 2022 – a catastrophic error of judgement by Unilever).

The idea for Pint-Sized Punk came during lockdown. What made you think of doing a fanzine?

ARLO: It was kind of my mum's idea, because she and my dad are really into music, and they order music magazines like Uncut and Mojo, stuff like that. And we've got a couple of friends who make zines – adult friends, Mikey and Nicola – but they didn't release theirs yet. But they had *awesome* parties!

Oh, okay . . . so they sort of worked on the zines, but they're still . . .

ARLO: . . . sending it to print. Yeah. Pint-Sized Punk was, like, sort of a home schooling project, to start with. And my mum just wanted to – she asked me what I wanted to write about, and I said I wanted to write about music. And then she came up with the idea to make a zine. Because we wanted to make a thing, not just writing for the sake of writing.

Yeah. So you've got a finished product, that you can keep . . .

ARLO: Yeah. We thought it would just be forty or fifty people buying it. I mean, we never thought we'd do more than one issue, really.

Had you read any zines, apart from these ones your friends were working on? Did you know about any others?

ARLO: Not really. I just thought it was writing about music, interviews and stuff.

Yeah. But did you have a clear idea of what it was going to look like, and how you were going to design it, and all that sort of thing?

ARLO: No, because if I had done, like, the cover and things, the zine would have been really messy! Like, if it weren't for Mum, this wouldn't be happening.

Yeah. So Mum's kind of acted like a sub-editor . . .

ARLO: She's like my vice president really!

I was amazed how quickly you got it out, because lockdown started at end of March, and issue 1 is for June, so you must have been really busy during April and May, doing all the interviews and stuff like that?

ARLO: Yeah. It took, like, a couple of months to do the first one, because we weren't really used to it yet. And we had no idea what we were doing! So the first one was quite hard. The second one was . . . a bit easier. But the third one was really fun.

Yeah, you were up and running by then.

ARLO: That was probably the best one yet.

And what was hard about the first one, was it working out how to get in touch with bands to interview them, and stuff like that?

ARLO: For the first one it was all people I knew or had met at gigs or festivals. So, the interviews, we just asked them, and they said 'Yeah, alright!' They thought it was just going to be a small thing. So I started off interviewing some small bands. Now sometimes I'm emailing bands, sometimes they're emailing me asking for interviews. Like, for the second issue, Bunf from SFA [Super Furry Animals] and a band called JOHN asked to be interviewed.

Did you not know who they were before that?

ARLO: I did know JOHN because my mum sees them at lots of gigs and she listens to them in the gym, and I know SFA, because . . . they're SFA!

So when you did the first one, you were thinking it might sell forty or fifty –

ARLO: Just a few really, we didn't think much was going to happen to it –

And you ran them off on your printer at home, and stapled them yourself?

ARLO: Yeah, this printer here.

Yeah, because by the time I went to buy one it was already sold out, but then you did another printing . . .

ARLO: Every time we finish printing them, more people order them, so we have to print another batch. And then another batch, and then another batch . . .

But you're still doing them on the printer at home . . .

ARLO: Yeah, we're sometimes running out of ink and having printer problems, printing so much. It's been a bit harder than when we first started. Because we sold a few hundred copies.

And when did you first start getting the media coverage? Because now if I search online, there's loads of articles – BBC, *Guardian*, *Times* – it's mentioned all over the place, and overseas. So how did that all begin?

ARLO: That started with a guy called Colin Paterson from BBC *Breakfast*, and he was going to pitch this little thing for BBC *Breakfast* in the morning, about how kids and people have made things good out of lockdown.

HANNAH: And how did Colin find it?

ARLO: Um . . .

HANNAH: So, Arlo sent a copy to Lauren Laverne –

ARLO: Oh yeah!

HANNAH: . . . at 6 Music . . .

ARLO: Oh yeah, *that* was where it started.

HANNAH: And she tweeted about it, so Colin saw her tweets. And he then pitched it to BBC *Breakfast*.

ARLO: Yeah, that's really where it started, when Lauren Laverne tweeted about it.

HANNAH: And that was about three weeks after the first copy.

Okay. So first copy had been out three weeks – what made you want to send one

Issue 1 (June 2020)

Issue 2 (July 2020)

Issue 3 (August 2020)

Issue 4 (September 2020)

Issue 5 (October 2020)

Issue 6 (November 2020)

to Lauren Laverne? Did you hear that she was interested in things like that, or did you just listen to her show?

ARLO: We listen to her show – Radio 6 is always on in the kitchen. It had been going quite good – like, we sold a hundred copies or so, and we thought that was amazing. That was double what we thought we'd sell.

That is good, for a fanzine . . .

HANNAH: He'd sold about 300 copies of that first issue before any media coverage. And he's sold about 900 now. So the poor printer is . . . struggling!

Yeah. I'm surprised you didn't send it to a press . . . you know, do a second edition of issue 1, or maybe that's, uh . . .

ARLO: I did think about that . . .

HANNAH: Oh, did you? Because . . . I didn't! Because we thought, 'Oh, we'll sell a few more, then we'll run off another 20.' And then it's another 20 . . .

ARLO: Yeah, we could send it off to that printing place?

HANNAH: I think what we hadn't anticipated is because it's still early on, the majority of orders we get at the moment are for all three. Because people want the back copies as well. We didn't really consider that they'd do that. But I think because it's so close to the beginning, that's realistic. Like, Arlo's just started subscribing to 2000 AD, and he said 'Oh, I want to go back to the beginning.' I said, 'Well, it started 42 years ago . . . It would cost you thousands!'

Well, if you keep reprinting, it's unlimited, isn't it? But some people like to make them a rarity, and just let it go out of print, and never reprint, just because then you create a bit of a collector's market.

ARLO: Yeah, that's what I thought, we could leave it a few issues – when we're on issue 7 or something – and go 'Limited edition! Rerun of issue 1!'

Yeah, yeah . . .

ARLO: And then just do 'Limited edition' on the cover . . . and then it's, like, one pound more . . .

So the Colin Paterson thing, was that on TV or radio?

ARLO: That was TV, for *BBC Breakfast*.

HANNAH: Well, in the interim, you were on Lauren Laverne's show, weren't you? Because she tweeted, and then her producer got in touch that day, to say, 'Actually, we want you on.' So we'd already arranged that, and then heard from Colin. So it was all very quick, wasn't it? It was a matter of a few days.

ARLO: And then after I was on *BBC Breakfast*, that day, I had, like, six radio interviews.

Wow!

HANNAH: It was all around the BBC, wasn't it? Because obviously, what we have no real knowledge of is that once the BBC have something, it's a vast network. So we got a

Issue 7   (Decmber 2020)

Issue 8   (January 2021)

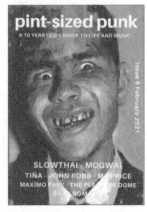

Issue 9   (February 2021)

Issue 10   (March 2021)

Issue 11   (April 2021)

Issue 12   (May 2021)

call the day before to say 'We know this is scheduled for tomorrow' –

ARLO: And we keep having people, like, 'Ooh, you've been in the papers! Ooh, you've been on *Newsround!*' Like, 'Have we?'

HANNAH: Yeah, we still get people contacting you every week, saying 'Oh, we saw you here . . .' So, that day, you were on Radio 5 Live first thing, weren't you? Because they wanted to beat breakfast TV and have you on earlier. So in that one day he was on Radio 5 Live, *BBC Breakfast*, on *The Today Show*, on Radio 4, and then Radio Bristol, BBC Radio Cymru . . . um . . .

ARLO: And BBC Radio Wales . . .

HANNAH: Yeah . . . that was Cymru . . . and Channel 4. All in one day. And then newspapers picked it up the following day. So for about a week we had things just appearing everywhere. And then *Newsround* was the following week, wasn't it?

ARLO: Yeah, and that was a big deal for me, because my teacher would, like, every week we'd have 'News Day Tuesday' and watch Newsround.

Oh, okay, so that was the big one for you.

ARLO: Yeah. That was my personal favourite.

HANNAH: And then it was global, because it went out on BBC World Service.

ARLO: Yeah. And I've done radio for . . . Dubai, I think?

HANNAH: Australia . . .

361

ARLO: That Australian interview was really good.

When you got all this media coverage, where were you getting the response from? Was it from, like, Twitter?

ARLO: It was really on Facebook. Before the media stuff we only had an email address and Facebook account. Now we're on Insta and Twitter as well.

And do you like doing stuff for that? Do you tweet a lot?

ARLO: I don't tweet as much, but it's better for getting bands. Last week, I did the listing part on Twitter. And I went tweet crazy!

Because I'm old school, my interest in fanzines is because I like physical things printed on paper, and that's what I was wondering – um, why you decided to do a fanzine rather than just doing a blog or . . .

ARLO: A blog wouldn't be as fun. You want to actually be able to hold something, and say 'I made this.' You can't really just go: 'I *made* this blog.' Like, it's not as good as, 'Oh, I made this magazine.'

HANNAH: I think . . . initially, from my perspective, this started as a replacement for a school project. The idea of making something physical was to try to motivate Arlo to actually do the work and finish it off. Because you're very similar to me, we're very good at starting a project but not so good at actually finishing it.

But now it's been so successful you must

Issue 13　(June/July 2021)

Issue 14　(November 2021)

Issue 15　(May 2022)

want to just keep on going as long as you can?

ARLO: Yeah . . . but sometimes, if I'm in a bad mood, I just go, 'Oh, I don't want to do this zine any more!'

HANNAH: You say that at least two or three times a week!

ARLO: And then I'll just go, like: [stomps out of the room]

HANNAH: It's catching you when you've got energy, isn't it? We don't want it to feel like a job.

No, of course.

HANNAH: But with the first one, it took you a good eight weeks to get it out, didn't it? And it was because of that fear of . . . it actually being finished. Fear of being judged.

Oh, really?

HANNAH: Yeah. So we started it perhaps beginning of April, but didn't get it out until . . . mid-June. And most of that was not – we had interviews all done, they were all edited – it was just that final hurdle of formatting it, getting it out, and saying 'Okay, we're finished.' But as soon as that went out and you got positive feedback, you were really excited for issue 2. And you've just got into the routine of doing it quite quickly, haven't you? That's what's really impressed me.

So your school was aware of it during the whole process?

ARLO: Yeah, my school's been really supportive.

In what way have they supported it?

ARLO: They've understood that I am, like, doing English, for doing the costs, and I have to write little notes to people, that's my handwriting . . . putting it together, I'm doing every subject.

HANNAH: So it got to the stage where you effectively stopped completing any work that school had set, didn't you? Because quite early on we contacted his teacher and said, 'Well, he's doing this . . .' We sent copies of your interviews to him, and he was like, 'That's absolutely fine.' And he said he could really see the difference in your writing. Because editing something is one of the skills that you don't work on so much at school, do you? And you find it quite difficult.

ARLO: It was really boring.

HANNAH: So it's been one of your target areas really, hasn't it?

ARLO: It was really boring at school because you don't have voice recordings and things like that. They make you work on the punctuation way more.

So the whole process of doing the interviews and typing them up and everything, did you actually type them up?

ARLO: We use a transcript place, called Rev, I think.

So that, like, listens to it and puts it into text?

ARLO: Yeah, it's done by computer, so it's really fast. Once we asked the band called JOHN if they like Marmite, and one of the guys' answers included 'Yes, I love Mama', 'hula', 'spunkie' and 'opiates'! It was really weird . . .

So you run the software, and then you have to read through it to look for mistakes, basically?

ARLO: Yeah, and we watch the Zoom interviews and stuff. It's so much easier for written ones, because you don't have to edit it. You just cut out questions.

I've never tried that, I've just been playing the tape recorder and typing it up. It takes so long.

ARLO: Yeah, the transcript is a bit better than typing it up.

HANNAH: Yeah, it's a good starting point, isn't it?

ARLO: If you use Rev it gives you one free one per email address, so we just switch email addresses all the time!

HANNAH: And then you've got a couple of people who contacted you to say, 'Well, actually I do this as my job. I'd be quite happy to transcribe for you.' So when it's more complex, when it's a band with several people, we've been asking for help and sending them off.

ARLO: And when I interviewed the drummer and bassist from Biffy Clyro – they're a Scottish band, and one of them had a really heavy accent –

HANNAH: Yes, it was an American lady who was doing the transcription, wasn't it? So there was quite a lot that she couldn't catch with the accent. But then it means you're only filling in single words or phrases rather than the whole thing.

Is that one you've just done then, Biffy Clyro?

ARLO: Yeah, that was last week.

So issue 4 is in the works already?

ARLO: Oh yeah, we've got all the interviews for issue 4. We just need to edit them.

Well, I'm glad there's more issues on the way. Because I was worried they were going to sort of stop when you go back to school.

ARLO: Oh, they won't stop, but they won't be out, like, once a month. They'll slow down.

And about the name, obviously I see why it's called Pint-Sized Punk, but I was wondering where you got the phrase from?

ARLO: That was actually my mum's idea, because she was like, 'You like punk music and you're pint-sized . . .'

HANNAH: Yes . . . English teachers like alliteration . . . But you've had a little bit of backlash, haven't you? Like, generally, people are really nice to you –

ARLO: There was this one guy who was like, 'How dare you call Super Furry Animals punk? How dare you?'

But you weren't, were you?

ARLO: No.

I mean, you're not saying everything in here is punk, you're just saying . . .

ARLO: Yeah, we're just saying 'I'm a punk . . . deal with it!'

HANNAH: That's it, it's just saying punk is the spirit of DIY.

ARLO: I remember . . . [laughs] there have been people going, like, 'Ooh, I like his hair!', and then there have been other people going 'Get your hair cut!'

HANNAH: That was what was interesting about the BBC coverage, was that it opened us up online to a whole different crowd of people.

Were you getting trolled?

ARLO: Yeah, there was this one guy who was like, 'Oh, she can get him on telly, but she can't cut his hair!'

Where did you hear that sort of thing, was it on social media? Twitter?

HANNAH: No, that was on the BBC website.

ARLO: And then Mum went back, like, 'Teaching a ten-year-old to write, interview, edit, illustrate and publish is in my skill, but cutting hair is not.' Something like that.

HANNAH: And he came back and said 'Sorry, I was only joking.'

But does any of it . . . does it hurt your feelings when you get negative stuff?

ARLO: Um . . . we haven't really got much negative stuff.

HANNAH: The only time you have had negative things – which I must admit I've shielded you from – because, obviously, of his age, all of his email and social media have to go through me – he's not allowed a Facebook or a Twitter account . . . we've had one – one and a half people, I would say – actually getting quite irate that they've asked you to review their band and you haven't. Just because of the sheer volume of people –

ARLO: We've had, like, ninety people asking that.

Are they all sort of local, or is it all over the country?

HANNAH: All over the world.

ARLO: They're bands I'd never heard of, really.

HANNAH: Yeah, some of it's directly from the bands themselves, we've got quite a few agents and PR companies and record labels that are now contacting Arlo, to say 'Would you like to review this?', 'Do you want to come and see this band in the studio?', 'Do you want to interview my acts?' . . . And it has been people who've been recommending their own family's band, and have got upset that you haven't got back to them.

You must have been interviewed more often than you've interviewed other people by now?

ARLO: Yeah. I miss interviewing people, because I'm not getting to do it as much now that it's really big. I have one interview every couple of weeks now.

Why can't you do it as much?

ARLO: We've got bands we know we can ask – we know we can get them, so we're, like, saving them for later.

HANNAH: Well, it's partly because you've got so many stacked up.

Oh, you've got loads that you've done, so they're all ready to go?

ARLO: I did loads of interviews.

HANNAH: It feels a bit strange interviewing people now, saying it won't be in the zine for three or four months.

Yeah, yeah, no, I see that, yeah. Unless you just do a bumper issue and get them all in? Or do them in smaller type . . .

ARLO: If we did a bumper issue, you'd probably pay more for postage than you do for the zine.

HANNAH: But we have discussed that, haven't we? Because we put it up to 48 pages. And then we spoke to the printing company about the weight of the paper. But we didn't think about the weight of the envelope! That then pushed it over, and it was costing us three times as much, four times as much to post. So we reduced the paper stock, which has worked okay. But we did talk about whether it's worth instead saying 'Well, every three months . . .' Then it will be more of a magazine . . . But I think, during lockdown, people have really valued it being monthly.

ARLO: It wouldn't be as fun. You want to say, 'Ooh, I've done five issues' [in five months], not, like, 'I've done four issues in a year . . .'

HANNAH: But a lot of other zines are quarterly. So there's only four a year. But they are much more substantial. But that's something you can decide as you go . . .

ARLO: What does substantial mean?

HANNAH: They're bigger.

Yeah. Well, I think a lot of zines only do one issue a year.

HANNAH: Well, it has to fit in around life, doesn't it?

Yeah. That's it, and you don't want it to become a chore. You just want to do it for fun, don't you? So issue 4, will that be –

ARLO: That will hopefully be out in September.

Yeah. And what would be your print run for that?

ARLO: What does that mean?

How many will you print?

ARLO: Oh! Probably, like . . . 1,000?

HANNAH: It's a difficult one.

ARLO: We printed loads for the third issue, but then people haven't bought it . . .

So, issue 2, how many did you print and how many did you sell?

ARLO: We got, like, 500. I'm like, 'We're never going to sell 500, Mum!'

HANNAH: But then we had to order, like, another 600.

So you sold through 500 and then printed another 600. That's amazing.

HANNAH: At the moment, of the first issue you've sold about 850. Still printing at home. The second issue, you've sold about . . . in between 1,000 and 1,100. The third issue, you've only sold 200. And obviously, second issue was when we had a lot of that media coverage. And it's only part way through the month. We haven't really considered for ongoing sales that we're still getting for the others.

Some are in shops, aren't they? And you work in a record shop?

ARLO: Yeah, I started a job.

Like, at weekends?

ARLO: Yeah. Sundays.

And you sell the fanzine there?

ARLO: Yeah. It's available in most record shops in Bristol and Bath.

HANNAH: And that's the other thing, people say 'Well actually I think this record shop in Brighton would like it' – or 'this record shop in Manchester' – so I think we probably need to spend a little bit of time, before you go back to school – a bit like you did with Lauren Laverne – just sending out copies and saying 'If you like it, let us know . . .'

Rough Trade in London, you could try . . .

HANNAH: Yes, they've had copies, and they've sold out, I think. Because you get on well with Rough Trade in Bristol, so they've been selling them online as well, Rough Trade, haven't they?

So sales dipped a bit for issue 3, which is not surprising, because it's after that massive media blitz . . .

HANNAH: Well, I think also it's slightly more niche bands you've got – even though we know it's the best edition so far, for content – they're not as mainstream, are they?

ARLO: Most people haven't heard of Beak. We probably should have put BC Camplight or Dream Wife [i.e. as main artist on the cover].

HANNAH: I don't know, you learn as you go, don't you? But again, with the cost of print, it's going through the economics – it's actually . . . it's okay for us to have 500 copies sitting in the loft. Because once you reach about 400 or 500, they don't cost very much to print. It's the first few hundred that are more expensive. So I'm not quite sure what we're going to do for the print run of issue 4.

One last question: are you named after Arlo Guthrie?'

ARLO: Yeah, I think so.

That doesn't really go with the punk thing, does it? He's more like folk music . . .

ARLO: I don't even know who he is.

HANNAH: Do you remember the story?

ARLO: Oh no, not the *story*! It's really long and boring . . .

HANNAH: When I was pregnant with you, we had friends over – we'd been out to a gig, actually, I was about six or seven months pregnant – so we'd all gone out, we were all back at our house, late night, and there was the film of Woodstock, the big festival, on TV. And we'd been talking about baby names all night, as you do, and we were all sitting there chatting, and then the announcer said: 'And next . . . Arlo Guthrie!' And all four of us looked at each other and went: 'Arlo . . . That's it!' So it was always Arlo or Rufus, after Rufus Wainwright. If you had red or black hair you would have been Rufus. But Rufus didn't feel right for a blond. So you became Arlo!

Well that wasn't too long . . .

HANNAH: Yeah! And his music's not awful. We should play you some.

ARLO: It was longer when you told it last time. It was, like, five or ten minutes. *Ages.*

AFTERWORD

Having completed the 20 interviews for this book, in August 2022 we met in Leicester to discuss our findings, reminisce about our own experiences as zine editors in the early nineties, and play a couple of rounds of crazy golf.

As noted in the preface, in our interviews we aimed to cover as broad a range as possible in terms of time period, subject matter and everything else. Even so, we inevitably ended up wishing we could have done more. One zine we aimed to cover is worth mentioning here: a publication called *Scabbin Crew News* produced by an anonymous British Airways cabin crew employee as a spoof of the company's official staff magazine, *Cabin Crew News*. The story of *Scabbin Crew News* is included in a fascinating book called *Cabin Crew Conflict: The British Airways Dispute 2009–11* by Phil Taylor, Sian Moore and Robert Byford (Pluto Press, 2019). *Scabbin Crew News* was 'a satirical magazine about pilots and managers . . . just taking the mickey out of them'. A British Airways pilot saw a copy, complained to management, and the editor was sacked for 'bullying and harassment' (a tribunal subsequently found the dismissal unfair). We were unable to track down the editor to request an interview.

One could argue about whether *Scabbin Crew News* was really a zine – this is indeed the sort of question that cropped up regularly in the four years we were working on this book, about many different kinds of publications. Without wanting to digress about that too much, we can certainly say that it's much easier to describe a paradigmatic zine than to adjudicate about outliers. Yet if *Scabbin Crew News* is not a paradigmatic zine, in one respect it exemplifies perhaps the most important factor that links all zines, which is that they are *lawless literature*. Even if not overtly political, by virtue of the fact that they operate *outside* the establishment, we would contend that they are *against* the establishment, and thus anti-corporate, even subversive. No professional writer has the freedom of expression of a zine writer, even down to the fact that they don't have to obey rules of grammar and spelling if they don't want to.

Besides *Scabbin Crew News*, there were other zines we would have liked to include in our book. Among others, we aimed to speak to Aggi of the Pastels about *Juniper Beri-beri* and *Pastelism*, and to John Bagnall about *Hairy Hi-Fi*. We tried to speak to someone from the collective behind the Oxford-based *Cuntry Living* feminist zine (albeit mainly because we liked the title). But ultimately there was only so much we could fit in, and this book is already about twice as long as we expected it to be when we started. Nevertheless, the conversation that follows (recorded in the garden of the Old Horse pub opposite Victoria Park) begins with us reflecting on other things we would have liked to shoehorn into this book.

HAMISH: One of the things that we didn't get into as much as I'd have liked to, in retrospect, was the design aspect of fanzines. What I started learning about quite late on in the process was how important Jamie Reid was in the design aspect of punk, and the fact that he's got this history that went back to before punk, to the early seventies, when he was involved in small-circulation magazines that were very like fanzines. I feel like that's a bit of a gap in the history that we haven't really been able to cover. We haven't tried to be too comprehensive, but there are always going to be gaps, given it's quite a big book. There's also all that whole area of things like Oz . . .

GAVIN: *International Times* . . .

HAMISH: Yeah, underground magazines of the sixties. Now, I don't think those as zines, but then I have to ask myself, 'Well, why not? Is it simply because they didn't call themselves fanzines?' In a way, I feel like it was because they always seemed like they had some money behind them, even though they weren't part of a big media corporation. They had some wealthy backer, and when they got involved in some court case they had someone who could pay . . .

GAVIN: Who could bail them out?

HAMISH: Yeah. And to me that's not what a typical fanzine could do, you know, so that's going a bit further away. But it's difficult to make these hard and fast distinctions, I think. There's a very good Routledge book about the sixties underground press [Nigel Fountain, Underground: The London Alternative Press 1966–74, Routledge, 1988], but it does feel almost more like part of the political anti-establishment movement than a sort of self-publishing kind of thing.

GAVIN: It's coming more from politics rather than being fan-based or music-based or whatever?

HAMISH: Yeah, and also, it's not part of the establishment, but it is part of a kind of funded project where there's like some organisation – editorial meetings – and they have, like, a backer who they're beholden to.

GAVIN: It's not one person in a bedroom somewhere.

HAMISH: No, that's it. Every time I think about it, even though a lot of fanzines became collaborative and things like that, in the purest sense, to me, it is one person in a bedroom, and probably someone who doesn't have much of a social life and doesn't have much money and is just working against every kind of inhibiting factor they could come up against.

GAVIN: If you think of the Platonic forms, that would be it, right? Someone working maybe in a northern town, in an attic bedroom, a typewriter, little money, quite shy.

HAMISH: We don't have to bring your northernisms into it! It could be a southern town.

GAVIN: Probably best northern . . . but yeah, okay, alright . . .

HAMISH: We're not all posh southerners you know.

GAVIN: All right, well, okay, maybe that's just me . . .

Hamish Ironside in the garden of the Old Horse, Leicester, perusing an issue of *Bag of Tricks and Candy Sticks*, edited by Gavin Hogg.

HAMISH: This guy who produced *My Name Is Larry* [one-off zine about Wild Man Fischer], you know, he's in the Orkneys . . . I don't suppose there are a lot of Wild Man Fischer fans in the Orkneys. I'm willing to bet he's the only one.

GAVIN: You're probably right.

HAMISH: And yet, you know, he's decided 'I'm gonna do this on paper'. You know, I suppose that partly is what our book's about, asking the question why. You know, what is the reason? Why do you do it on paper? I mean, I like paper because I hate all things digital and you know paper is, if not completely permanent, more permanent than anything else. Maybe that's what Jake Parappa Hainey [editor of *My Name is Larry*] thinks.

Gavin Hogg in the garden of the Old Horse, Leicester, perusing an issue of *Saudade*, edited by Hamish Ironside.

GAVIN: There is something about, I guess, the kind of artist that's covered in music fanzines. I don't know, but there probably wasn't a fanzine for, back in the day, a band like Coldplay or Elton John, do you know what I mean?

HAMISH: Yeah. Can you imagine a U2 fanzine? How awful would that be?

GAVIN: I probably would have bought that, to be honest! But why is that?

HAMISH: I feel like there may be a sort of inversely proportional relationship between the popularity of an artist and the intensity of the fans' feeling towards them.

GAVIN: Yeah, that's interesting, I think you're probably right. So what were your favourite bits from being a fanzine editor? Looking back, how has it informed things that have happened since?

HAMISH: Well, the thing I remember is . . . I was incredibly shy as a teenager. I didn't have a circle of friends. We lived in a village. You know, I'd got my brother, who was like my best friend, and we both had very intense interest in music. And we produced little magazines. Before I ever did a published fanzine I was making little magazines just for fun.

But the thing is, I was producing my zine about Sparks I was 17, and then *Saudade* when I was 18. What I keep thinking about is, if you're of that age, and you don't really have a social life, these things become so important. And when I discovered these other fanzines – more general fanzines, like *Dregs* and *Grim Humour* – dozens and dozens of them – what I remember is getting familiar with the fact that they were sometimes writing not just about bands but about social issues. And I think your political views, when you're that age, they're not fully formed, and they can't really be until you've had more experience of, like, what it's like to have to earn money, and pay rent . . . all those things inform your political views. But I was already getting a sort of . . . advance notice of all these issues I was going to have to confront through the pages of fanzines. And I'm really grateful for those things, because a lot of fanzines, you know, they're very very left wing, and a lot of them are anarchist. And I am just really grateful for being exposed to those things at that age. That's probably the lasting thing, more than all the musical things I was reading about, was the fact that it shaped my political outlook.

I was reading my diaries and I made some notes about how many I produced and things like that. So, the *Tacky Tiger*, I printed it in November '88. Basically, we knew these people in the village where I grew up – Blewbury – they produced the *Blewbury Bulletin* on a Gestetner. My mum and dad both actually helped to produce the *Blewbury Bulletin*. I think it was monthly. But it was just a village magazine produced on a Gestetner. And I saw the Gestetner in action every now and then, because I'd come along once or twice to see it all happen. When I came to do my first fanzine we went over to Roger Cambray's house, and Roger very kindly made the plates and printed it up on his Gestetner.

GAVIN: Oh, that's amazing!

HAMISH: Did 500 copies . . . collated and stapled them myself . . . how many did I get rid of? I don't know – I feel like I knew every Sparks fan in the country at the time, but that was probably about 20 people! In fact every Sparks fan in the world, because there was one in Finland, one in Holland that I was in touch with regularly . . . but it was like – I produced my Sparks fanzine at their lowest ebb in popularity of their entire career. I don't even know how many I sold. I've only got about two or three copies now, but I think I must have thrown away a few hundred.

So that's the *Tacky Tiger* – that's '88 . . . and I was thinking of doing a second issue of *Tacky Tiger*, but at the same time I was starting to get more into other bands, especially They Might Be Giants. So I decided to do a general music fanzine, and that was *Saudade*. I took it to the printer in December '89 – I'd have been 18 then. I got 1200 copies printed!

GAVIN: The hubris! Why did you . . . I mean, I like your ambition, but why did you think 1200 was a good number to print?

HAMISH: I don't know. I mean, at the time . . . I took a year out before going to university, I guess I was earning money and living at home . . . so I put my own money into it. I don't think I had any idea how I was going to sell them. I don't know what I was thinking when I came up with that number. The only thing I can think of is I was looking at how much money I'd got saved up, and I went to the printer and said something like, 'I've got six hundred pounds, how many copies can you do for that?'

GAVIN: Jesus . . .

HAMISH: I don't know, I can't understand it myself . . . I don't think I even sold 50. I mean, maybe 20, something like that? A lot of them, they didn't even get recycled, they went in a skip. Years later, when my parents moved.

GAVIN: But then I presume you didn't get as many printed for subsequent issues?

HAMISH: Issue 2, it didn't say how many I got done, which is a bit annoying, but that was June 1990. So that's about six months later. That's not too bad a gap, really.

GAVIN: No, that's good, you were very quick at getting them out. The first issue is where our paths intersected for the first time, because I remember you put an advert in the *Melody Maker*, I think, or the *NME*, or something? It probably would have been Morrissey and Captain Beefheart that would have attracted me. £1.50, at the time, that was quite expensive for a zine, wasn't it?

HAMISH: Thank you!

GAVIN: But that's because the quality was so high, Hamish! But I remember being impressed straight away because – I'd not read a lot of zines at that point, and you had stuff, you know, about Muriel Spark, who I'd never heard of at the time, and Jack Kerouac – who I had – but you didn't see those kind of things in zines. And rummy! And you were always very good on the merch stuff as well, like the Mr Brownstone cassette.

HAMISH: Yeah – no one ever ordered any of that stuff!

GAVIN: You had a key fob! [Quoting] 'Oddities-cum-commodities' . . . But that was very impressive – there was a real attention to detail that I liked. So we kind of became friends quite quickly after this. Because I thought, 'I should hitch my wagon to this guy's train, he seems to be going places!'

HAMISH: So, first issue of *Bag of Tricks and Candy Sticks*, uh . . . seems to be undated . . .

GAVIN: Ah, sorry, sorry! It would have been around '91, I guess . . .

HAMISH: How old were you then?

GAVIN: I would have been 21. So I was maybe a little bit older than most people when they do their first one.

HAMISH: And what were you doing at that time?

GAVIN: Was I still a student? Yeah, I think I started it when I was probably still a student. Probably published it just around the time I was doing my finals. And then – that's it – I think I got them ready just before I went to Reading in '91. That would have been the summer that I'd finished my course. Yeah, so – yeah! I'd just turned 21. And the first fanzine I got was Pete Paphides's *Perturbed* when I was 17, 18. I didn't really have a frame of reference for it – I didn't quite know what I was reading, but it looked kind of interesting . . . I think it really wasn't until I got yours, and we started to become friends, that I thought, 'Oh, actually I could get involved in this world as well, myself.' I was a little bit older by then, and I just had a bit more confidence maybe. You know, 'I love music and I'm passionate about things and I could get a part of this for myself', you know?

HAMISH: Talking about prices, yours are both 60p – that's good value – £1.50 for mine, yeah, that's a lot! And *Tacky Tiger* also £1.50. But if you look at the ones after that . . .

GAVIN: They're great value!

HAMISH: Second issue of *Saudade*: 75p. Price is halved, but you get more pages. And then issue 3: it's a pound for ninety-six pages. Ninety-six pages, Gavin!

GAVIN: But *Saudade* issue 1 was 32 pages and it's £1.50, so what was going on with your pricing structure there?

HAMISH: I don't know . . . I was losing money on this one [*Saudade* issue 3] . . . I think my unit cost must have been more than a pound per copy.

GAVIN: Yeah, for sure. I mean, I remember mine were . . . I worked out the price per issue exactly. I did a hundred . . . I think I worked out that if I sold every issue, I'd break even, so that's the price I put it at. Obviously I sold about a tenth of what I'd paid for.

HAMISH: Absolutely no wish to make any money on it?

GAVIN: No.

HAMISH: So how were you selling it?

GAVIN: Really badly! I think I put an advert in *Record Collector* and maybe they reviewed a copy. I sent a copy to John Peel and he read out my name and address for the first one. So Dave Gedge [singer with the Wedding Present] bought a copy.

HAMISH: I don't know why I never thought of doing that because it seems like everyone who sent to Peel he did mention.

GAVIN: He did, yeah. He was really sweet. I mean, I don't know, I probably sold like three or four on the back of that but it was nice to do anyway. I think I put one maybe in the NME as well and did little flyers that I would trade with other fanzine editors. I probably sold, I don't know 10, 20, no more than that. And I had 100 done. But then, you know, I traded some for other fanzines, so that was good.

HAMISH: Yeah. In issue 2, in the editorial, you actually mention: 'For those of you unaware, there exists a first edition of this zine, of which I have copious copies in my bedroom'!

GAVIN: [laughs] Yeah ... yeah, because I think I'd been ... I went to Reading Festival in 1991 and I remember putting a load in my bag, I probably had about 40 of the copies with me, thinking, 'It's fine, I'll sell them at Reading Festival'. But what I'd forgotten is that I was actually quite shy, and I didn't like going up to strangers.

HAMISH: You forgot that you were shy?

GAVIN: Yeah! Well, I think in my head –

HAMISH: You were thinking, 'I'm a gregarious type – I'll just sell them all!'

GAVIN: I think maybe I thought there was a new possibility for me at the music festival. I could reinvent myself, and suddenly become very confident ... But it didn't happen. I remember taking them all, carrying them around with me, never approaching anyone, and coming home with the exact same number that I'd taken with me. I couldn't even give them away.

HAMISH: Anyway ... so I got 400 done of *Saudade* issue 3 in '91. I'm at university at this point, in Canterbury, but I still took them back to the printer in Reading – got 400 done ... this is the really thick one, 96 pages ... folded and stapled them myself ... took 120 back to Canterbury ... gave my sister 20, not sure why ... I think quite a lot of them went, because at that point I was ... I wasn't *selling* so much as trading. I was in touch with a lot of people at that point. And I was trading my zine for theirs, and quite a few did go to these zine distributors as well.

Never saw any money from anyone, as far as I recall, for those. But I did send them copies of my fanzine. So I did get rid of it, at least!

Saudade issue 4, March '92: I got them done at Catford Copy Centre this time, and they were already stapled and folded, which was a blessing.

GAVIN: That's where I got mine done. I'm sure you told me about Catford Copy Centre. Because I didn't know anyone else, so you must have told me about them.

HAMISH: This is my favourite issue because it's got the best bands in, the best interviews. And I did it all by hand – no word processor or typewriter, I wrote everything out. Now, this one I did take to Reading, and even though I'm, if anything, even more shy than you, I did go round selling it to people. Sold 30 in three hours on 28th August 1992 . . . then sold 40 the next day . . . that's 70 in two days, Gavin!

GAVIN: That's incredible!

HAMISH: And then the following day I sold 10, but it was waterlogged on that day and I'd had enough and went home. That was the year Nirvana were at Reading, as well as several other bands I'd like to have seen, but I decided not to spend my money on seeing them. That's another of my regrets from that period.

GAVIN: But you weren't spending money seeing them, because – were you not already there?

HAMISH: No, I was selling it in the, like, the bit outside . . .

GAVIN: Oh, I see what you mean. But that's quite impressive, that you did that. Did you find that quite tricky early on?

HAMISH: Well, it was really instructive. And that was quite late in my fanzine-producing career. But . . . if I'd known it earlier – or had the confidence to try that earlier – it would have made a big difference, because then you can make money on your fanzine, doing that. I mean, the classic thing where that still works is the football fanzine. If you can more than cover your costs, it's a nice hobby to do.

When you get 1200 copies done and say 'I'm only selling them mail order', you know . . . it's a total disaster. If you're only doing it mail order, nobody's going to hear about it unless you place an advert, you're

Six fanzines edited by Hamish Ironside: the only issue (thus far) of *The Tacky Tiger* (1989) and *Saudade* issues 1–5 (1990–1994).

never going to cover the cost of a single advert through sales of the fanzine. So it's a loss maker from the beginning, even before you take into account the print cost.

Anyway, to conclude the *Saudade* story: *Saudade* 4 was in March '92 ... *Saudade* 5 was in June '94, and it's just a collection of things I did for the university magazine, mostly interviews with bands, and I just put them all together.

GAVIN: You went small here, didn't you?

HAMISH: Yeah, I went A6, and I think it's quite a cute little format.

GAVIN: It's a nice little thing, yeah.

HAMISH: It's kind of a shame, in a way, because all the others are A5, so it's ... it's an inconsistency. But as far as I remember, I never made any effort to sell any copies of that to anyone. It was a purely vanity publication.

GAVIN: It's strange that you wouldn't try to sell this one, really, because you've got some quite big names ... well, you've got, like, Sultans of Ping, who were fairly well known at the time. Voice of the Beehive ... Silverfish ...

HAMISH: The interview with David Icke is in there as well, which is the really interesting one.

GAVIN: Yeah – 'Goalkeepers Are Different'.

HAMISH: Then again, who's going to buy that? David Icke fans aren't going to ever hear of it.

GAVIN: So you don't know how many you did of number 5?

HAMISH: No, but it would have been a reasonably modest amount. But I do still have loads of copies left! Because I never tried to sell it to anyone.

GAVIN: I think this is the first fanzine I saw in this size, actually.

HAMISH: Well, it seems to be quite popular now. I'm seeing a lot of A6 ones, I've got a stack here.

GAVIN: You led the way on this!

HAMISH: Yeah, I was influential. They're all copying *Saudade* 5!

GAVIN: Whether they know it or not ...

HAMISH: We both crammed quite a lot of stuff into our pages. I mean I'm noticing that when I look at *Bag of Tricks and Candysticks*. It's not just down to, like, how many pages there are, it's the fact that you stuff loads of stuff in, you're writing in the margins and everything.

GAVIN: Yeah. Every inch of paper was ...

HAMISH: ... was precious.

GAVIN: Yeah, it was.

HAMISH: I mean I think it's superb for 60p.

GAVIN: Thank you.

The whole Hogg: *Bag of Tricks and Candy Sticks* issue 1 (1991) and issue 2 (1992), edited by Gavin Hogg.

HAMISH: Fantastic value for money. By the way, is this Letraset on the cover?

GAVIN: Yes, it was.

HAMISH: Because this looks like Cooper Black. Lovely use of Cooper Black. You know, it's beautiful. It's a shame you blew that fucking beer all over it.

GAVIN: Sorry, I was just freaked out by the wasp. Yes, Letraset, I used a lot. It was very precious stuff. You used to buy sheets, didn't you, like in WHSmith's? And you'd run out ... quite quickly you'd run out of certain letters, wouldn't you?

HAMISH: Oh God, my memory of Letraset's really grim, it really is. You've really got to have a lot of patience to use it.

GAVIN: You'd have to line it up right and make sure you really pressed down enough. Often it would kind of split on the thing and you get letters that were kind of broken.

HAMISH: Well, there are blemishes, to be honest, look at that 'r'.

GAVIN: Yes, that was another letter and then I kind of, I think, I just used a bit of an 'a' – I don't know . . .

HAMISH: Like some of these characters, they don't look like proper Cooper Black . . .

GAVIN: No, there's all sorts going on. And I think I kind of wanted to do this all in the same font, but then I run out of letters, so as you get like random letters from other fonts in there, I ran out of esses very quickly . . . that was awful.

You got a lot of record reviews in *Saudade*. Particularly in issue 3, there are pages of reviews. How did you get those?

HAMISH: I had a policy of like, reviewing everything I received. I got on a mailing list for certain companies, agencies or whatever. I got everything Shimmy Disc did, which was the really great thing. I was still using my parents' address. I remember coming home and just finding stacks of records. It was like a chore eventually, the amount of records I got. It was almost like being a professional journalist and it got to the point where I was thinking 'When am I going to get time to listen to all these and review them?' It lost a bit of its lustre due to that, I think. But I probably did think at that time I might have wanted to be a journalist myself and it maybe put it put me off that a little bit because it's sort of . . . you feel a bit pulled two different ways because you want to be listening to music for pleasure and when you're listening to it just to come up with some copy, it kind of impinges on the pleasure.

GAVIN: Yeah. I think that's a thing I always thought. In my head, as a kid, I always thought maybe one day I'd like to be music journalist. But then it's that thing of writing about things you don't like or just having to churn something out. The nice thing about doing a zine is you can choose exactly what you want to write about, isn't it?

HAMISH: I kind of shot myself in the foot a little bit, because I said I would review absolutely everything. But then I think I kind of liked slagging things off as well. I took some kind of a pleasure in doing that, but when I read it back . . . I don't know, I don't really enjoy reading back, like, one-star reviews where I'm just saying how terrible something is.

GAVIN: Is that because you know how much effort has gone into something now, now that you're a bit older and a bit more experienced and you just feel a bit bad?

HAMISH: Yeah, I do feel that a little bit about the fanzines I slagged off, but the music? No, not so much that, I was just doing it out of an obligation.

I'm amazed that I did some of the things I did for the fanzine. When I was reading my diary about putting some of these issues of Saudade together, it was . . . like, to get the interview with the Pastels and Jad Fair, I was going to the venue, banging on the door and stuff. I'd never have the balls to do that now. I was surprised I'd done that, you know, how did that happen? I just turned up and I interviewed them. I was banging on the door until someone let me in.

GAVIN: 'Someone speak to this kid for 20 minutes just to get rid of him.'

HAMISH: Mostly I think it was arranged in advance, but the way you read it from the diary entry, I was just turning up and banging on the door.

GAVIN: So it's almost a sense of you having, like, a different persona as a zine editor.

HAMISH: Yeah. I mean, why not? It's in their interests to be in my fanzine, you know? It's the right attitude really. That's the way you should be.

GAVIN: It's a certain cockiness of youth, isn't it?

HAMISH: Exactly, it's the cockiness of youth. I mean, one of the things I loved about doing our interviews was talking to Mark Hodkinson about how people decry adolescence as if it's a phase you go through and you grow out of it. You know, all these sort of feelings and views of adolescence are valid . . . it's not something you have to grow out. That's what I think about doing fanzines. Even though people do end up using it as a springboard to go into journalism or something like that, it's not just that. It's a valid experience in itself.

FURTHER READING

This is not supposed to be an exhaustive list, but we think it includes most of the tomes worth reading, and perhaps one or two that aren't really worth reading but are included anyway since we went to the trouble of buying the damn things. An important caveat is that we only list books about zines in general, so we don't list the compilations of original issues that have been published for specific zines such as *Sniffin' Glue*, *Ripped & Torn*, *Jamming!*, *Ablaze!*, *Pynk Moon* and *Grim Humour*, to name just the ones we are aware of.

The list is arranged in chronological order of publication date. Several of the books are out of print, but second-hand copies should be reasonably affordable for all but a couple of titles.

Fredric Wertham, The World of Fanzines: A Special Form of Communication (Carbondale, IL: Southern Illinois University Press, 1973), 235 × 178 mm, 160 pp.
This is the only title on this list that we have not been able to read. Copies are very scarce and hence very expensive (too expensive for us). Wertham has a bad reputation among comics fans, having been a prime instigator behind the Comics Code (see page 19 of our own book for more on that); but let us cut the guy some slack. In the 1940s he was an outspoken critic of mainstream psychiatry in the US and its assumption that criminal behaviour is biologically determined, rather than a result of poverty and neglect. He also took action against the overt racism that he recognised within the psychiatric world, opening a free community psychiatric clinic in Harlem with interracial staff, at a time when segregation was still widespread. All his theories about violence seem sound until you come to the undue emphasis he placed on a link between reading comics that depicted violence and re-enacting that violence. He later wrote more positively about comics, but by then the Comics Code was in full swing. *The World of Fanzines* is his final book; having read extracts and reviews of it online, it is clear that he saw the free expression they afforded as

a good thing, representing 'a constructive and healthy exercise of creative drives'.

In fact, in the extracts we've seen, Wertham comes across as perceptive and even rather lyrical:

> Behind much that appears as free expression in strictly commercial magazines and publications we have to visualize some 'stone-faced business tycoon' (*Fantasy Advertiser* 33). Those whose names are printed as creators may be more like marionettes, with the guiding threads invisible – though every once in a while the threads show. Whatever one may think about fanzines, they are not guided in any way by such invisible threads. This is one of the secrets of fanzines.

May we submit that Wertham is a good egg after all?

Mike Gunderloy, *How to Publish a Fanzine* (Port Townsend, WA: Loompanics Unlimited, 1988), 206 × 124 mm, 99 pp.

We only discovered this little gem rather late in the day, so have not had the chance to give it much of a read, but it is a captivating snapshot of the practicalities of producing a zine over 30 years ago. Mike Gunderloy is something of a hero for having founded *Factsheet Five*, and he is a very engaging writer. Although *Factsheet Five* listed zines on every subject, Gunderloy emerged from SF fandom, and it is interesting to learn that terms like 'perzine' were devised by the SF community as long ago as this. Original copies of this book are now collectors' items, but it is freely available to download from www.zinebook.com/resource/fanzine.pdf.

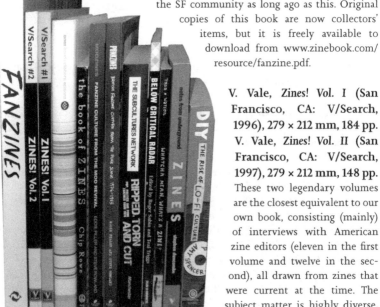

V. Vale, *Zines! Vol. I* (San Francisco, CA: V/Search, 1996), 279 × 212 mm, 184 pp. V. Vale, *Zines! Vol. II* (San Francisco, CA: V/Search, 1997), 279 × 212 mm, 148 pp.

These two legendary volumes are the closest equivalent to our own book, consisting (mainly) of interviews with American zine editors (eleven in the first volume and twelve in the second), all drawn from zines that were current at the time. The subject matter is highly diverse, with zines on washing dishes for a living, Arthur Cravan, fat pride and eight-track cassettes, among others. You won't find these books on Amazon (not that you should be looking there anyway!), but if you can't find second-hand copies they are still available direct from RE/Search at www.researchpubs.com at a cost of $75 including postage to Britain from the States.

Chip Rowe (ed.), *The Book of Zines: Readings from the Fringe* (New York: Henry Holt, 1997), 233 × 186 mm, 192 pp.
This is another very American volume, comprising selections of actual excerpts from zines. I feel a bit ambivalent about this one; there's a sense that the zines from which they are drawn are those that come closest to mainstream journalism, and when it's all professionally typeset it doesn't feel very ziney at all. It's the sort of book that would form the ideal companion on a long train journey, yet if you were to read it in the privacy of your own home you'd probably start feeling like you should be reading Dostoevsky instead.

Stephen Duncombe, *Notes from Underground: Zines and the Politics of Alternative Culture* (London: Verso, 1997), 234 × 156 mm, 250 pp.
Like all the previous books in this list, *Notes from Underground* is by an American author and nearly all the examples are American. Yet the sort of ethical and political issues that are discussed here are of a universal kind, and will certainly be recognised by British zine readers: 'purity' versus 'selling out'; anarchism versus capitalism; alienation versus community; and so on. The book is exceptionally well researched, well written and well organised; each chapter examines a distinct theme (e.g. identity, work, consumption), and it doesn't need to be read from cover to cover in order to follow the argument – you can dip into it anywhere and find something of interest. For example, the section on the history of *Factsheet Five* covers a huge amount of ground in the space of six pages, drawing on first-hand research from interviews with Mike Gunderloy and Seth Friedman (the subsequent editor) to depict the difficulty in knowing where to draw the line between integrity and commercialism. This is essential reading for anyone with an academic interest in zines. But we also commend it to 'anybody who just reads and runs', as Salinger put it.

Roger Sabin and Teal Triggs (eds), *Below Critical Radar: Fanzines and Alternative Comics from 1976 to Now* (Hove: Slab-O-Concrete, undated [c.2001]), 251 × 216 mm, 116 pp.
This is now a collector's item, and we are grateful to Elias Nebula for letting us know about the copy at the MVE bookshop in Notting Hill, which we obtained by trading in a bunch of dross from that pile in the corner. I'm sorry to say you'll probably have to pay over £50 for a copy online. There is an appealing scrapbook quality to the book, which has five main chapters, interspersed with unrelated pages devoted to a specific publication or topic. The content seems fairly evenly balanced between

UK and US zines and comics. The distinguishing feature of the book is its claim that fanzines and alternative comics have more in common than do fanzines and mainstream magazines, or alternative comics and mainstream comics. That would be more convincing if 'alternative comics' were understood to mean purely self-published ones, but here it includes comics published by the likes of Fantagraphics (indeed Gary Groth contributes one of the five chapters), which are certainly an alternative to Marvel and DC, but a good deal more commercial than a typical zine. No biggie, though – it's all good stuff!

Liz Farrelly (ed.), Zines (London: Booth-Clibborn Editions, 2001), 264 × 214 mm, 256 pp.
This is a luxurious art book, printed in full colour on glossy paper, in hardback with a dust jacket that folds out into a poster. So it's surprising that second-hand copies are available at prices far below what its original retail price must have been (there's a copy available on Abe for £1.69, if you're quick). There is very little text, and the book chiefly consists of very high-quality reproductions of images from a selection of artzines from around the world. It's interesting in that it covers publications beyond the UK and USA, and it's quite different from any of the other books on this list, but it is a book for looking at rather than reading.

Mark Todd and Esther Pearl Watson, Whatcha Mean, What's a Zine? The Art of Making Zines and Mini-Comics (Boston, MA: Houghton Mifflin, 2006), 228 × 178 mm, 112 pp.
This guide to the nuts and bolts of producing zines and comics is itself laid out like a cross between the two forms, with many illustrations and strips throughout, and the text is all either hand-lettered or typed on a manual typewriter. At least half the book is by contributors other than the authors, which adds a good deal of variety to the graphics. My favourite item is a spread devoted to staplers, including the following exchange with Chuck Johnson ('the Staple Guy'):

Q: 'Have you ever stapled yourself by accident?'
A: 'Once.'

Amy Spencer, DIY: The Rise of Lo-fi Culture (London: Marion Boyars, 2008), 196 × 130 mm, 358 pp.
This is a revised edition of a book originally published in 2005, from an American author (but a British publisher); the content covers both sides of the Atlantic, but mainly the US. A small-format paperback, it has very few illustrations, and unfortunately the poor quality of the paper stock is already evident in my copy. The book covers lo-fi and self-produced music as well as zines, plus sections on online publishing, crafting and DIY radio, among other things. It seems like it's been cobbled together in rather a hurry: it covers a lot of ground, but not in much depth, and the leaps from one paragraph to the next sometimes feel disjointed. But the good news is that second-hand copies can be found at very low prices!

Teal Triggs, *Fanzines* (London: Thames & Hudson, 2010), 340 × 242 mm, 256 pp.

This whopper is mainly pictorial, with hundreds of colour images of zine covers from the full spectrum of zine history, a fair number of which are from outside the UK and US. It's a beautiful book to browse through, and when you do so you find that there is actually a surprising amount of text lurking among the images, making this seem more substantial than a mere coffee table book. The book is organised into six chapters mainly covering specific periods (including one chapter on 'e-zines', but we won't hold that against her). Each chapter opens with an excellent, concise overview, and the book is very well annotated and indexed. A second-hand copy should cost you around £25 to £30, which is a little more than its original retail price, but still well worth it.

The Subcultures Network (ed.), *Ripped, Torn and Cut: Pop, Politics and Punk Fanzines from 1976* (Manchester: Manchester University Press, 2018), 234 × 156 mm, 342 pp.

Ripped, Torn and Cut is an edited collection of 18 chapters, and every one of them is fascinating. The starting point is punk, but the book traces the various paths that led from there, including anarcho-punk, industrial, goth and indie, culminating in the riot grrrl movement of the early 1990s. Each chapter tackles a distinct theme: Cazz Blase discusses the 'invisible women' involved in punk zine creation; Nicholas Bullen (a founding member of Napalm Death) reminisces about producing his first fanzine, *Antisocial*, in 1980, at the age of 12; Clare Wadd recounts how producing her zine *Kvatch* led to co-founding Sarah Records; Tom Vague offers a memoir of his experiences of producing the legendary *Vague* through the 1980s; and so on. One of my favourite chapters is by Kirsty Lohman, regarding the Dutch fanzine *Raket*, and how it negotiated the dichotomy of supporting free speech while opposing fascism. At £16.99, the book is exceptionally good value, so what are you waiting for? Order it now!

Eddie Piller and Steve Rowland, *Modzines: Fanzine Culture from the Mod Revival* (London: Omnibus, 2018), 268 × 213 mm, 176 pp.
Eddie Piller and Steve Rowland, *Punkzines: British Fanzine Culture from the Punk Scene 1976–1983* (London: Omnibus, 2021), 268 × 213 mm, 176 pp.

Although they were published three years apart, these two volumes appear as a matching pair in terms of design and production. Like Triggs's *Fanzines*, both are beautifully illustrated with an abundance of full-colour reproductions of zine covers, but here the ratio of text to images is roughly half and half. Contrary to what you might expect, the volume on modzines came first, and is perhaps the more notable of the two for covering a genre that no one else has covered. I was amazed to discover how many modzines there were, and they are documented here with the authority that comes from having been immersed in the scene (Eddie Piller founded one of the most prominent modzines, *Extraordinary Sensations*). In contrast, punkzines have already been written about extensively elsewhere, and I did wonder what this book might add to the existing literature, but once I started reading it became clear that it's a story that bears repeating any amount of times, if the research is original and well carried out, as is the case here. Both volumes benefit from original interviews with pivotal figures, including Mark Perry, Steve Micalef and Tony Drayton in the case of *Punkzines*. It's also worth mentioning that both books have that irresistible smell I tend to associate with American zines – every time I pick one of them up I can't resist burying my nose in it and giving it a good sniff. Overall, at £16.99 each, both books are excellent value.

Matthew Worley, *Zerox Machine: Punk, Post-Punk and Fanzines in Britain, 1976–1988* (forthcoming)

This book is still being written as we go to press, but the author kindly shared the introduction chapter with us, and that in itself is a captivating and meticulously researched history that whets the appetite for what is to follow. The book is due for publication in 2023, and looks set to become the definitive work on what was arguably the most creative and diverse period of British zine culture.

RESOURCES

Much as we despise the internet, we have to acknowledge that almost all current information about zines is online. Even where there is a physical shop, festival, workshop or archive, unless it's right on your doorstep you'll probably need the internet to find it. The difficulty is finding good information. As we know, search engines are constructed to funnel you towards the sites that have the most money behind them, not the best information. When I searched 'punk fanzines' today, the top result was 'Low prices on punk fanzines – Amazon.co.uk'.

The resources that are listed below are divided into two categories, based on the assumption that you either want to read a zine or buy a zine. Of course you may instead want to collaborate on a zine, trade a zine, discuss zines, go to a zine fest, attend a zine workshop or even commission a zine, but several of these resources offer those options too, even if they are primarily either an archive or a distro.

For online resources in particular, what we list below is somewhat selective, but the ones we have chosen are included partly because they include good links to other resources, so do check their sites even if they are not obviously what you are looking for.

Libraries and archives

One thing we note about the zine archives is that there are good resources for the SF zines produced from the 1930s onwards, and also for very recent or contemporary zines on all subjects, but very little on the kinds of zine covered in the majority of this book: the music and other fanzines produced from the start of punk to the start of the internet era. I began this paragraph intending to lament this state of affairs; on the other hand, suppose in ten years' time every zine produced between 1976 and 2000 was available to download on the internet, is that what we want? No! Let's face it, there is something we quite like about them being hard to find. And, as we keep mentioning, we do loathe the internet. What has it done to deserve our hypothetical hoard of zines?

Rob Hansen's Fan Stuff

www.fiawol.org.uk

'FIAWOL' stands for 'fandom is a way of life', and Rob Hansen's site is a gateway to the entire world of SF fandom covered in Chapter 1 of this book. In addition to collecting much of Rob's own writing, his site links to many other meticulously compiled resources, notably including fanac.org, which is the biggest archive of SF zines by far: at last count it contained 16,634 issues of 991 fanzine titles, totalling 286,845 pages. These are high-quality scans of every SF zine they could find – a monumental project that stands as an example of what can be done by a well-connected and like-minded community if they are prepared to put the time in just for the love of it. Most of the Fanac archive comprises American zines, but there's a page on Rob's site that links directly to the UK zines to make it easier to find them.

Norwich Zine Library

This is a physical archive on the first floor of Norfolk & Norwich Millennium Library, the main public library in Norwich. Librarian Rachel Ridealgh tells us the archive holds 200–300 zines, many from local makers, and the collection is growing all the time.

There are similar zine libraries at other locations around the country – those we know of include Glasgow (www.glasgow zinelibrary.com, located at 636 Cathcart Road), Edinburgh (www.edinburghzinelibrary.com, in Edinburgh Central Library), Scarborough (www.crescentarts.co.uk/whats_on/scarborough-zine-library), Hull (www.instagram.com/hullzinelibrary), Derbyshire (www.instagram.com/derbyshirezinelibrary), and yet more are listed in our next resource . . .

UK and Ireland Zine Librarians

https://uizl.wordpress.com

Not an archive in itself, but an excellent listing of collections around the country.

56a Infoshop

https://56a.org.uk

Founded in 1991, 56a Infoshop is a volunteer-run, unfunded, DIY social centre at 56

Crampton Street in Walworth (south London). It is open for limited hours Thursday to Saturday only, so check those hours on their website before dropping in. They have an archive of around 70,000 zines, pamphlets and other papers, plus almost 1500 books, and you are welcome to drop in to browse – they even provide free tea and coffee. A hub for radical left-wing politics, they provide a squatters' noticeboard to meet other squatters, post info on empty buildings, read legal advice, and so on. They also have a selection of books and zines for sale.

Madzines

https://madzines.org

This is a research project running from June 2020 to October 2023. In their own words, they explore how zines 'craft contention' about mental health. The website includes details of related workshops and events, as well as an archive of zines produced through the project.

Zineopolis

https://zineopolis.blogspot.com

Zineopolis opened in June 2007 after a project by students at the University of Portsmouth. Their archive focuses on 'zines heavy with visual content, now more commonly referred to as Art-zines'.

Shops and distros

Here again we may distinguish between recent zines and older zines. As far as we are aware, there are no dedicated sellers of older zines, and your only real option is eBay, where you will usually (but not always) have to pay through the nose for what you want, if you are lucky enough to find it at all.

For contemporary zines, in addition to the resources below, there's no escaping the fact that the single best place to find the zine you want is Etsy. If you search, say, 'riot grrrl zines' on Etsy, you currently get 389 results, of wildly varying relevance, but a fair number are very enticing.

But we encourage you to go first to the distros listed below, which are all eminently worth supporting.

Pen Fight

https://penfightdistro.com

Pen Fight is a queer and feminist distro selling zines and books, plus a few other items (such as a badge declaring 'Straight White Boys Don't Own Punk'). They have a superb range of zines, covering subjects from birding to punk and anarchist squats in Poland, at prices that can't be beat: we bought eleven zines (including several by Janet Brown, co-star of Chapter 15) for under £20, including postage. If you are interested in exploring the world of contemporary zines, we reckon this is the best place to start.

AK Press

https://akuk.com

AK is a worker-owned and worker-led anarchist publishing and distribution service that has been going since long before the internet came along and ruined everything (okay, I'll stop that now). The interesting thing here is that their website has no 'Zines' section – the zines are all listed under 'Pamphlets', which perhaps does reflect the fact that contemporary zines are more like pamphlets, and less like periodicals, than they used to be 'back in the day'. In any case, the zines/pamphlets listed here are plentiful, mostly very interesting and unlikely to be found at any of the other distros, so their website is well worth a browse.

Coin Operated Press

https://coinoperatedpress.com

A Scottish, queer-led social enterprise that produces and distributes collaborative zines, among other things. You can even commission them to make a zine!

Common Threads

www.commonthreadspress.co.uk

Common Threads is dedicated to 'putting feminist, queer and radical craft histories on your bookshelf'. We discovered them at the 2022 Latitude Festival, where they were running a 'zine shed' that proved to be a welcome relief from Marcus Brigstocke on the comedy stage.

Mark Pawson

http://markpawson.uk

Mark Pawson's website is worth looking at as a kind of gallery in itself. It is hard to navigate, but worth any amount of effort to find your way around it. The zine-related items are few, but they include fascinating items such as a reprint of a 1980 listing of fanzines for sale from Rough Trade.

Shelf Life Books and Zines

www.shelflifebookshop.com

A not-for-profit radical bookshop in Cardiff working with independent publishers and DIY zine-makers to 'make space for marginalised and under-represented voices'. Their stock is also available on their website, which includes details of several community action initiatives they have set up.

Interesting Books + Zines

https://interestingbooks.co.uk

This bookshop in Berwick-upon-Tweed has a carefully chosen stock aiming to 'champion the work of talented, creative and emerging writers, artists, independent publishers and small presses', with an appealing website for those of us not within striking distance of Berwick.

INDEX

Note: italic page numbers indicate illustrations.

INDEX